10,⁷⁰

DRUG LEGALIZATION
For and Against

DRUG
LEGALIZATION
For and Against

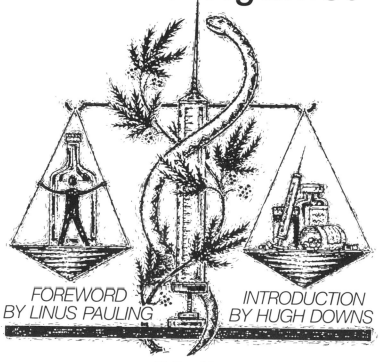

FOREWORD BY LINUS PAULING

INTRODUCTION BY HUGH DOWNS

Edited by

Rod L. Evans and Irwin M. Berent

Open ✳ Court

La Salle, Illinois 61301

Volume 1 in the series, 'For and Against'

OPEN COURT and the above logo are registered in the U.S. Patent and Trademark Office.

© 1992 by Open Court Publishing Company

First printing 1992
Second printing 1993
Third printing 1994
Fourth printing 1996

Printed and bound in the United States of America.

Library of Congress Cataloging-in-Publication Data

Drug legalization: for and against/edited by Rod L. Evans and Irwin
    M. Berent; foreword by Linus Pauling; introduction by Hugh Downs.
        p.   cm.—(For and against; v. 1)
    Includes bibliographical references (p.   ) and index.
    ISBN 0-8126-9183-0 (cloth).—ISBN 0-8126-9184-9 (paper)
    1. Drug legalization—United States. 2. Drug abuse—United
States.   I. Evans, Rod L., 1956–   . II. Berent, Irwin M.
III. Series.
KF3890.D79   1992
364.1′77′0973   dc20
                                                              92-1626
                                                              CIP

CONTENTS

Contents

Contents

About the Contributors

MARGUERITE A. BENNETT is special agent supervisor of the Education/Communication Arts Unit, Federal Bureau of Investigation Academy, Quantico, Virginia.

WILLIAM JOHN BENNETT is former Director of the White House Office of Drug Control Policy (1988–1990). He holds a Ph.D. from the University of Texas (1970) and a J.D. from Harvard University (1971). He has served as chairman of the National Endowment for the Humanities (1981–1985) and secretary of the U.S. Department of Education (1985–1988). He has also served as assistant to the president at Boston University (1972–1976) and as executive director (1976–1979) and president and director (1979–1981) at the National Humanities Center, Research Triangle Park, North Carolina. He was an associate professor at North Carolina State University (1979–1981) and at the University of North Carolina (1979–1981).

IRWIN M. BERENT is a historian, archivist, and genealogist who has written many articles on the history of the South. With Dr. Rod L. Evans, he co-authored *Fundamentalism: Hazards and Heartbreaks* (1988) and *The Right Words* (1992).

TAYLOR BRANCH is a freelance writer and author of biographies of Bill Russell (*Second Wind*, with Bill Russell, Ballantine) and Martin Luther King Jr. (*Parting the Waters: America in the King Years, 1954–1963*, Simon and Schuster, 1988).

TODD AUSTIN BRENNER received his J.D. (1990) from Capital

University and was Notes Editor for the *Capital University Law Review*. He is an attorney in private practice in Columbus.

WILLIAM FRANK BUCKLEY JR. is editor-in-chief (from 1955) and syndicated columnist (from 1962) of *National Review*. He is also host of the weekly television show, 'Firing Line'. Mr. Buckley is the author of numerous books and articles, including *Airborne: A Sentimental Journey* (New York: MacMillan, 1976), *Four Reforms: A Guide for the Seventies* (New York: Putnam, 1973), *The Governor Listeth: A Book of Inspired Political Revelations* (New York: Putnam, 1970), *God and Man At Yale* (Washington: Regnery Gateway, 1977), and *Up From Liberalism* (New Rochelle: Arlington House, 1951), as well as several best-selling spy thrillers.

WILLIAM HODDING CARTER III is a columnist for the *Wall Street Journal* and president of MainStreet TV Production Company. He has received four Emmy awards for public affairs television (1984–85). He served as department spokesman for the Department of State, Washington, D.C. (1977–1980), and he was a member of the campaign staffs of Johnson for President (1964) and Carter for President (1976). He was anchorman and chief correspondent of 'Inside Story' (Public Broadcasting System, 1981–84) and chief correspondent and executive editor of 'Capitol Journal' (P.B.S., 1985–86).

HUGH MALCOLM DOWNS has been host of NBC's 'Today' show (1962–1971) and '20/20' (1978 to the present). He began his TV career as staff announcer of WLOK (Lima, Ohio) in 1939, then WWJ (Detroit, 1940), and WMAQ (Chicago, 1943). He hosted the TV game show 'Concentration' (1958–1968) and 'Over Easy' (1977–1980), for which he won an Emmy in 1981. He has been chairman of the National Space Institute, a board member of Planned Parenthood World Population, visiting fellow at the Center for the Study of Democratic Institutions, and special consultant to the United Nations on refugee problems in the Middle East. His published books include *Yours Truly* (1960), *A Shoal of Stars* (1967), *Potential: The Way to Emotional Maturity* (1973), and *The Best Years Book* (1980).

ROD L. EVANS has a Ph.D. in philosophy from the University of Virginia and teaches philosophy at Old Dominion University. With Irwin Berent he has written *Fundamentalism: Hazards and Heartbreaks* (1988) and *The Right Words* (1992).

DARYL FRAZELL served as editor of the perspective section of the *St. Petersburg (Florida) Times*. He is currently associate professor of journalism at the University of Nebraska, Lincoln.

MILTON FRIEDMAN is Senior Research Fellow at Hoover Institute, Stanford University. He holds a Ph.D. from Columbia University (1946). He is the recipient of the 1976 Nobel Memorial Prize in Economic Science. He was Paul Snowden Russell distinguished service professor of economics at the University of Chicago (1962–1981) and a member of the research staff of the National Bureau of Economic Research, New York City (1937–1945, 1948–1981). In 1981 he was appointed to the President's Economic Policy Advisory Board. Dr. Friedman was a columnist for *Newsweek* (1966–1984) and a contributing editor of *Newsweek* (1971–1984). He is the author of numerous books and articles, including *Capitalism and Freedom* (with Rose D. Friedman; Chicago: University of Chicago Press, 1962), *Free to Choose: A Personal Statement* (with Rose Friedman; New York: Harcourt Brace Jovanovich, 1980), *A Monetary History of the United States, 1867–1960* (with Anna J. Schwartz; Princeton: Princeton University Press, 1963), *Tyranny of the Status Quo* (with Rose Friedman; San Diego: Harcourt, Brace, Jovanovich, 1984), and *Milton Friedman's Monetary Framework: A Debate with his Critics* (edited by Robert J. Gordon; Chicago Press, 1974).

MICHAEL S. GAZZANIGA is the Andrew W. Thomson Jr. professor of psychiatry (Neuroscience) at Dartmouth Medical School. He is also editor-in-chief of the *Journal of Cognitive Neuroscience* and the author of *Mind Matters* (Houghton Mifflin, 1988) and several other books.

JOHN LAWRENCE HILL is professor of law at Western State University College of Law at Irvine, California. He holds a J.D. and a

Ph.D. (Philosophy) from Georgetown University. He was visiting assistant professor at the Illinois Institute of Technology Chicago-Kent College of Law. He has written numerous law journal articles, including 'What Does It Mean to be a Parent?' (*New York University Law Review,* May 1991).

MORTON MATT KONDRACKE is Senior Editor of *The New Republic* (from 1986) and a television commentator for The McLaughlin Group (from 1981). He has been a correspondent for the *Chicago Sun Times* (1963–1977), executive editor of *The New Republic* (1977–1985), a columnist for the *Wall Street Journal* (1980–85) and United Features Syndicate (1983–85), and the Washington bureau chief of *Newsweek* (1985–86).

MARK H. MOORE is professor of criminal justice at the John F. Kennedy School of Government, Harvard University. In the mid-1970s he was chief planning officer of the D.E.A., and wrote *Buy and Bust: The Effective Regulation of an Illicit Market in Heroin* (Lexington, Ma.: Lexington Books, 1977).

DAVID FRANKLIN MUSTO is professor of psychiatry (Child Study Center) and of the history of medicine at the Yale School of Medicine. He received his M.D. from the University of Washington. He has served as Special Assistant to the Director of the National Institute of Mental Health and as Program Director of the National Humanities Institute at Yale. He was also a member of the White House Strategy Council (1978–1981). Dr. Musto is the author of *The American Disease: Origins of Narcotic Control* and other books.

ETHAN AVRAM NADELMANN is assistant professor of politics and public affairs at the Woodrow Wilson School of Public and International Affairs, Princeton University. He received his J.D. (1984) and Ph.D. (in political science, 1987) from Harvard University. He was founding co-ordinator of the Harvard Study Group on Organized Crime (1986), and a consultant to both the Public Agenda Foundation's National Issues Forum (1988–89) and the Bureau of International Narcotics Matters, Department of State (1984–85). He has been an assistant editor of the *Journal of Drug Issues* and a contributing editor of the *International Journal on Drug Policy* (since 1989).

GABRIEL G. NAHAS is professor of anesthesiology at the College of Physicians and Surgeons of Columbia University, adjunct professor at the University of Paris, and consultant to the United Nations Commission on Narcotics. Dr. Nahas is the author of *Cocaine: The Great White Plague* (in collaboration with Helene Peters), *How to Save Your Child from Drugs* (with Harold M. Vuth), *Keep off the Grass*, and other books.

LINUS PAULING was awarded the 1954 Nobel Prize for chemistry and the 1962 Nobel Prize for peace. In the 1950s he was harassed by the U.S. government because he claimed that fallout from nuclear weapons tests was harmful. He has been the recipient of over 40 honorary degrees from universities around the world. For the past 25 years he has been campaigning for the medical recognition of well-established research findings in nutrition. He is best known for his immensely popular works, *Vitamin C and the Common Cold* (1970) and *How to Live Longer and Feel Better* (1986).

CHARLES BERNARD RANGEL is a member of the House of Representatives, 16th New York District (previously, the 19th District, from 1970). He is a member of the House Ways and Means Committee and chairman of the Select Committee on Narcotics Abuse and Control (from 1983). He holds a J.D. from St. John's University School of Law (1960). He has served as an Assistant U.S. Attorney, Southern District, New York (1961–62), and as a member of the New York State Assembly (1960–1970).

KURT LIDELL SCHMOKE is Mayor of the city of Baltimore, Maryland (from 1987). He was a Rhodes Scholar at Oxford University and received his law degree from Harvard University. He has served as assistant director, White House Domestic Policy Staff (1977); Assistant United States Attorney in Baltimore (1978–1982); and State's Attorney for Baltimore City (1982–87). He has served on the Maryland Governor's Commission on Prison Overcrowding, the Maryland Criminal Justice Co-ordinating Council, and the Task Force to Reform the Insanity Defense. He established a Narcotics Unit to prosecute drug cases in Baltimore.

MERRILL A. SMITH was Chief of Probation, Administrative Office of the United States Courts.

THOMAS S. SZASZ is professor of psychiatry at the State University of New York, Syracuse (Health Science Center). He received his M.D. from the University of Cincinnati. Dr. Szasz serves on the editorial boards of the *Journal of Law and Human Behavior* and other scholarly journals. He is the author of *Ceremonial Chemistry: The Ritual Persecution of Drugs, Addicts, and Pushers; Insanity: The Idea and Its Consequences; Law, Liberty, and Psychiatry: An Inquiry into the Social Uses of Mental Health Practices; The Untamed Tongue: A Dissenting Dictionary*, and several other books.

ARNOLD S. TREBACH is a professor in the School of Justice at the American University, and president of the Drug Policy Foundation. He holds a Ph.D. (politics) from Princeton University and a J.D. from the New England School of Law. He has been Chief, Administration of Justice Section, U.S. Commission on Civil Rights; Administrator, National Defender Project, National Legal Aid and Defender Association; Chief Consultant, White House Conference on Civil Rights; founder and President, University Research Corporation; and co-founder and Chairman, National Committee on the Treatment of Intractable Pain. Dr. Trebach is the author of several books, including *The Heroin Solution* and *The Great Drug War*, and is editor of *Drugs, Crime, and Politics*. He was also lead author of the *1961 Justice Report* (U.S. Commission on Civil Rights).

EDWARD J. TULLY is Unit Chief of the Education/Communication Arts Unit, Federal Bureau of Investigation Academy, Quantico, Virginia.

JAMES QUINN WILSON is Collins professor of management and public policy at U.C.L.A. He is also chairman of the Police Foundation and a member of the council of academic advisors of the American Enterprise Institute. He has served as chairman of the National Advisory Council for Drug Abuse Prevention, and he was the director of the Joint Center for Urban Studies M.I.T and Harvard. Dr. Wilson is the author of *Thinking About Crime* (1977), *Crime and Human Nature* (with Richard Hernstein, 1986), *Bureaucracy* (1989), and other books.

STEVEN WISOTSKY is a professor of Law at the Nova University Law Center and the editor of the proceedings of the University's War on Drugs Symposium. Dr. Wisotsky is the author of *Breaking the Impasse in the War on Drugs* and *Beyond the War on Drugs: Overcoming a Failed Public Policy.*

Foreword

One of the greatest problems that we are now facing is that of the damage done by and the cost of psychoactive drugs. The annual cost for the United States alone may be over 200 billion dollars: 100 billion the direct cost of the drugs, 10 billion for government efforts to enforce the laws, and many billions lost because of drug-related crimes and punishment of criminals. This book, edited by Rod L. Evans and Irwin M. Berent, provides information and arguments both for and against legalization, as presented by many scholars and other authorities. It is my opinion that this anthology should be studied by every person who is concerned about the well-being of men, women, and children and about the future of the United States and the world as a whole.

Now that the cold war has come to an end, and the United States and the Soviet Union have begun to co-operate, there is an increased chance of controlling the international trade in these substances. As some of the contributors have argued, the best solution to the problem during the immediate future is probably neither that of legalizing all drugs all over the world nor that of increasing the legal restrictions on them and the military and police power needed to enforce them, that is, to expand the war on drugs. A reasonable course might be to legalize some drugs (marijuana, cocaine) and to continue to outlaw the more dangerous ones. Reference is made to the system in the Netherlands as an example.

It is my own opinion that a policy of this sort, the legalization of some drugs, should be adopted in the United States. I shall not attempt to review the arguments underlying this opinion; almost all of them are presented in this book. I shall, however, mention one argument that is not well known.

I have for 22 years pointed out that substances that may enter the human body may be divided into two classes. First, we have *orthomolecular substances*, which are substances that are normally present in the human body, with many of them, such as the vitamins, required for life. On the other hand there are the *drugs*, substances that may be introduced into the human body, often with pronounced physiological effects, but that are not normally present in it.

A principal difference between these two kinds of substances is that the orthomolecular substances are often essentially non-toxic or at any rate have toxic or lethal doses far larger than the doses that produce significant physiological effects, whereas the drugs are toxic at the physiologically effective intakes and cause much suffering and many deaths. A possible explanation of this difference is that human beings and their forerunners have been exposed to the orthomolecular substances for hundreds of thousands or millions of years and have through mutations and other evolutionary processes developed a tolerance for them, at any rate at the dosages available to early man and his predecessors. This tolerance would not have been developed for the other substances, the drugs.

Ethanol, the principal constituent of alcoholic beverages, is an orthomolecular substance, available to human beings and their predecessors for thousands of generations. It is produced in nature by the fermentation of fruits and grains, and these fermented foods were eaten by early man, who thus was supplied with a moderate intake of ethanol. It is not surprising that most human beings now tolerate alcoholic drinks, if not excessive. A moderate alcohol intake has value as a natural tranquillizer and a way of preventing high blood pressure. This evolutionary mechanism has not operated to accustom the human body to high intakes of ethanol, however, because large amounts of the substance were not available to primitive man; the high-proof beverages became available only a few hundred years ago, when the alchemists invented distillation. We can accordingly understand why an excessive intake of alcohol leads to drunkenness and to severe damage to the human body.

There are some narcotic drugs that probably have been available to primitive man for such a long time that they may be considered to be orthomolecular substances. Among these are marijuana and cocaine, and perhaps also peyote. Recognition of these different classes of psychoactive substances may be helpful in formulating legislation about drugs.

Linus Pauling

Linus Pauling Institute of Science and Medicine
440 Page Mill Road
Palo Alto, CA 94306

Introduction

This selection of essays is both timely and important. It is timely because the debate over legalization has recently intensified, and it shows no signs of passing out of American legal and social thought. It is important because the drug laws affect millions of people, and we must be careful in drafting and executing the law. The arguments for and against the legalization of drugs deserve our attention.

Drug laws affect many more people than merely the large number of those who get arrested. There is little disagreement, for example, that drug laws contribute to, and indeed define, the black market, in which the prices of drugs are artificially inflated. Because of the inflated market, many drug users resort to robberies and burglaries, endangering or destroying the lives of ordinary citizens; they may also resort to encouraging others to buy drugs from them. The black market also creates an environment in which drug traffickers and dealers fight, often lethally, over turf. Further, it is in the interests of dealers and manufacturers of illegalized drugs to adulterate the drugs to produce the maximum number of dosages, at times putting the user at serious risk beyond the usual hazards involved in drug use.

The present system forces many of those who want to use currently illegal drugs to form associations with the underworld to get the drugs. What's more, current drug laws stigmatize and punish millions of people, especially minorities, in whose communities drug use is prevalent. In short, treating the use of certain drugs as illegal often substitutes the force of law for the guidance of education and the healing of medical treatment.

Yet if the considerations described above were the only considerations, there would be no need for this book or indeed for a debate at all. Unfortunately, the issues are too complex simply to dismiss arguments against legalization. In evaluating the merits of the different arguments, people need to weigh the evils of the current system against the estimated consequences of a more liberal system. People will need to try to understand a number of questions, including the following: How 'addictive' are particular drugs? Former Surgeon General Koop once stated that nicotine was a more powerful addiction than heroin. And there is still debate over whether cannabis is at all addictive. How much control do most people have over addictions? (In particular, does a given drug create a need for increased dosage to achieve the same level of 'high'?) How much would the incidence of drug use in a liberalized system increase, both in the short run and in the long run? Repeal of liquor prohibition did result in increase of alcohol consumption. How effective is education in reducing drug use? The Partnership for a Drug-Free America reports a drop of 46 percent in the number of teenage cocaine users since 1987. Much of this they attribute to education such as the public service spots on television showing the dangers of drug use. Does making drug use legal automatically imply approval on the part of government? Will it make young people think that drug use is acceptable? (Cigarette smoking remains legal under the same government that requires warning labels—an implicit disapproval.) Are the current costs of cigarette smoking (such as lung cancer and heart disease) and alcohol drinking (such as alcoholism and auto accidents) predictors of the probable costs of drug use under a legalized system, or are they merely proof that cigarette and alcohol problems will always be proportionately much greater problems than the problems associated with the legalized use of other drugs? Put simply, what would be the probable social costs and benefits of a legalized system as compared to the costs and benefits of our present 'War On Drugs'? This question has not been adequately looked into. Many other questions need to be carefully entertained.

Evans and Berent have selected an excellent series of essays from a growing and almost bewilderingly large literature on the pros and cons of legalization. Together, those essays encompass virtually every major argument in the debate and represent a wide variety of fields, including law, medicine, psychiatry, sociology, economics, and philosophy. Because it represents an extraordinarily large number of opinions and fields, the book will most likely largely define the debates to come.

Whatever your views about legalization, you can profit from reading this book, which goes out of its way to present impartially the major arguments both for and against legalization. The questions raised here are not simple, but they can be answered only by well-informed people who are familiar with the major relevant arguments.

The issue of legalization, once taboo and entertained largely by those outside the American 'mainstream', is now considered an appropriate topic of debate. Indeed, even a glance at the book will reveal many of the eminent participants in the debate. Advocates of legalization, such as William F. Buckley, Baltimore Mayor Kurt Schmoke, economist Milton Friedman, and former Secretary of State George Schultz are hardly 'eccentrics' or 'radicals'. Likewise, the opponents of legalization are obviously also serious, well-informed people. Indeed, noting the highly sophisticated participants, one cannot avoid the view that the issue of legalization is extremely complex, calling for a careful presentation of a wide variety of opinions. And that is exactly what Messrs. Evans and Berent give the reader.

Hugh Downs

The Background to the Debate

I. Making up our Minds on a Complex Issue

The drug legalization debate is not a discussion that should interest only scholars and policy-makers. It concerns all of us, since all of us are affected by the use, sale, and distribution of drugs as well as by laws governing drugs. Both the legal and illegal drug industries involve billions of dollars, and the use and regulation of drugs have profound social, political, medical, legal, and moral implications.

Thus, although this book is organized around a central theme, namely drug legalization, it covers a wide variety of opinions and points of view, touching on law, morality, history, sociology, psychology, pharmacology, and political philosophy. Readers need to appreciate that variety to understand the rich texture of the debate on drug legalization. In this debate, as in any other debate on complex, controversial topics, readers need patiently to hear out representatives of all viewpoints to discover the reasons and evidence for their positions. However intimidated some readers may feel about certain subjects, they must, in the end, come to their own conclusions, based on their assessments of the most reliable data and arguments.

Further, in this debate, as in many other debates, people in one field, for example, law, will sometimes use arguments borrowed from another field, for example, economics or psychology. Thus, readers will have to judge how well the arguments are represented and how strong they are. For, again, the readers must decide whom to believe and who has most cogently presented evidence and arguments.

This book is unlike most other anthologies on complex issues, since the essays in this book were selected for their capacity to represent the delicate shadings and nuances of the various positions, not for their capacity either to promote or to oppose a particular position. In short, the book reflects the editors' conviction that the legalization debate is *not* neatly divided into *only* two sides. For example, some people who want to relax or liberalize the drug laws favor legalizing only certain drugs, such as marijuana and cocaine, and want to retain laws against other drugs, such as PCP. Some other people who want to liberalize the drug laws favor a system under which certain drugs could be personally used and grown but not for sale or distribution. Indeed, on some issues both opponents and proponents of legalization will agree: both will often agree, for instance, on criminalizing drug sales to children. While we have tried to maintain a balance of 'pro' and 'con' essays, the readers will soon discover that one 'pro' position may, on certain points, sharply disagree with another. So also with the 'con' positions.

Readers will also soon discover a striking fact: liberalizers and their adversaries will often appeal to the same data. For example, both will appeal to the historical example of Prohibition, which will sometimes be condemned by liberalizers who will say it strengthened organized crime, but which will sometimes be praised by opponents of legalization who will say it reduced the consumption of alcohol and consequent evils, such as the incidence of cirrhosis of the liver.

II. A Historical Overview of Media Coverage

The articles in this anthology capture the beginning of an important American debate. Whatever the eventual results of the debate, most of what will follow in years, even decades, to come will evolve largely from the views originally expressed in the few years commencing in 1988.

While there have been occasional critics of U.S. drug policy in the approximately 80 years of drug prohibition, not until the 1960s were the loudest calls for legalization first heard. At that time, however, the main concern of legalizers was with marijuana. Further, the 'hippies' were largely not taken seriously.

Before 1988, calls for legalization, especially beyond the legalization of marijuana, were only seldom heard and seldom discussed in the media.

David D. Friedman called for legalization of all drugs in the April 1969 issue of *New Guard* (reprinted in his 1973 book *The Machinery of Freedom*, which appeared in an enlarged second edition in 1989). His more celebrated father, distinguished economist Milton Friedman, advocated legalization of all drugs in the May 1st, 1972, issue of *Newsweek*. Criminologist Ernest van den Haag wrote an article in the *New York Times* of August 8th, 1985, 'Legalize Those Drugs We Can't Control'. Also in 1985, Sid Bernstein, publisher of *Advertising Age*, began calling for general legalization (he repeated the plea in his August 14th, 1989, column). The December 5th, 1986, issue of the conservative *National Review* contained two articles sharply criticizing the drug war and suggesting some form of legalization. For the most part, however, the media ignored the question of legalization (which really was not yet a live issue at all, since few people gave enough credence to the question even to discuss it).

Ultimately, the event that more than anything else attracted the media and, in effect, ushered in the era of serious debate over legalization took place at the U.S. Conference of Mayors on April 25th, 1988, when Baltimore mayor Kurt Schmoke called for Congress to hold hearings on the issue, saying that the drug problem should be treated as a health concern, not a criminal justice concern. He repeated his sentiments on a May 10th broadcast of ABC's 'Nightline' and in the May 15th issue of the *Washington Post*.

In April of the previous year (1987), the Drug Policy Foundation, a reformist think-tank opposed to the war on drugs in America and other countries, had been formally begun by Dr. Arnold S. Trebach. At its meeting in London in July 1987, the Foundation, while not calling for legalization, resolved that "the war on drugs should be declared terminated, everywhere" and that "less law enforcement attention should be paid to small dealers and simple users, who should be virtually ignored by the police unless they commit other crimes . . ." Also in 1987, Nova University held a conference debating the issue of legalization, much of it later being published in the Spring 1987 issue of the *Nova Law Review*. In the August 17th issue of *Business Week*, Gary S. Becker, professor of economics and sociology at the University of Chicago, argued for legalization in his article, 'Should Drug Use be Legalized?' On

October 12th, *USA Today* carried an opinion piece by H. Schwartz, 'We Can't Win the War: Let's Make Drugs Legal'. Late in 1987, the New York County Lawyers Association Committee on Law Reform published a report advocating the decriminalization of heroin, cocaine, and marijuana.

By the beginning of 1988, William F. Buckley, the editor of the *National Review*, had changed his earlier stand against the idea of legalization, now arguing for legalization in his column of February 5th, 1988. The *Miami Herald* of February 23rd reported that the Attorney General of Colombia believed that the government "may have to consider" legalization in the future. Edwin M. Yoder Jr. criticized prohibition in the *Washington Post* (March 4th, 1988), and Richard Cohen expressed sentiments favoring legalization in the *Los Angeles Times* (March 10th, 1988). David Boaz, Vice President for Public Policy at the Cato Institute, wrote 'Let's Quit the Drug War' in the *New York Times* (March 17th, 1988). The British weekly, *The Economist*, advocated legalization in April, May, and June commentaries (April 12th, May 21st, June 4th).[1] On April 18th, New York State Senator Joseph L. Galiber, from a district in Bronx, introduced a bill in the New York State legislature "to decriminalize the possession, distribution, sale, and use of all forms of controlled substances under the aegis of a State Controlled Substance Authority."

Soon after Mayor Schmoke's call for Congressional hearings, others joined his call, including congressmen Fortney H. (Pete) Stark (California democrat, chairman of the Health Subcommittee of the House Ways and Means Committee) and Steny H. Hoyer (Maryland democrat) and mayors Donald M. Fraser (of Minneapolis) and Marion S. Barry Jr. (Washington, D.C.); only Mayor Barry favored some form of legalization.

Soon virtually all major newspapers and magazines were running articles that either debated the issue or, at least, devoted some space to

---

[1] In that same period, editorials supporting legalization were published in the *New York Times* (March 17th, 1988), the *Los Angeles Times* (April 8th), *Federal Probation* (March), and elsewhere, while editorials opposing legalization were published in the *New York Times* (April 1st), the *Washington Post* (April 16th), and elsewhere.

reporting that there was a debate taking place.[2] In addition, news shows on network TV were beginning to cover the debate (for example, 'Nightline', 'This Week with David Brinkley', 'CBS Evening News', 'Good Morning America', and others).

The British medical journal *The Lancet* discussed the legalization question in its April 30th, 1988, issue. The Spring 1988 issue of *Foreign Policy* magazine contained a detailed scholarly essay favoring legalization by Ethan A. Nadelmann.[3] The *National Catholic Reporter* of May 20th, 1988, published on its opinion page an article entitled 'Legalizing drugs might do good by eliminating evils'. An editorial in *El Pais*, the most influential Spanish newspaper, recommended 'La Legalizacion de la Droga' (May 22nd, 1988). The May 30th, 1988, issues of both *Newsweek* and *Time* featured stories on the growing debate over the question of legalization. On June 6th, 1988, although it opposed legalization, the Police Executive Research Forum, composed of law enforcement execu-tives from the nation's largest jurisdictions, endorsed the call for national debate, welcoming the debate in hopes that it "may shift attention to an old problem in need of fresh perspectives and new ideas." The British science journal, *Nature*, on June 9th, 1988, suggested that legalization

---

[2]Some of the articles and editorials supporting legalization included those in *Christian Science Monitor* (May 20th, 1988), the *Los Angeles Times* (June 22nd) and *Business Week* (June 27th).

Time (June 6th, 1988) and *Fortune* (June 20th) included articles favoring legalization of marijuana only.

Articles and editorials opposing legalization included those in the *Baltimore Sun* (April 30th, 1988), *New York Times* (May 17th), *Los Angeles Times* (May 19th), *Washington Post* (May 20th, 31st; June 11th; July 20th), *Insight* (May 30th), *Journal of the Florida Medical Association* (June), *Christian Science Monitor* (June 20th), *The New Republic* (June 27th), and the *Wall Street Journal* (July 11th).

Other magazines and newspapers covering the debate included *Jet* (May 23rd, June 6th, 1988), *St. Petersburg Times* (June 5th), *MacLean's* (June 20th), *Black Enterprise* (August), and *Science* (September 2nd).

[3]Dr. Nadelmann's *Foreign Policy* article was later reprinted or excerpted in *Annual Editions: Drugs, Society and Behavior* (1989) and the *Philadelphia Inquirer* (May 1st and 2nd, 1988). Other articles (or reprints or excerpts) by Dr. Nadelmann that promoted legalization appeared in *Public Interest* (Summer 1988), *Chicago Lawyer* (October 1988), *The New Republic* (June 13th, 1988), *Boston Globe* (October 2nd, 1988), *Dialogue* (USIA journal, March 1989), *Debate Agrario* (Peru, July/December 1989), *Princeton International Review* (Spring 1989), *Science* (September 1st, 1989), *Los Angeles Times* (September 6th, 1989; March 20th, 1990), *Washington Post* (October 8th, 1989), *Law Enforcement News* (November 30th, 1989), *U.S. Journal of Drug and Alcohol Dependence* (December 1989), *Harvard International Review* (Spring 1990), *State Legislatures* (July 1990), and other periodicals.

"could lessen the social evils of abuse". In September 1988, 'Nightline' broadcast a three-hour 'National Town Forum' with 13 panelists debating the issue.

On September 29th and 30th, the U.S. House of Representatives Select Committee on Narcotics Abuse and Control, under the chairmanship of Congressman Charles Rangel, held hearings on the question of drug legalization. The idea of legalization was evidently abhorrent to every congressman who testified except for New York Congressman James H. Scheuer. Congressman Rangel set the official tone of the hearings in his introductory remarks when he stated, "I am unalterably opposed to even the notion that we should legalize illicit drugs . . ." The hearings, carried live over public television and public radio, did, however, give advocates of various forms of legalization an opportunity to present their case. Those testifiers included Senator Galiber, Mayor Schmoke, Mayor Barry, Mayor Donald Master (Charlestown, West Virginia), Dr. Nadelmann, Dr. Trebach, Dr. Tod Mikuriya (psychiatrist at U.C. Berkeley), David Boaz, Professor William Chamblis (George Washington University), Professor Steven Wisotsky (Nova University), and Marvin Miller (NORML, the National Organization to Reform Marijuana Laws).

About the same time as the hearings, National Families In Action's *Drug Abuse Update* featured a special section, 'Arguments Against Legalization', which contained the views of 25 influential persons, each opposed to legalization, including Nancy Reagan, congressmen, professors, scientists, national and regional drug policy-makers, law enforcement officials, and others involved in drug law policy or enforcement.

As Jerelyn Eddings described it in an October 3rd, 1988, article in the *Baltimore Sun*, it seemed as though no one but Schmoke supported legalization:

> As debates go, this one is not exactly an even match-up. On the one side there's Kurt Schmoke. . . . On the other side, there [are] . . . the U.S. Congress . . . ; the executive branch of the federal government . . . ; the International Association of Chiefs of Police; the National District Attorneys' Association; Jesse Jackson; New York Mayor Ed Koch, Scotty McGregor's Athletes Against Drugs and a cast of thousands.

About the time of the hearings, Gallup polls were reporting that only about 16 percent of all adult Americans favored legalization. An ABC News poll reported that 25 percent favored legalizing marijuana, 7 percent cocaine, and 6 percent heroin.

Yet by early 1990, a *Los Angeles Times* poll reported that 30 percent of American adults favored legalizing drugs. Between the time of the hearings and 1990, other influential persons came out in support of the legalization idea, including former Secretary of State George Schultz, New York District Court Judge Robert W. Sweet, and *Harper's* magazine editor Lewis Lapham. And Milton Friedman reiterated his stand for legalization in an open letter to William Bennett in the *Wall Street Journal* of September 12th, 1989.

Some people, though not supporting legalization, were growing wary of current drug policy and therefore becoming more willing at least to consider it worthy of debate. Columnist Anthony Lewis, for example, writing in the *New York Times* (December 14th, 1989), said that, while he was opposed to legalization, he thought "the Government ought to be studying that alternative seriously instead of rejecting it with contempt as weak and unpatriotic." Similarly, *Science* magazine editor Daniel E. Koshland Jr. wrote in the September 22nd, 1989, issue that the current 'get-tough' policy of the Government should be regarded as an "experiment", and that "The experiment will be acceptable only if accompanied by a scientific detachment that says, 'The get-tough experiment is under way. If it fails, legalization is next.'" A *New York Times* article (November 27th, 1989) quoted a Miami federal customs official as saying that, although he did not support legalization, he was "appalled when members of Congress indicated it would be unthinkable to debate such a thing." Policy analyst Charles Murray, who had been edging toward legalization, suggested in *The New Republic* (May 21st, 1990) that we should "Forget about eradicating drug use everywhere" but rather establish certain drug-free zones, as in the schools, neighborhoods, and workplaces. Columnist William Raspberry went from concluding that legalization "looks less like a solution than an admission of failure" *(Washington Times,* May 14th, 1988) to concluding that proponents of legalization may be right, "but if they aren't, their proposal could end up making

America's drug problem irretrievably worse" *(Washington Post,* May 26th, 1989). Finally, in his October 9th editorial *(Washington Post),* Raspberry concluded, "He [Schmoke] hasn't persuaded me yet, but his argument is making more and more sense."

The legalization debate was becoming a topic considered at least worthy of debate and news coverage. For example, the *American Behavioral Scientist* (January-February 1989) devoted an entire issue to the debate that included six articles by opponents and supporters of legalization.[4] And in May 1989, the Cato Institute released its pro-legalization policy analysis, 'Thinking About Legalization', which was written by Buffalo attorney James Ostrowski, and which further fueled the debate.

In an early 1990 'Cato Policy Report', David Boaz submitted that "the media are slowly coming to recognize the validity of the argument", noting what he considered a subtle but significant shift: *Newsweek* had stated in May 1988 that legalization would be "a nightmare" that would create millions of new drug addicts; yet, by December 1989 *"Newsweek* had retreated to the position that 'legalization *could* become the national disaster [drug czar] Bennett predicts' (emphasis added)."

---

[4]Some of the other articles and editorials supporting legalization at that time included those in *The New Republic* (October 24th, 1988), *National Review* (October 28th, 1988; May 5th, October 13th, November 10th, 1989; February 5th, May 28th, 1990), *Humanistic Psychologist* (Autumn 1988), *New Perspectives Quarterly* (Summer 1989), *Capital University Law Review* (Summer 1989), *Wall Street Journal* (July 13th, 1989), *Los Angeles Times* (September 6th, 1989), *Newsweek* (January 1st, 1990), *Mother Jones* (February/March 1990), *US Catholic* (May 1990), and *Rolling Stone* (July 26th, 1990).

Articles and editorials opposing legalization included those in *Christianity Today* (December 9th, 1988), *FBI Law Enforcement Bulletin* (February 1989), *New York Times* (March 14th, September 26th, October 16th, 17th, 20th, 29th, December 14th, 15th, 1989), *Police Chief* (August 1989), *U.S. News and World Report* (September 11th, November 13th, 1989), *Wall Street Journal* (October 6th, 1989), *Los Angeles Times* (December 12th, 1989), *Washington Post* (December 15th, 1989), *Washington Times* (December 15th, 1989), *Journal of the National Medical Association* (January 1990), *Commentary* (February 1990), and *Reader's Digest* (March 1990).

Other magazines and newspapers covering the debate included *Mademoiselle* (November 1988), *Glamour* (January 1989), *Playboy* (February 1989), *Challenge* (March/April 1989), *Omni* (April 1989), *Journal of the American Medical Association* (April 28th, 1989), *New York Times* (May 15th, November 27th, 1989), *Human Rights* (Spring 1989), *Washington Post* (June 4th, August 31st, 1989), *Barron's* (June 26th, 1989), *Ebony* (August 1989), *Financial World* (October 3rd, 1989), *Economist* (November 18th, 1989), *Los Angeles Times* (November 20th, 1989), *USA Today* (December 15th, 1989), *New York Daily News* (December 17th, 1989), *Washington Journalism Review* (January/February 1990), *U.S. News and World Report* (January 22nd, April 9th, 1990), *British Journal of Addiction* (January 1990), *Security Management* (February 1990), and *Issues in Science and Technology* (Summer 1990).

III. Our Selection of Articles

Out of the hundreds of pieces written from 1988 to 1990, we have selected for this anthology those articles written by people who are generally knowledgeable in fields pertinent to the current debate, such as law, law enforcement, psychology, political science, history, psychiatry, pharmacology, economics, and philosophy. We have been careful to avoid using articles whose authors do not offer adequate evidence for their assertions, such as numerous dogmatic op-ed columns containing personal attacks.

In addition, we have made sure to include several articles written by people who have led this debate, especially Congressman Charles Rangel, former 'Drug Czar' William Bennett, Baltimore mayor Kurt Schmoke, and Nobel Prize-winning economist Milton Friedman. We have also taken from the unprecedented 1988 Congressional hearings on legalization the testimony of psychiatrist David F. Musto (an opponent of legalization) and the testimony of professor Steven Wisotsky (an advocate of legalization).

IV. An Aid in Forming Your Own Conclusions

As editors of this anthology, we have not attempted to favor either the pro-legalization argument or the anti-legalization argument. We do believe, however, that the debate is a worthy one, and it will require making difficult moral, economic, political, and medical decisions.

Some questions the reader will need to consider are questions of moral and political values, such as 'Where does an individual's right to autonomy end and the state's right to regulate conduct begin?' Other questions are straightforwardly scientific, though perhaps difficult to answer: 'What would be the likely medical and social consequences of legalizing or decriminalizing certain drugs?'

Whether moral, political, or economic, the questions pertinent to legalization require clarity of thought and reliable data. We hope that this anthology will help thousands of individuals to grasp the significant issues in the debate and thereby to form their own opinions in an enlightened, responsible, and rational manner.

1

QUESTIONS TO
CONSIDER

INTRODUCTION

We begin this anthology with an article written shortly before the House Select Committee on Narcotics Abuse and Control held its hearings on the question of legalization. The article, written by the Committee's chairman, Charles Rangel, was originally intended, in part, to establish some ground rules for the hearings. For Rangel presented what he considered the questions that must be answered before rationally discussing whether to legalize drugs.

While there are many questions you will do well to ask yourself as you read this anthology, Mr. Rangel's list is, we believe, a good place to start. We are not suggesting that answering those questions will necessarily lead to dismissing the legalization argument (Mr. Rangel's claim). Rather, we believe that keeping these kinds of questions in mind will help you make rational decisions about drug policy, *whatever* those decisions may be.

Legalizing Drugs:
A Dangerous Idea

Charles B. Rangel

Congressman Charles Rangel (Democrat, 16th District, New York City) argues against legalization by presenting a series of questions that, when honestly and knowledgeably answered, might, he submits, "put to rest once and for all" the "very dangerous idea of legalization."

Mr. Rangel strongly believes that serious attempts to answer those questions should lead advocates of legalization to rethink their position.

On the surface, the call by Baltimore Mayor Kurt Schmoke (May 15th) and others for a national debate on decriminalizing illicit narcotics seems reasonable. Schmoke is clearly right that more narcotics entering the United States are generating more addicts and more crime.

The answer, however, is not surrender before we have even fought the war. When we consider that the administration has no one in charge, full-time, of the Number One problem facing the nation, and that the person the president has placed in charge, Attorney General Edwin Meese, is obviously concerned with other personal as well as substantive issues, the lack of seriousness of the national effort to date is obvious. Top administration officials, including Office of Management and Budget Director James Miller and Secretary of Education William Bennett, have testified that drug use, drug-related crime and school-based prevention are "state and local" problems, not national issues. To me, this is absurd, considering that practically not one ounce of cocaine or heroin is grown

'Legalizing Drugs: A "Dangerous Idea"' by Charles B. Rangel (*Washington Post*, June 11th, 1988). Used by permission.

in any community in the United States. We clearly have a national and international crisis mandating a federal commitment.

To be given serious consideration, the advocates of a "debate" on legalization or decriminalization of drugs would have to bring some answers to the table. I would ask the following questions:

1. Which narcotic and psychotropic drugs should be legalized? On what criteria should this decision be based?

2. Should narcotic and psychotropic drugs be made available to anyone who wishes to try them—or just to people already dependent on them?

3. Would an unlimited supply of drugs be made available to habitual users or addicts? Or would they have to pay the market price, even for drugs for which an increasing tolerance would require the purchase of ever larger quantities? Could those who were heavily dependent or addicted work or even hold a job? Or would they resort to crime to support their legal habit and to provide livelihoods for themselves and their dependents?

4. Who would provide drugs? Private companies? The government? Would they be provided at cost or for a profit—or be subject to a tax? If taxed, what would be a fair rate?

5. Where would these drugs be made available? Pharmacies? Supermarkets? Special shops? Dispensaries? Clinics?

6. Would use of legalized drugs by employees in certain occupations be prohibited? Since marijuana can remain in the body for weeks after use, would marijuana use by employees in jobs in which security and safety are at issue be forbidden even off duty? What about airline pilots, surgeons, police, firefighters, military personnel, railroad engineers, bus drivers, cross-country truckers, nuclear reactor operators—even Wall Street brokers and teachers?

7. What rate of addiction and dependency would one project if drugs were legalized and thereby made cheaper and more readily available? Wouldn't cheap and readily available legal drugs result in more people using more drugs? What would one project the accidental drug-related death rate to be?

8. What is the opinion of medical experts as to the potential effects of legalization? And of drug-treatment experts?

9. Would legalization affect medical insurance rates and the overall cost of health care?

10. Would we be adding to the spread of AIDS by having more addicts using more needles?

It just may be that when these questions are answered, the very dangerous idea of legalization of drugs will be put to rest once and for all. Then I hope we can get on with the battle with a true federal commitment to confronting our greatest crisis.

2

INTRODUCTORY
ARGUMENTS

INTRODUCTION

Two excellent summaries of the arguments for legalization and the arguments against legalization are those of Ethan A. Nadelmann and James Q. Wilson, respectively.

The Case for Legalization

Ethan A. Nadelmann

While granting that legalization will increase the use and misuse of drugs, social scientist Dr. Ethan A. Nadelmann argues that there are compelling reasons for taking those risks. He argues that the present policy in which people seek to interdict drugs and apprehend smugglers is a failure: "we can safely assume that there will never be a shortage of producers and smugglers."

Dr. Nadelmann argues that, while drug arrests have "swamped court dockets", those arrested represent fewer than 2 percent of the 35 to 40 million Americans estimated to consume illegal drugs. He further submits that, while currently between $10 and $50 billion per year goes to members of organized crime, much of that money could be used for a large tax base if drugs were legal.

*Nadelmann is most disturbed by "the moral cost of drug prohibition." In essence, he argues that "overzealous law enforcement" threatens to create a society of informers. By labeling 40 million Americans who illegally consume drugs as criminals, the current drug policy "m*kes a mockery of an essential principle of a free society: that those who do no harm to others should not be harmed by others, particularly the state."*

He argues that because drugs are illegal, the underground market is exceptionally profitable—in fact, so profitable that law-abiding residents of urban ghettos must often fear gunfire from dealers protecting their turfs, the glamorization of wealthy drug dealers, and the recruitment of juveniles into the drug trade.

'Drugs: The Case For Legalization' by Ethan A. Nadelmann (*Washington Post*, October 8th, 1989). Used by permission. This article is based on 'Drug Prohibition in the United States: Costs, Consequences, and Alternatives', *Science*, vol. 245 (September 1989), pp. 939–947, which gives the argument more fully, with more detail and documentation.

Ethan A. Nadelmann

Dr. Nadelmann suggests that the sale of currently illegal drugs be treated in the way that alcohol and tobacco are treated. He proposes, for example, that those drugs be taxed, that they be subject to restrictions on time and place of sale and consumption, that their use be subject to insurance adjustments, and that their use among drivers be seriously punished.

He believes that, while legalization is risky, most Americans will not seriously misuse drugs and that the minority of people who will misuse them need treatment and education but not punishment.

The nation has now committed itself to a prolonged and costly 'war on drugs', the outcome of which is far from certain, without giving fair consideration to a radical but promising alternative: controlled legalization or decriminalization of drugs. But unless law-enforcement efforts prove dramatically more successful than they have in the past, legalization may soon be recognized as a highly attractive policy option.

Even with strict controls, legalization would almost certainly increase the availability of drugs, decrease their price and remove the deterrent power of the criminal sanction—all of which may well invite increased use and abuse. There are compelling reasons, however, why these risks are worth taking: Drug-control strategies that rely primarily on criminal-justice measures are significantly and inherently limited. Many are increasingly costly and highly counterproductive. And legalization may well be far less hazardous than most people assume.

Few law-enforcement officials any longer contend that their efforts can do much more to reduce drug abuse in the United States. International action to discourage drug exports and attempts at interdiction have met with scant success and show few indications of succeeding in the future. Marijuana and opium can be grown in a wide variety of locales; and coca grows in practically any subtropical region with suitable rainfall, temperature range and drainage. Even where eradication efforts prove relatively successful in one country, others stand ready to emerge as new producers, as has occurred with both the international marijuana and heroin markets during the past two decades.

Moreover, the foreign export price is such a tiny fraction of the retail

20

price in the United States (approximately 4 percent with cocaine, 1 percent with marijuana, and much less than 1 percent with heroin) that international control efforts have failed even to raise the cost of illicit drugs to U.S. consumers. During the past decade, the U.S. wholesale price of cocaine has dropped by 80 percent even as the retail purity has quintupled from 12 to about 60 percent. Coast Guard and Customs Service officials concede that they will never seize more than a small percentage of total shipments. The financial incentives are so great, and drugs such a large source of income and employment to undeveloped countries, that we can safely assume that there will never be a shortage of producers and smugglers.

The High Price of Failure

On the domestic front, criminalization of the drug market has proven as counterproductive as did Prohibition 60 years ago—at costs that are becoming insupportable.

Between 1981 and 1987, federal expenditures on anti-drug law enforcement more than tripled, from less than $1 billion per year to about $3 billion. Next year, they will total close to $6 billion. In addition, state and local governments spent some $5 billion in 1986 alone. Drug cases currently account for more than one-third of the 50,000 federal prison inmates, and a significant proportion of the approximately 300,000 in municipal jails. Nationwide, drug offenses accounted for 135,000 (23 percent) of the 583,000 felony convictions in state courts in 1986. State and local agencies laid out at least $2 billion last year to incarcerate drug offenders. The expense of housing this growing population is rising at an astronomical rate. Other costs—alternative social expenditures foregone, non-drug criminals not imprisoned—are perhaps even more severe.

All this effort, however, has had little impact on either drug dealers or the general public. Police now make about 750,000 arrests per year for violations of the drug laws. But over three-quarters of these have been solely for possession, typically of marijuana. Those arrested represent less than 2 percent of the 35 to 40 million Americans estimated to consume illegal drugs. The arrest deluge has swamped court dockets: In Washington, drug-law violations accounted for some 52 percent of all felony indictments in 1986, up from 13 percent in 1981.

Ironically, the greatest beneficiaries of drug laws are traffickers. The criminalization of the drug market effectively imposes a de facto value-added tax paid to dealers. More than half of all organized crime revenues are believed to derive from the illicit drug business; estimates of the dollar value range between $10 and $50 billion per year. If those markets were legal, state and federal governments would collect billions of dollars annually in tax revenues. Instead, they expend billions in a virtual subsidy of organized criminals.

Legalization would slash those costs as well as reduce the number of crimes committed to buy drugs at artificially high prices. Despite its many limitations, our current methadone maintenance system represents a form of quasi-legalization that has proven effective in reducing the criminal behavior and improving the lives of thousands of addicts.

The commission of violent and other crimes by people under the influence of illicit drugs obsesses the popular imagination. Clearly, certain drugs do 'cause' some people to commit crimes by reducing normal inhibitions, unleashing aggressive and other antisocial tendencies; and cocaine may be somewhat more incitatory than marijuana and heroin, although evidence has yet to substantiate media depictions. But in fact, as during Prohibition, most drug-related violence stems from disputes among dealers or shoot-outs with police. Furthermore, no drug is as strongly associated with violent behavior as is alcohol. According to Justice Department statistics, 54 percent of all jail inmates convicted of violent crimes in 1983 reported having used alcohol just prior to committing their offense. Numerous studies confirm this relationship.

There is also the health cost of unregulated drug production and sale. Many marijuana smokers are worse off for having smoked cannabis that was grown with dangerous fertilizers, sprayed with paraquat or mixed with more dangerous substances. Consumers of heroin and cocaine face fatal overdoses and poisonings from unexpectedly potent or impure drug supplies. Drug enforcement operations that succeed in temporarily disrupting supply networks are thus a double-edged sword: They encourage some addicts to seek treatment, but they oblige others to search out new and less reliable suppliers, resulting in more drug-related emergencies and deaths. In addition, about 25 percent of all AIDS cases here and in Europe, as well as the large majority of human immunodeficiency virus (HIV)-infected heterosexuals, children and infants, are believed to have contracted the disease from illegal intravenous drug use.

Finally, and most disturbing, is the moral cost of drug prohibition. Overzealous law enforcement puts our democratic ethic of tolerance at risk and threatens to create a society of informers. Directing criminal sanctions at the nearly 40 million Americans who illegally consume drugs every year—the vast majority of whom injure no one but themselves in doing so—makes a mockery of an essential principle of a free society: that those who do no harm to others should not be harmed by others, particularly the state. This may be the greatest societal cost of our current drug prohibition system.

So far, those paying the highest price in all the above categories have been the law-abiding residents of urban ghettos, whose streets are prey to gunfire and whose children often perceive dealers as heros and role models. At the same time, increasingly harsh criminal penalties imposed on adult drug dealers have led to the widespread recruiting of juveniles.

Risks and Rewards

Repeal of drug prohibition laws clearly promises tremendous advantages. Between reduced government expenditures and new tax revenue from legal production and sales, public treasuries would enjoy a net benefit of at least $10 billion per year and possibly much more; thus billions in new revenues would be available for much-needed drug-treatment, educational and job-training programs. The quality of urban life would rise, the rate of homicide and other crimes would decline, and U.S. foreign policy would be freed to pursue more realistic goals.

All these benefits, however, would be for naught if millions more people were to become drug abusers. Our experience with legal drugs provides ample warning. Alcohol is consumed by 140 million Americans and tobacco by 50 million. In 1986, alcohol was a contributing factor in 10 percent of work-related injuries and 40 percent of both suicide attempts and traffic fatalities. As many as 18 million Americans are

23

reported to be alcoholics or alcohol abusers, and they cost society some $100 billion annually. Estimates of the number of deaths linked to alcohol use vary from 50,000 to 200,000 per year; tobacco is responsible for an estimated 320,000 premature deaths per year in the United States alone.

By comparison, the National Council on Alcoholism reported that only 3,562 people were known to have died in 1985 from use of all illegal drugs combined. Even if we assume that thousands more such deaths went unreported, it is still clear that the combined health costs of marijuana, cocaine and heroin amount to only a tiny fraction of those caused by alcohol or tobacco.

Demand-Side Dangers

But if drugs were decriminalized, would they become as popular as alcohol? And how much damage would result? The logic of legalization depends in part upon two assumptions: that most illegal drugs are not as dangerous as is commonly believed, and that the most risky of them are unlikely to prove widely appealing precisely because of the obvious danger. Consider marijuana. Among the roughly 60 million Americans who have smoked it, not one has died from an overdose (a striking contrast with alcohol, which is involved in some 10,000 overdose deaths annually, half in combination with other drugs). Although there are good health reasons for people not to smoke marijuana daily, and for children, pregnant women and some others not to smoke at all, there still appears to be little evidence that occasional marijuana consumption does much harm. It is not notably addictive, and in fact recent research suggests that heavy marijuana use is typically a phase through which most users pass.

Cocaine, heroin and other illicit substances are more hazardous, but not nearly so dangerous as generally believed. For example, heroin—which may be as highly addictive as nicotine—causes relatively little physical harm. Consumed on an occasional or regular basis under sanitary conditions, its worst side effect, apart from addiction, is constipation. As for cocaine, NIDA reported in 1986 that over 20 million Americans had tried it, that 12.2 million had consumed it at least once during 1985 and that nearly 5.8 million had used it within the past month. Among 18- to 25-year-olds, 8.2 million had tried cocaine, 5.3 million had used it within the past year, 2.5 million had used it within the past month; and 250,000 had used it on the average weekly. One could extrapolate from these figures that a quarter of a million young Americans are potential problem users. But one could also conclude that only 3 percent of those 18- to 25-year-olds who had ever tried the drug fell into that category, and that only 10 percent of monthly users were at risk.

All of this is not to say that cocaine is not a potentially dangerous drug. Many tens of thousands of Americans have suffered severely from it, and a tiny fraction have died. But there is overwhelming evidence that most users of cocaine do not get into trouble with the drug. In one survey of high school seniors' drug use, respondents were asked whether they had ever tried to stop using cocaine and found they couldn't. Only 3.8 percent responded affirmatively, in contrast to almost 7 percent of marijuana smokers and 18 percent of cigarette smokers.

Much of the damage caused by illegal drugs today stems from their consumption in particularly potent and dangerous ways. There is good reason to doubt that many Americans would inject heroin or cocaine into their veins even if given the legal opportunity. And just as the dramatic growth in the heroin-consuming population during the '60s leveled off for reasons apparently having little to do with law enforcement, we can expect (if it has not occurred already) a similar plateau in crack-smoking.

Perhaps the most reassuring aspect of legalization is what we have learned from our experience with alcohol and tobacco. We now know that consumption taxes are effective in limiting use. So, it seems, are advertising regulations, restrictions on time and place of sale and consumption, prohibitions of use in public places, packaging require-ments, mandated adjustments in insurance policies, crackdowns on driving while under the influence, and laws holding bartenders and hosts responsible for the drinking of customers and guests. Finally, Americans are switching from hard liquor to beer and wine, from high tar-and-nicotine cigarettes to lower levels and even from caffeinated to decaffein-ated beverages. Legalization might produce a similar trend in drug use.

There is no question that legalization is risky. But risk is not certainty. One thing, however, is certain: Current drug-control policies have produced little progress and have proven highly counterproductive. The administration's 'war on drugs' promises only to be more costly and more repressive. Unless we are willing to honestly evaluate all our options, we may never find the best solutions.

Against the Legalization of Drugs

James Q. Wilson

Dr. James Q. Wilson, Collins Professor of Management and Public Policy at UCLA, argues against legalization. Wilson maintains, by appeal to history, that the easier illegal drugs are to obtain, the more widespread is their use. According to his analysis, most Vietnam veterans who regularly used heroin in Southeast Asia gave up the habit in the United States because heroin here is less available and sanctions against its use are more pronounced. He accordingly submits that the worst thing the United States government could do would be to legalize all currently illegal drugs, markedly reducing their price and increasing their availability and use.

Dr. Wilson submits that, while the social costs of criminalization may be high, the social costs of legalization might be higher, especially if there were a great increase in the number of addicts. According to him, legalizing drugs would very likely remove the stigma attached to habits that are damaging to not only physical health but also moral personality. Accordingly, he writes: "Tobacco shortens one's life, cocaine debases it. Nicotine alters one's habits, cocaine alters one's soul."

He argues that legalization would be an extremely risky social experiment whose potential negative consequences might be difficult to reverse, the power of addiction being so great: "there is no way to put the genie back in the bottle, and it is not a kindly genie."

He reasons that the consequences of continuing on our current path of prohibition are, at worst, "heavy costs in law enforcement and some forms of

'Against the Legalization of Drugs' by James Q. Wilson (*Commentary*, February 1990, pp. 21–28). Reprinted by permission.

criminality," while the worst consequences of legalization are quite unacceptable: that millions of additional people may have their lives degraded or destroyed.

In 1972, the President appointed me chairman of the National Advisory Council for Drug Abuse Prevention. Created by Congress, the Council was charged with providing guidance on how best to co-ordinate the national war on drugs. (Yes, we called it a war then, too.) In those days, the drug we were chiefly concerned with was heroin. When I took office, heroin use had been increasing dramatically. Everybody was worried that this increase would continue. Such phrases as "heroin epidemic" were commonplace.

That same year, the eminent economist Milton Friedman published an essay in *Newsweek* in which he called for legalizing heroin. His argument was on two grounds: as a matter of ethics, the government has no right to tell people not to use heroin (or to drink or to commit suicide); as a matter of economics, the prohibition of drug use imposes costs on society that far exceed the benefits. Others, such as the psychoanalyst Thomas Szasz, made the same argument.

We did not take Friedman's advice. (Government commissions rarely do.) I do not recall that we even discussed legalizing heroin, though we did discuss (but did not take action on) legalizing a drug, cocaine, that many people then argued was benign. Our marching orders were to figure out how to win the war on heroin, not to run up the white flag of surrender.

That was 1972. Today, we have the same number of heroin addicts that we had then—half a million, give or take a few thousand. Having that many heroin addicts is no trivial matter; these people deserve our attention. But not having had an increase in that number for over 15 years is also something that deserves our attention. What happened to the 'heroin epidemic' that many people once thought would overwhelm us?

The facts are clear: a more or less stable pool of heroin addicts has been getting older, with relatively few new recruits. In 1976 the average age of heroin users who appeared in hospital emergency rooms was about 27; ten years later it was 32. More than two-thirds of all heroin users appearing in emergency rooms are now over the age of 30. Back in the early 1970s, when heroin got onto the national political agenda, the typical heroin addict was much younger, often a teenager. Household surveys show the same thing—the rate of opiate use (which includes heroin) has been flat for the better part of two decades. More fine-grained studies of inner-city neighborhoods confirm this. John Boyle and Ann Brunswick found that the percentage of young blacks in Harlem who used heroin fell from 8 percent in 1970–71 to about 3 percent in 1975–76.

Why did heroin lose its appeal for young people? When the young blacks in Harlem were asked why they stopped, more than half mentioned "trouble with the law" or "high cost" (and high cost is, of course, directly the result of law enforcement). Two-thirds said that heroin hurt their health; nearly all said they had had a bad experience with it. We need not rely, however, simply on what they said. In New York City in 1973–75, the street price of heroin rose dramatically and its purity sharply declined, probably as a result of the heroin shortage caused by the success of the Turkish government in reducing the supply of opium base and of the French government in closing down heroin-processing laboratories located in and around Marseilles. These were short-lived gains for, just as Friedman had predicted, alternative sources of supply—mostly in Mexico—quickly emerged. But the three-year heroin shortage interrupted the easy recruitment of new users.

Health and related problems were no doubt part of the reason for the reduced flow of recruits. Over the preceding years, Harlem youth had watched as more and more heroin users died of overdoses, were poisoned by adulterated doses, or acquired hepatitis from dirty needles. The word got around: heroin can kill you. By 1974 new hepatitis cases and drug-overdose deaths had dropped to a fraction of what they had been in 1970.

Alas, treatment did not seem to explain much of the cessation in drug use. Treatment programs can and do help heroin addicts, but treatment did not explain the drop in the number of *new* users (who by definition had never been in treatment) nor even much of the reduction in the number of experienced users.

No one knows how much of the decline to attribute to personal observation as opposed to high prices or reduced supply. But other evidence suggests strongly that price and supply played a large role. In 1972 the National Advisory Council was especially worried by the prospect that U.S. servicemen returning to this country from Vietnam would bring their heroin habits with them. Fortunately, a brilliant study by Lee Robins of Washington University in St. Louis put that fear to rest. She measured drug use of Vietnam veterans shortly after they had returned home. Though many had used heroin regularly while in Southeast Asia, most gave up the habit when back in the United States. The reason: here, heroin was less available and sanctions on its use were more pronounced. Of course, if a veteran had been willing to pay enough—which might have meant traveling to another city and would certainly have meant making an illegal contact with a disreputable dealer in a threatening neighborhood in order to acquire a (possibly) dangerous dose—he could have sustained his drug habit. Most veterans were unwilling to pay this price, and so their drug use declined or disappeared.

Reliving the Past

Suppose we had taken Friedman's advice in 1972. What would have happened? We cannot be entirely certain, but at a minimum we would have placed the young heroin addicts (and, above all, the prospective addicts) in a very different position from the one in which they actually found themselves. Heroin would have been legal. Its price would have been reduced by 95 percent (minus whatever we chose to recover in taxes). Now that it could be sold by the same people who make aspirin, its quality would have been assured—no poisons, no adulterants. Sterile hypodermic needles would have been readily available at the neighborhood drugstore, probably at the same counter where the heroin was sold. No need to travel to big cities or unfamiliar neighborhoods—heroin could have been purchased anywhere, perhaps by mail order.

There would no longer have been any financial or medical reason to avoid heroin use. Anybody could have afforded it. We might have tried to prevent children from buying it, but as we have learned from our efforts to prevent minors from buying alcohol and tobacco, young people have a way of penetrating markets theoretically reserved for adults. Returning

Vietnam veterans would have discovered that Omaha and Raleigh had been converted into the pharmaceutical equivalent of Saigon.

Under these circumstances, can we doubt for a moment that heroin use would have grown exponentially? Or that a vastly larger supply of new users would have been recruited? Professor Friedman is a Nobel Prize-winning economist whose understanding of market forces is profound. What did he think would happen to consumption under his legalized regime? Here are his words: "Legalizing drugs might increase the number of addicts, but it is not clear that it would. Forbidden fruit is attractive, particularly to the young."

Really? I suppose that we should expect no increase in Porsche sales if we cut the price by 95 percent, no increase in whiskey sales if we cut the price by a comparable amount—because young people only want fast cars and strong liquor when they are "forbidden". Perhaps Friedman's uncharacteristic lapse from the obvious implications of price theory can be explained by a misunderstanding of how drug users are recruited. In his 1972 essay he said that "drug addicts are deliberately made by pushers, who give likely prospects their first few doses free." If drugs were legal it would not pay anybody to produce addicts, because everybody would buy from the cheapest source. But as every drug expert knows, pushers do not produce addicts. Friends or acquaintances do. In fact, pushers are usually reluctant to deal with non-users because a non-user could be an undercover cop. Drug use spreads in the same way that any fad or fashion spreads: somebody who is already a user urges his friends to try, or simply shows already-eager friends how to do it.

But we need not rely on speculation, however plausible, that lowered prices and more abundant supplies would have increased heroin usage. Great Britain once followed such a policy and with almost exactly those results. Until the mid-1960s, British physicians were allowed to prescribe heroin to certain classes of addicts. (Possessing these drugs without a doctor's prescription remained a criminal offense.) For many years this policy worked well enough because the addict patients were typically middle-class people who had become dependent on opiate painkillers while undergoing hospital treatment. There was no drug culture. The British system worked for many years, not because it prevented drug abuse, but because there was no problem of drug abuse that would test the system.

All that changed in the 1960s. A few unscrupulous doctors began passing out heroin in wholesale amounts. One doctor prescribed almost 600,000 heroin tablets—that is, over 13 pounds—in just one year. A youthful drug culture emerged with a demand for drugs far different from that of the older addicts. As a result, the British government required doctors to refer users to government-run clinics to receive their heroin.

But the shift to clinics did not curtail the growth in heroin use. Throughout the 1960s the number of addicts increased—the late John Kaplan of Stanford estimated by fivefold—in part as a result of the diversion of heroin from clinic patients to new users on the streets. An addict would bargain with the clinic doctor over how big a dose he would receive. The patient wanted as much as he could get, the doctor wanted to give as little as was needed. The patient had an advantage in this conflict because the doctor could not be certain how much was really needed. Many patients would use some of their 'maintenance' dose and sell the remaining part to friends, thereby recruiting new addicts. As the clinics learned of this, they began to shift their treatment away from heroin and toward methadone, an addictive drug that, when taken orally, does not produce a 'high' but will block the withdrawal pains associated with heroin abstinence.

Whether what happened in England in the 1960s was a mini-epidemic or an epidemic depends on whether one looks at numbers or at rates of change. Compared to the United States, the numbers were small. In 1960 there were 68 heroin addicts known to the British government; by 1968 there were 2,000 in treatment and many more who refused treatment. (They would refuse in part because they did not want to get methadone at a clinic if they could get heroin on the street.) Richard Hartnoll estimates that the actual number of addicts in England is five times the number officially registered. At a minimum, the number of British addicts increased thirtyfold in ten years; the actual increase may have been much larger.

In the early 1980s the numbers began to rise again, and this time nobody doubted that a real epidemic was at hand. The increase was estimated to be 40 percent a year. By 1982 there were thought to be

20,000 heroin users in London alone. Geoffrey Pearson reports that many cities—Glasgow, Liverpool, Manchester, and Sheffield among them—were now experiencing a drug problem that once had been largely confined to London. The problem, again, was supply. The country was being flooded with cheap, high-quality heroin, first from Iran and then from Southeast Asia.

The United States began the 1960s with a much larger number of heroin addicts and probably a bigger at-risk population than was the case in Great Britain. Even though it would be foolhardy to suppose that the British system, if installed here, would have worked the same way or with the same results, it would be equally foolhardy to suppose that a combination of heroin available from leaky clinics and from street dealers who faced only minimal law-enforcement risks would not have produced a much greater increase in heroin use than we actually experienced. My guess is that if we had allowed either doctors or clinics to prescribe heroin, we would have had far worse results than were produced in Britain, if for no other reason than the vastly larger number of addicts with which we began. We would have had to find some way to police thousands (not scores) of physicians and hundreds (not dozens) of clinics. If the British civil service found it difficult to keep heroin in the hands of addicts and out of the hands of recruits when it was dealing with a few hundred people, how well would the American civil service have accomplished the same tasks when dealing with tens of thousands of people?

Back to the Future

Now cocaine, especially in its potent form, crack, is the focus of attention. Now as in 1972 the government is trying to reduce its use. Now as then some people are advocating legalization. Is there any more reason to yield to those arguments today than there was almost two decades ago?[1]

I think not. If we had yielded in 1972 we almost certainly would have

---

[1] I do not here take up the question of marijuana. For a variety of reasons—its widespread use and its lesser tendency to addict—it presents a different problem from cocaine or heroin. For a penetrating analysis, see Mark Kleiman, *Marijuana: Costs of Abuse, Costs of Control* (Greenwood Press, 217 pp.).

had today a permanent population of several million, not several hundred thousand, heroin addicts. If we yield now we will have a far more serious problem with cocaine.

Crack is worse than heroin by almost any measure. Heroin produces a pleasant drowsiness and, if hygienically administered, has only the physical side effects of constipation and sexual impotence. Regular heroin use incapacitates many users, especially poor ones, for any productive work or social responsibility. They will sit nodding on a street corner, helpless but at least harmless. By contrast, regular cocaine use leaves the user neither helpless nor harmless. When smoked (as with crack) or injected, cocaine produces instant, intense, and short-lived euphoria. The experience generates a powerful desire to repeat it. If the drug is readily available, repeat use will occur. Those people who progress to "bingeing" on cocaine become devoted to the drug and its effects to the exclusion of almost all other considerations—job, family, children, sleep, food, even sex. Dr. Frank Gawin at Yale and Dr. Everett Ellinwood at Duke report that a substantial percentage of all high-dose, binge users become uninhibited, impulsive, hypersexual, compulsive, irritable, and hyperactive. Their moods vacillate dramatically, leading at times to violence and homicide.

Women are much more likely to use crack than heroin, and if they are pregnant, the effects on their babies are tragic. Douglas Besharov, who has been following the effects of drugs on infants for twenty years, writes that nothing he learned about heroin prepared him for the devastation of cocaine. Cocaine harms the fetus and can lead to physical deformities or neurological damage. Some crack babies have for all practical purposes suffered a disabling stroke while still in the womb. The long-term consequences of this brain damage are lowered cognitive ability and the onset of mood disorders. Besharov estimates that about 30,000 to 50,000 such babies are born every year, about 7,000 in New York City alone. There may be ways to treat such infants, but from everything we now know the treatment will be long, difficult, and expensive. Worse, the mothers who are most likely to produce crack babies are precisely the ones who, because of poverty or temperament, are least able and willing to obtain such treatment. In fact, anecdotal evidence suggests that crack mothers are likely to abuse their infants.

The notion that abusing drugs such as cocaine is a 'victimless crime' is not only absurd but dangerous. Even ignoring the fetal drug syndrome, crack-dependent people are, like heroin addicts, individuals who regularly victimize their children by neglect, their spouses by improvidence, their employers by lethargy, and their co-workers by carelessness. Society is not and could never be a collection of autonomous individuals. We all have a stake in ensuring that each of us displays a minimal level of dignity, responsibility, and empathy. We cannot, of course, coerce people into goodness, but we can and should insist that some standards must be met if society itself—on which the very existence of the human personality depends—is to persist. Drawing the line that defines those standards is difficult and contentious, but if crack and heroin use do not fall below it, what does?

The advocates of legalization will respond by suggesting that my picture is overdrawn. Ethan Nadelmann of Princeton argues that the risk of legalization is less than most people suppose. Over 20 million Americans between the ages of 18 and 25 have tried cocaine (according to a government survey), but only a quarter of a million use it daily. From this Nadelmann concludes that at most 3 percent of all young people who try cocaine develop a problem with it. The implication is clear: make the drug legal and we only have to worry about 3 percent of our youth.

The implication rests on a logical fallacy and a factual error. The fallacy is this: the percentage of occasional cocaine users who become binge users *when the drug is illegal* (and thus expensive and hard to find) tells us nothing about the percentage who will become dependent when the drug is legal (and thus cheap and abundant). Drs. Gawin and Ellinwood report, in common with several other researchers, that controlled or occasional use of cocaine changes to compulsive and frequent use "when access to the drug increases" or when the user switches from snorting to smoking. More cocaine more potently administered alters, perhaps sharply, the proportion of "controlled" users who become heavy users.

The factual error is this: the federal survey Nadelmann quotes was done in 1985, *before* crack had become common. Thus the probability of becoming dependent on cocaine was derived from the responses of users who snorted the drug. The speed and potency of cocaine's action increases dramatically when it is smoked. We do not yet know how greatly the advent of crack increases the risk of dependency, but all the clinical evidence suggests that the increase is likely to be large.

It is possible that some people will not become heavy users even when the drug is readily available in its most potent form. So far there are no scientific grounds for predicting who will and who will not become dependent. Neither socio-economic background nor personality traits differentiate between casual and intensive users. Thus, the only way to settle the question of who is correct about the effect of easy availability on drug use, Nadelmann or Gawin and Ellinwood, is to try it and see. But that social experiment is so risky as to be no experiment at all, for if cocaine is legalized and if the rate of its abusive use increases dramatically, there is no way to put the genie back in the bottle, and it is not a kindly genie.

Have We Lost?

Many people who agree that there are risks in legalizing cocaine or heroin still favor it because, they think, we have lost the war on drugs. 'Nothing we have done has worked' and the current federal policy is just 'more of the same.' Whatever the costs of greater drug use, surely they would be less than the costs of our present, failed efforts.

That is exactly what I was told in 1972—and heroin is not quite as bad a drug as cocaine. We did not surrender and we did not lose. We did not win, either. What the nation accomplished then was what most efforts to save people from themselves accomplish: the problem was contained and the number of victims minimized, all at a considerable cost in law enforcement and increased crime. Was the cost worth it? I think so, but others may disagree. What are the lives of would-be addicts worth? I recall some people saying to me then, "Let them kill themselves." I was appalled. Happily, such views did not prevail.

Have we lost today? Not at all. High-rate cocaine use is not commonplace. The National Institute on Drug Abuse (NIDA) reports that less than 5 percent of high-school seniors had used cocaine within the last 30 days. Of course this survey misses young people who have dropped out of school and miscounts those who lie on the questionnaire, but even if we inflate the NIDA estimate by some plausible percentage, it is still not much above 5 percent. Medical examiners reported in 1987 that about 1,500 died from cocaine use; hospital emergency rooms reported about 30,000 admissions related to cocaine abuse.

These are not small numbers, but neither are they evidence of a nationwide plague that threatens to engulf us all. Moreover, cities vary greatly in the proportion of people who are involved with cocaine. To get city-level data we need to turn to drug tests carried out on arrested persons, who obviously are more likely to be drug users than the average citizen. The National Institute of Justice, through its Drug Use Forecasting (DUF) project, collects urinalysis data on arrestees in 22 cities. As we have already seen, opiate (chiefly heroin) use has been flat or declining in most of these cities over the last decade. Cocaine use has gone up sharply, but with great variation among cities. New York, Philadelphia, and Washington, D.C., all report that two-thirds or more of their arrestees tested positive for cocaine, but in Portland, San Antonio, and Indianapolis the percentage was one-third or less.

In some neighborhoods, of course, matters have reached crisis proportions. Gangs control the streets, shootings terrorize residents, and drug-dealing occurs in plain view. The police seem barely able to contain matters. But in these neighborhoods—unlike at Palo Alto cocktail parties—the people are not calling for legalization, they are calling for help. And often not much help has come. Many cities are willing to do almost anything about the drug problem except spend more money on it. The federal government cannot change that; only local voters and politicians can. It is not clear that they will.

It took about ten years to contain heroin. We have had experience with crack for only about three or four years. Each year we spend perhaps $11 billion on law enforcement (and some of that goes to deal with marijuana) and perhaps $2 billion on treatment. Large sums, but not sums that should lead anyone to say, 'We just can't afford this any more.'

The illegality of drugs increases crime, partly because some users turn to crime to pay for their habits, partly because some users are stimulated by certain drugs (such as crack or PCP) to act more violently or ruthlessly than they otherwise would, and partly because criminal organizations seeking to control drug supplies use force to manage their markets. These also are serious costs, but no one knows how much they would be reduced if drugs were legalized. Addicts would no longer steal to pay black-market prices for drugs, a real gain. But some, perhaps a great deal, of that gain would be offset by the great increase in the number of addicts. These people, nodding on heroin or living in the delusion-ridden high of cocaine, would hardly be ideal employees. Many would steal simply to support themselves, since snatch-and-grab, opportunistic crime can be managed even by people unable to hold a regular job or plan an elaborate crime. Those British addicts who get their supplies from government clinics are not models of law-abiding decency. Most are in crime, and though their per-capita rate of criminality may be lower thanks to the cheapness of their drugs, the total volume of crime they produce may be quite large. Of course, society could decide to support all unemployable addicts on welfare, but that would mean that gains from lowered rates of crime would have to be offset by large increases in welfare budgets.

Proponents of legalization claim that the costs of having more addicts around would be largely if not entirely offset by having more money available with which to treat and care for them. The money would come from taxes levied on the sale of heroin and cocaine.

To obtain this fiscal dividend, however, legalization's supporters must first solve an economic dilemma. If they want to raise a lot of money to pay for welfare and treatment, the tax rate on the drugs will have to be quite high. Even if they themselves do not want a high rate, the politicians' love of 'sin taxes' would probably guarantee that it would be high anyway. But the higher the tax, the higher the price of the drug, and the higher the price the greater the likelihood that addicts will turn to crime to find the money for it and that criminal organizations will be formed to sell tax-free drugs at below-market rates. If we managed to keep taxes (and thus prices) low, we would get that much less money to pay for welfare and treatment and more people could afford to become addicts. There may be an optimal tax rate for drugs that maximizes revenue while minimizing crime, bootlegging, and the recruitment of new addicts, but our experience with alcohol does not suggest that we know how to find it.

The Benefits of Illegality

The advocates of legalization find nothing to be said in favor of the current system except, possibly, that it keeps the number of addicts smaller than it would otherwise be. In fact, the benefits are more substantial than that.

First, treatment. All the talk about providing 'treatment on demand' implies that there is a demand for treatment. That is not quite right. There are some drug-dependent people who genuinely want treatment and will remain in it if offered; they should receive it. But there are far more who want only short-term help after a bad crash; once stabilized and bathed, they are back on the street again, hustling. And even many of the addicts who enroll in a program honestly wanting help drop out after a short while when they discover that help takes time and commitment. Drug-dependent people have very short time horizons and a weak capacity for commitment. These two groups—those looking for a quick fix and those unable to stick with a long-term fix—are not easily helped. Even if we increase the number of treatment slots—as we should—we would have to do something to make treatment more effective.

One thing that can often make it more effective is compulsion. Douglas Anglin of UCLA, in common with many other researchers, has found that the longer one stays in a treatment program, the better the chances of a reduction in drug dependency. But he, again like most other researchers, has found that drop-out rates are high. He has also found, however, that patients who enter treatment under legal compulsion stay in the program longer than those not subject to such pressure. His research on the California civil-commitment program, for example, found that heroin users involved with its required drug-testing program had over the long term a lower rate of heroin use than similar addicts who were free of such constraints. If for many addicts compulsion is a useful component of treatment, it is not clear how compulsion could be achieved in a society in which purchasing, possessing, and using the drug were legal. It could be managed, I suppose, but I would not want to have to answer the challenge from the American Civil Liberties Union that it is wrong to compel a person to undergo treatment for consuming a legal commodity.

Next, education. We are now investing substantially in drug-education programs in the schools. Though we do not yet know for certain what will work, there are some promising leads. But I wonder how credible such programs would be if they were aimed at dissuading children from doing something perfectly legal. We could, of course, treat drug education like smoking education: inhaling crack and inhaling tobacco are both legal, but you should not do it because it is bad for you. That tobacco is bad for you is easily shown; the Surgeon General has seen to that. But what do we say about crack? It is pleasurable, but devoting yourself to so much pleasure is not a good idea (though perfectly legal)? Unlike tobacco, cocaine will not give you cancer or emphysema, but it will lead you to neglect your duties to family, job, and neighborhood? Everybody is doing cocaine, but you should not?

Again, it might be possible under a legalized regime to have effective drug-prevention programs, but their effectiveness would depend heavily, I think, on first having decided that cocaine use, like tobacco use, is purely a matter of practical consequences; no fundamental moral significance attaches to either. But if we believe—as I do—that dependency on certain mind-altering drugs *is* a moral issue and that their illegality rests in part on their immorality, then legalizing them undercuts, if it does not eliminate altogether, the moral message.

That message is at the root of the distinction we now make between nicotine and cocaine. Both are highly addictive; both have harmful physical effects. But we treat the two drugs differently, not simply because nicotine is so widely used as to be beyond the reach of effective prohibition, but because its use does not destroy the user's essential humanity. Tobacco shortens one's life, cocaine debases it. Nicotine alters one's habits, cocaine alters one's soul. The heavy use of crack, unlike the heavy use of tobacco, corrodes those natural sentiments of sympathy and duty that constitute our human nature and make possible our social life. To say, as does Nadelmann, that distinguishing morally between tobacco and cocaine is "little more than a transient prejudice" is close to saying that morality itself is but a prejudice.

The Alcohol Problem

Now we have arrived where many arguments about legalizing drugs begin: is there any reason to treat heroin and cocaine differently from the way we treat alcohol?

There is no easy answer to that question because, as with so many human problems, one cannot decide simply on the basis either of moral principles or of individual consequences; one has to temper any policy by a common-sense judgment of what is possible. Alcohol, like heroin, cocaine, PCP, and marijuana, is a drug—that is, a mood-altering substance—and consumed to excess it certainly has harmful consequences: auto accidents, bar-room fights, bedroom shootings. It is also, for some people, addictive. We cannot confidently compare the addictive powers of these drugs, but the best evidence suggests that crack and heroin are much more addictive than alcohol.

Many people, Nadelmann included, argue that since the health and financial costs of alcohol abuse are so much higher than those of cocaine or heroin abuse, it is hypocritical folly to devote our efforts to preventing cocaine or drug use. But as Mark Kleiman of Harvard has pointed out, this comparison is quite misleading. What Nadelmann is doing is showing that a *legalized* drug (alcohol) produces greater social harm than *illegal* ones (cocaine and heroin). But of course. Suppose that in the 1920s we had made heroin and cocaine legal and alcohol illegal. Can anyone doubt that Nadelmann would now be writing that it is folly to continue our ban on alcohol because cocaine and heroin are so much more harmful?

And let there be no doubt about it—widespread heroin and cocaine use are associated with all manner of ills. Thomas Bewley found that the mortality rate of British heroin addicts in 1968 was 28 times as high as the death rate of the same age group of non-addicts, even though in England at the time an addict could obtain free or low-cost heroin and clean needles from British clinics. Perform the following mental experiment: suppose we legalized heroin and cocaine in this country. In what proportion of auto fatalities would the state police report that the driver was nodding off on heroin or recklessly driving on a coke high? In what proportion of spouse-assault and child-abuse cases would the local police report that crack was involved? In what proportion of industrial accidents would safety investigators report that the forklift or drill-press operator was in a drug-induced stupor or frenzy? We do not know exactly what the proportion would be, but anyone who asserts that it would not be much higher than it is now would have to believe that these drugs have little appeal except when they are illegal. And that is nonsense.

An advocate of legalization might concede that social harm—perhaps harm equivalent to that already produced by alcohol—would follow from making cocaine and heroin generally available. But at least, he might add, we would have the problem 'out in the open' where it could be treated as a matter of 'public health.' That is well and good, *if* we knew how to treat—that is, cure—heroin and cocaine abuse. But we do not know how to do it for all the people who would need such help. We are having only limited success in coping with chronic alcoholics. Addictive behavior is immensely difficult to change, and the best methods for changing it—living in drug-free therapeutic communities, becoming faithful members of Alcoholics Anonymous or Narcotics Anonymous—require great personal commitment, a quality that is, alas, in short supply among the very persons—young people, disadvantaged people—who are often most at risk for addiction.

Suppose that today we had, not 15 million alcohol abusers, but half a million. Suppose that we already knew what we have learned from our long experience with the widespread use of alcohol. Would we make whiskey legal? I do not know, but I suspect there would be a lively debate. The Surgeon General would remind us of the risks alcohol poses to pregnant women. The National Highway Traffic Safety Administration would point to the likelihood of more highway fatalities caused by drunk drivers. The Food and Drug Administration might find that there is a non-trivial increase in cancer associated with alcohol consumption. At the same time the police would report great difficulty in keeping illegal whiskey out of our cities, officers being corrupted by bootleggers, and alcohol addicts often resorting to crime to feed their habit. Libertarians, for their part, would argue that every citizen has a right to drink anything he wishes and that drinking is, in any event, a 'victimless crime'.

However the debate might turn out, the central fact would be that the problem was still, at that point, a small one. The government cannot legislate away the addictive tendencies in all of us, nor can it remove completely even the most dangerous addictive substances. But it can cope with harms when the harms are still manageable.

Science and Addiction

One advantage of containing a problem while it is still containable is that it buys time for science to learn more about it and perhaps to discover a cure. Almost unnoticed in the current debate over legalizing drugs is that basic science has made rapid strides in identifying the underlying neurological processes involved in some forms of addiction. Stimulants such as cocaine and amphetamines alter the way certain brain cells communicate with one another. That alteration is complex and not entirely understood, but in simplified form it involves modifying the way in which a neurotransmitter called dopamine sends signals from one cell to another.

When dopamine crosses the synapse between two cells, it is in effect carrying a message from the first cell to activate the second one. In certain parts of the brain that message is experienced as pleasure. After the message is delivered, the dopamine returns to the first cell. Cocaine apparently blocks this return, or 'reuptake', so that the excited cell and others nearby continue to send pleasure messages. When the exaggerated high produced by cocaine-influenced dopamine finally ends, the brain cells may (in ways that are still a matter of dispute) suffer from an extreme lack of dopamine, thereby making the individual unable to experience any pleasure at all. This would explain why cocaine users often feel so depressed after enjoying the drug. Stimulants may also affect the way in which other neurotransmitters, such as serotonin and noradrenaline, operate.

Whatever the exact mechanism may be, once it is identified it becomes possible to use drugs to block either the effect of cocaine or its tendency to produce dependency. There have already been experiments using desipramine, imipramine, bromocriptine, carbamazepine, and other chemicals. There are some promising results.

Tragically, we spend very little on such research, and the agencies funding it have not in the past occupied very influential or visible posts in the federal bureaucracy. If there is one aspect of the 'war on drugs' metaphor that I dislike, it is its tendency to focus attention almost exclusively on the troops in the trenches, whether engaged in enforcement or treatment, and away from the research-and-development efforts back on the home front where the war may ultimately be decided.

I believe that the prospects of scientists in controlling addiction will be strongly influenced by the size and character of the problem they face. If the problem is a few hundred thousand chronic, high-dose users of an illegal product, the chances of making a difference at a reasonable cost will be much greater than if the problem is a few million chronic users of legal substances. Once a drug is legal, not only will its use increase but many of those who then use it will prefer the drug to the treatment: they will want the pleasure, whatever the cost to themselves or their families, and they will resist—probably successfully—any effort to wean them away from experiencing the high that comes from inhaling a legal substance.

If I Am Wrong . . .

No one can know what our society would be like if we changed the law to make access to cocaine, heroin, and PCP easier. I believe, for reasons given, that the result would be a sharp increase in use, a more widespread degradation of the human personality, and a greater rate of accidents and violence.

I may be wrong. If I am, then we will needlessly have incurred heavy costs in law enforcement and some forms of criminality. But if I am right, and the legalizers prevail anyway, then we will have consigned millions of people, hundreds of thousands of infants, and hundreds of neighborhoods to a life of oblivion and disease. To the lives and families destroyed by alcohol we will have added countless more destroyed by cocaine, heroin, PCP, and whatever else a basement scientist can invent.

Human character is formed by society; indeed, human character is inconceivable without society, and good character is less likely in a bad society. Will we, in the name of an abstract doctrine of radical individualism, and with the false comfort of suspect predictions, decide to take the chance that somehow individual decency can survive amid a more general level of degradation?

I think not. The American people are too wise for that, whatever the academic essayists and cocktail-party pundits may say. But if Americans today are less wise than I suppose, then Americans at some future time will look back on us now and wonder, what kind of people were they that they could have done such a thing?

3

A CLASSIC CORRESPONDENCE: THE ECONOMIST VERSUS THE 'DRUG CZAR'

INTRODUCTION

One of the central figures—if not the central figure—in the initial period of highly publicized debate on legalizing drugs, was William J. Bennett, then Director (or 'Czar') of the government's Office of Drug Control Policy; it was he who perhaps more than anyone else represented the government's stand against legalization. He consequently became a target for much of the criticism of the government's drug policy. Here we present a published correspondence between Bennett and one of the most outspoken and well-known critics of drug policy, Nobel-laureate economist Milton Friedman.

An Open Letter to Bill Bennett

Milton Friedman

Dr. Friedman's open letter to Dr. Bennett appeared in the September 7th, 1989, issue of the Wall Street Journal. *Dr. Friedman proposes that the way to respond to the current drug situation is to legalize drugs instead of enlarging police forces, building more jails, imposing harsher penalties, and so on. He submits that Dr. Bennett is right in the end he wants to achieve (namely, to decrease the destructive force of drugs), but that he is mistaken in the means he chooses to effect that end. Dr. Friedman maintains that the legalization of drugs is the only solution to the problem, since it alone can both reduce violence and respect individual liberty.*

Dear Bill:

In Oliver Cromwell's eloquent words, "I beseech you, in the bowels of Christ, think it possible you may be mistaken" about the course you and President Bush urge us to adopt to fight drugs. The path you propose of more police, more jails, use of the military in foreign countries, harsh penalties for drug users, and a whole panoply of repressive measures can only make a bad situation worse. The drug war cannot be won by those tactics without undermining the human liberty and individual freedom that you and I cherish.

You are not mistaken in believing that drugs are a scourge that is devastating our society. You are not mistaken in believing that drugs are

---

'An Open Letter to Bill Bennett' by Milton Friedman (*Wall Street Journal,* September 7th, 1989, p. A16). Used by permission.

tearing asunder our social fabric, ruining the lives of many young people, and imposing heavy costs on some of the most disadvantaged among us. You are not mistaken in believing that the majority of the public share your concerns. In short, you are not mistaken in the end you seek to achieve.

Your mistake is failing to recognize that the very measures you favor are a major source of the evils you deplore. Of course the problem is demand, but it is not only demand, it is demand that must operate through repressed and illegal channels. Illegality creates obscene profits that finance the murderous tactics of the drug lords; illegality leads to the corruption of law enforcement officials; illegality monopolizes the efforts of honest law forces so that they are starved for resources to fight the simpler crimes of robbery, theft and assault.

Drugs are a tragedy for addicts. But criminalizing their use converts that tragedy into a disaster for society, for users and non-users alike. Our experience with the prohibition of drugs is a replay of our experience with the prohibition of alcoholic beverages.

Prohibition Has Increased Addiction

I append excerpts from a column that I wrote in 1972 on 'Prohibition and Drugs.' The major problem then was heroin from Marseilles; today, it is cocaine from Latin America. Today, also, the problem is far more serious than it was 17 years ago: more addicts, more innocent victims; more drug pushers, more law enforcement officials; more money spent to enforce prohibition, more money spent to circumvent prohibition.

Had drugs been decriminalized 17 years ago, 'crack' would never have been invented (it was invented because the high cost of illegal drugs made it profitable to provide a cheaper version) and there would today be far fewer addicts. The lives of thousands, perhaps hundreds of thousands of innocent victims would have been saved, and not only in the U.S. The ghettos of our major cities would not be drug-and-crime-infested no-man's lands. Fewer people would be in jails, and fewer jails would have been built.

Colombia, Bolivia and Peru would not be suffering from narco-terror, and we would not be distorting our foreign policy because of narco-terror. Hell would not, in the words with which Billy Sunday welcomed Prohibition, "be forever for rent", but it would be a lot emptier.

Decriminalizing drugs is even more urgent now than in 1972, but we must recognize that the harm done in the interim cannot be wiped out, certainly not immediately. Postponing decriminalization will only make matters worse, and make the problem appear even more intractable.

Alcohol and tobacco cause many more deaths in users than do drugs. Decriminalization would not prevent us from treating drugs as we now treat alcohol and tobacco: prohibiting sales of drugs to minors, outlawing the advertising of drugs and similar measures. Such measures could be enforced, while outright prohibition cannot be. Moreover, if even a small fraction of the money we now spend on trying to enforce drug prohibition were devoted to treatment and rehabilitation, in an atmosphere of compassion not punishment, the reduction in drug usage and in the harm done to the users could be dramatic.

This plea comes from the bottom of my heart. Every friend of freedom, and I know you are one, must be as revolted as I am by the prospect of turning the United States into an armed camp, by the vision of jails filled with casual drug users and of an army of enforcers empowered to invade the liberty of citizens on slight evidence. A country in which shooting down unidentified planes 'on suspicion' can be seriously considered as a drug-war tactic is not the kind of United States that either you or I want to hand on to future generations.

Milton Friedman
Senior Research Fellow
Hoover Institution
Stanford University

Postscript

(The following is a truncated version of a column in Newsweek's *May 1st, 1972, issue, as President Nixon was undertaking an earlier 'drug war'.)*

"The reign of tears is over. The slums will soon be only a memory. We will turn our prisons into factories and our jails into storehouses and corncribs. Men will walk upright now, women will smile, and the children will laugh. Hell will be forever for rent."

That is how Billy Sunday, the noted evangelist and leading crusader against Demon Rum, greeted the onset of Prohibition in early 1920.

We know now how tragically his hopes were doomed.

Prohibition is an attempted cure that makes matters worse—for both the addict and the rest of us.

Consider first the addict. Legalizing drugs might increase the number of addicts, but it is not clear that it would. Forbidden fruit is attractive, particularly to the young. More important, many drug addicts are deliberately made by pushers, who give likely prospects that first few doses free. It pays the pusher to do so because, once hooked, the addict is a captive customer. If drugs were legally available, any possible profit from such inhumane activity would disappear, since the addict could buy from the cheapest source.

Whatever happens to the number of addicts, the individual addict would clearly be far better off if drugs were legal. Addicts are driven to associate with criminals to get the drugs, become criminals themselves to finance the habit, and risk constant danger of death and disease.

Consider next the rest of us. The harm to us from the addiction of others arises almost wholly from the fact that drugs are illegal. It is estimated that addicts commit one third to one half of all street crime in the U.S.

Legalize drugs, and street crime would drop dramatically.

Moreover, addicts and pushers are not the only ones corrupted. Immense sums are at stake. It is inevitable that some relatively low-paid police and other government officials—and some high-paid ones as well—will succumb to the temptation to pick up easy money.

Legalizing drugs would simultaneously reduce the amount of crime and raise the quality of law enforcement. Can you conceive of any other measure that would accomplish so much to promote law and order?

In drugs, as in other areas, persuasion and example are likely to be far more effective than the use of force to shape others in our image.

A Response to Milton Friedman

William J. Bennett

William Bennett responded to Milton Friedman's public charges against the policies he was promoting with a letter of his own in the Wall Street Journal, *September 19th, 1989. In the letter, Dr. Bennett charges that Friedman's call for legalization is "unrealistic", implying that it naively overlooks undesirable consequences, which would be "a public policy disaster". For Bennett submits that, whenever drugs have been cheaper and more easily obtained, drug addiction "has skyrocketed".*

He agrees with Dr. Friedman that the costs of drug prohibition are enormous, but he argues that the "toll" of legalization would probably be greater, as "measured in lost productivity, in rising health insurance costs, in hospitals flooded with drug overdose emergencies, in drug caused accidents, and in premature death . . ." Further, he declares that the legalization debate is a "distraction from the genuine debate on national drug policy."

Dear Milton,

There was little, if anything, new in your open letter to me calling for the legalization of drugs. As the excerpt from your 1972 article made clear, the legalization argument is an old and familiar one, which has recently been revived by a small number of journalists and academics who insist that the only solution to the drug problem is no solution at all. What surprises me is that you would continue to advocate so unrealistic a proposal without pausing to consider seriously its consequences.

'A Response to Milton Friedman' by William J. Bennett (*Wall Street Journal,* September 19th, 1989). Used by permission.

If the argument for drug legalization has one virtue it is its sheer simplicity. Eliminate laws against drugs, and street crime will disappear. Take the profit out of the black market through decriminalization and regulation, and poor neighborhoods will no longer be victimized by drug dealers. Cut back on drug enforcement, and use the money to wage a public health campaign against drugs, as we do with tobacco and alcohol.

Counting Costs

The basic premise of all these propositions is that using our nation's laws to fight drugs is too costly. To be sure, our attempts to reduce drug use do carry with them enormous costs. But the question that must be asked—and which is totally ignored by the legalization advocates—is: what are the costs of *not* enforcing laws against drugs?

In my judgment, and in the judgment of virtually every serious scholar in this field, the potential costs of legalizing drugs would be so large as to make it a public policy disaster.

Of course, no one, including you, can say with certainty what would happen in the U.S. if drugs were suddenly to become a readily purchased product. We do know, however, that wherever drugs have been cheaper and more easily obtained, drug use—and addiction—has skyrocketed. In opium and cocaine producing countries, addiction is rampant among the peasants involved in drug production.

Professor James Q. Wilson tells us that during the years in which heroin could be legally prescribed by doctors in Britain, the number of addicts increased forty-fold. And after the repeal of Prohibition—an analogy favored but misunderstood by legalization advocates—consumption of alcohol soared by 350 percent.

Could we afford such dramatic increases in drug use? I doubt it. Already the toll of drug use on American society—measured in lost productivity, in rising health insurance costs, in hospitals flooded with drug overdose emergencies, in drug caused accidents, and in premature death—is surely more than we would like to bear.

You seem to believe that by spending just a little more money on treatment and rehabilitation, the costs of increased addiction can be avoided. That hope betrays a basic misunderstanding of the problems facing drug treatment. Most addicts don't suddenly decide to get help. They remain addicts either because treatment isn't available or because they don't seek it out. The National Drug Control Strategy announced by President Bush on September 5th goes a long way in making sure that more treatment slots are available. But the simple fact remains that many drug users won't enter treatment until they are forced to—often by the very criminal justice system you think is the source of the problem.

As for the connection between drugs and crime, your unswerving commitment to a legalization solution prevents you from appreciating the complexity of the drug market. Contrary to your claim, most addicts do not turn to crime to support their habit. Research shows that many of them were involved in criminal activity before they turned to drugs. Many former addicts who have received treatment continue to commit crimes during their recovery. And even if drugs were legal, what evidence do you have that the habitual drug user wouldn't continue to rob and steal to get money for clothes, food, or shelter? Drug addicts always want more drugs than they can afford, and no legalization scheme has yet come up with a way of satisfying that appetite.

The National Drug Control Strategy emphasizes the importance of reclaiming the streets and neighborhoods where drugs have wrought havoc because, I admit, the price of having drug laws is having criminals who will try to subvert them. Your proposal might conceivably reduce the amount of gang- and dealer-related crime, but it is fanciful to suggest that it would make crime vanish. Unless you are willing to distribute drugs freely and widely, there will always be a black market to undercut the regulated one. And as for the potential addicts, for the school children and for the pregnant mothers, all of whom would find drugs more accessible and legally condoned, your proposal would offer nothing at all.

So I advocate a larger criminal justice system to take drug users off the streets and deter new users from becoming more deeply involved in so hazardous an activity. You suggest that such policies would turn the country "into an armed camp". Try telling that to the public housing tenants who enthusiastically support plans to enhance security in their buildings, or to the residents who applaud police when a local crack house is razed. They recognize that drug use is a threat to the individual liberty and domestic tranquility guaranteed by the Constitution.

I remain an ardent defender of our nation's laws against illegal drug use and our attempts to enforce them because I believe drug use is wrong. A true friend of freedom understands that government has a responsibility to craft and uphold laws that help educate citizens about right and wrong. That, at any rate, was the Founders' view of our system of government.

Liberal Ridicule

Today this view is much ridiculed by liberal elites and entirely neglected by you. So while I cannot doubt the sincerity of your opinion on drug legalization, I find it difficult to respect. The moral cost of legalizing drugs is great, but it is a cost that apparently lies outside the narrow scope of libertarian policy prescriptions.

I do not have a simple solution to the drug problem. I doubt that one exists. But I am committed to fighting the problem on several fronts through imaginative policies and hard work over a long period of time. As in the past, some of these efforts will work and some won't. Your response, however, is to surrender and see what happens. To my mind that is irresponsible and reckless public policy. At a time when national intolerance for drug use is rapidly increasing, the legalization argument is a political anachronism. Its recent resurgence is, I trust, only a temporary distraction from the genuine debate on national drug policy.

William J. Bennett
Director
Office of National Drug Control Policy

Bennett's "Public Policy Disaster" is Already Here

Milton Friedman

William Bennett is entirely right that "there was little, if anything, new in" my open letter to him—just as there is little, if anything, new in his proposed program to rid this nation of the scourge of drugs. That is why I am so disturbed by that program. It flies in the face of decades of experience. More police, more jails, more stringent penalties, increased efforts at interception, increased publicity about the evils of drugs—all this has been accompanied by more, not fewer, drug addicts; more, not fewer, crimes and murders; more, not less, corruption; more, not fewer, innocent victims.

Like Mr. Bennett, his predecessors were "committed to fighting the problem on several fronts through imaginative policies and hard work over a long period of time." What evidence convinces him that the same policies on a larger scale will end the drug scourge? He offers none in his response to me, only assertion and the conjecture that legalizing drugs would produce "a public policy disaster"—as if that is not exactly what we already have.

Legalizing drugs is not equivalent to surrender in the fight against drug addiction. On the contrary, I believe that legalizing drugs is a precondition for an effective fight. We might then have a real chance to prevent sales to minors; get drugs out of the schools and playgrounds; save crack babies and reduce their number; launch an effective educational campaign on the personal costs of drug use—not necessarily conduct-

From 'Letters to the Editor', *Wall Street Journal*, 29th September, 1989. Reprinted by permission.

ed, I might add, by government; punish drug users guilty of harming others while "under the influence"; and encourage large numbers of addicts to volunteer for treatment and rehabilitation when they could do so without confessing to criminal actions. Some habitual drug users would, as he says, "continue to rob and steal to get money for clothes, food or shelter." No doubt also there will be "a black market to undercut the regulated one"—as there now is bootleg liquor thanks to high taxes on alcoholic beverages. But these would be on a far smaller scale than at present. Perfection is not for this world. Pursuing the unattainable best can prevent achievement of the attainable good.

As Mr. Bennett recognizes, the victims of drugs fall into two classes: those who choose to use drugs and innocent victims—who in one way or another include almost all the rest of us. Legalization would drastically reduce the number of innocent victims. That is a virtual certainty. The number of self-chosen victims might increase, but it is pure conjecture that the number would, as he asserts, skyrocket. In any event, while both groups of victims are to be pitied, the innocent victims surely have a far greater claim on our sympathy than the self-chosen victims—or else the concept of personal responsibility has been emptied of all content.

A particular class of innocent victims generally overlooked is foreigners. By what right do we impose our values on the residents of Colombia? Or, by our actions undermine the very foundations of their society and condemn hundreds perhaps thousands of Colombians to violent death? All because the U.S. government is unable to enforce its own laws on its own citizens. I regard such actions as indefensible, entirely aside from the distortions they introduce into our foreign policy.

Finally, he and I interpret the "Founders' view of our system of government" very differently. To him, they believed "that government has a responsibility to . . . help educate citizens about right and wrong." To me, that is a totalitarian view opening the road to thought control and would have been utterly unacceptable to the Founders. I do not believe, and neither did they, that it is the responsibility of government to tell free citizens what is right and wrong. That is something for them to decide for themselves. Government is a means to enable each of us to pursue our own vision in our own way so long as we do not interfere with the right of others to do the same. In the words of the Declaration of Indepen-

dence, "all Men are . . . endowed by their Creator with certain unaliena-
ble Rights, that among these are Life, Liberty, and the pursuit of
Happiness. That to secure these Rights Governments are instituted
among Men, deriving their just powers from the consent of the
Governed." In my view, Justice Louis Brandeis was a "true friend of
freedom" when he wrote: "Experience should teach us to be most on our
guard to protect liberty when the government's purposes are beneficial.
Men born to freedom are naturally alert to repel invasions of their liberty
by evil-minded rulers. The greater dangers to liberty lurk in insidious
encroachment by men of zeal, well meaning, but without understanding."

MILTON FRIEDMAN
Hoover Institution
Stanford, California

4

LAW ENFORCEMENT
RESPONSES

INTRODUCTION

We present here two articles written by persons involved in the law enforcement end of drug policy, each reaching a different conclusion. In the first article, F.B.I. chief Edward J. Tully and F.B.I. special agent Marguerite A. Bennett argue against legalization. In the second article, a retired Chief of Probation in the U.S. Courts argues for legalization.

Pro-Legalization Arguments Reviewed and Rejected

Edward J. Tully and Marguerite A. Bennett

Arguing from the perspective of many (though not all) law enforcement officers, Edward J. Tully and Marguerite A. Bennett hold that legalization would most likely produce "no significant benefit to anyone in society."

They reject the arguments of many legalizers that drug laws encourage criminal violence, asserting that such a view "requires acceptance of the implausible claim that individuals who choose to use or distribute drugs, and subsequently become involved in additional unlawful activities, somehow bear no responsibility."

They also doubt whether drug users who have become used to committing crime would give up crime if drugs were legalized, and they argue that even if legalization reduced some crime now due to high drug prices, it would most likely increase other crime, such as assault and child abuse, which would grow because of the greater use of drugs.

To the argument that legalization is needed to undermine the black market, they respond that there will always be a black market unless proponents of legalization intend to sell any drug, to any person, at any time, in any amount desired. Further, they doubt that the government would find it at all easy to undersell illegal drug cartels, especially without government subsidies, "themselves a drain on economic resources."

In short, Chief Tully and Agent Bennett support retaining the drug laws

---

'A Law Enforcement Response to Legalizing Illicit Drugs' by Edward J. Tully and Marguerite A. Bennett (*Police Chief*, August 1989, pp. 57–64). Used by permission. This article was unanimously endorsed by the Major City Chiefs of Police at their October 6th, 1988, meeting in Portland, Oregon.

to stabilize if not reduce intemperate drug use, which "is a significant threat to our common welfare". "The problem incurred by removing current sanctions would", they say, "only make the threat more pronounced."

> Those who cannot remember the past are condemned to repeat it.
> —George Santayana
> *Life of Reason*, Volume 1

When the question of legalizing illicit drugs was raised at the October 1988 meeting of the Major City Chiefs (an organization consisting of 48 chief executive officers of the largest law enforcement organizations in the United States and Canada), the chiefs responded with disappointment, having believed that the merits of this issue had long since been settled. Their next step was to encourage the preparation of an appropriate response, reflecting the general thinking of the law enforcement community.

The objective of the following article is to present the reasonable legalization arguments and provide the persuasive rebuttals known to law enforcement officials. Our purpose is not to chill debate, or to demean those who are, in good faith, calling for some aspect of legalization. Neither should this be viewed as an attempt to glorify, justify or rationalize law enforcement's efforts to control drug problems during the past 20 years or so. We have made many mistakes in the past and will probably make more in the future. When these errors occur, we encourage the community to call them to our attention so that we can make appropriate corrections and adjustments.

Both sides of the legalization argument agree that North America has a serious drug abuse problem that involves both legal and illegal substances. The stated goals of both sides are to protect individual rights, reduce general and violent crime, promote the mental and physical health of the people and ensure a better quality of life for all citizens. Thus, the discussion should center on the path we take to ensure that our mutual objectives are met. The law enforcement community argues that legalization advocates propose dangerous experiments in social policy. In our view, the legalization of illicit drugs promises no significant benefit to anyone in our society. Therefore, we view the experiments as risks that we should not entertain.

Following are basic arguments presented by proponents of legalization.

The Protection of Individual Rights

The central, underlying theme of many arguments to legalize illicit drugs is that individuals in a free society have a right to make their own choices, even if their exercise of liberty leads to their own destruction. This argument was offered by Dr. Ethan Nadelmann in the Summer 1988 issue of *Public Interest*. "Legalization is . . . a recognition of the right to make . . . choices free of the fear of criminal sanction." Once again, as often in the past, the debate over legalization centers on the delicate balance between the liberty and rights of individuals and the well-being of the community. Americans have frequently held that as long as an individual's behavior does not adversely affect others, then he ought to be free to do as he chooses. This position safeguards free speech, freedom of religion, freedom of association and the freedom to live a reasonable lifestyle. The conflict comes when an individual's action threatens the community. If the community decides that the potential threat to the citizenry legitimately overrides the freedom exercised by the individual, it handles the problem through laws or cultural norms, or both.

In order for the 'individual rights' argument to succeed, the proponents of legalization must successfully argue that the abuse of currently illicit drugs does not pose a significant threat. In practice, proponents offer the rationale that drugs are not harmful; that many individuals who use them are perfectly competent; that users and addicts are not primarily to blame for their actions while under the influence; that actions of the community to protect itself are more of a threat to the public good than the actions of drug abusers; and, finally, that there would be fewer social problems if current criminal sanctions were lifted and education and treatment were emphasized instead.

No one denies the importance of drug prevention, education and treatment. But the real issues are: 1. whether society and government have the authority to protect the public from the harmful acts of drug abusers and other persons who would do it harm either intentionally or otherwise; 2. whether society should protect an individual from himself; and 3. what measure—or combination of measures—is acceptable in terms of diminished individual rights, to promote the common welfare?

In response to the first issue, all sides agree, in general terms, that certain aspects of drug abuse (violence to others, for example) pose a significant threat to our society and that, in these cases, society does have a fundamental right to take measures to protect itself from danger.

Second, American and Canadian societies have a long history of taking appropriate measures to protect people from their own unwise actions. They have established mandatory social security regulations, seat belt laws, and child labor laws, among others.

Finally, America's traditions of government and social policy are based on the recognition that individuals are responsible for the consequences of their actions. Some legalization advocates have sought to shift responsibility from the individual, blaming society for drug use. Thus, a person who freely chooses to become drug dependent is excused of any blame for act or consequences. Usually the first to be blamed are the poor parents, who must obviously have erred in parenting. Next in line are the schools, churches, and the individual's peers. Finally, the laws are blamed. If this argument is accepted, it follows that the drug-induced actions should be legalized on the logical assumption that the attendant problems will fade.

Proponents of 'individual rights' have used this argument in the past with respect to sexual conduct, speech, and a host of other issues, successfully at times and unsuccessfully at others. In the case of drug abuse, however, it is difficult to accept the argument that individuals must not be held accountable for their lifestyles. A large number of our citizens have freely chosen to ignore the law and to engage in activities that are a threat not only to themselves, but also to the community.

In this situation, the law was not wrong, unjust or an unacceptable infringement on individual rights. The responsibility of government is to do what it can do to ensure that its citizens are able to enjoy and exercise their very considerable freedoms. Government "of the people, by the people, and for the people" requires a population physically and mentally able to make prudent decisions.

Punitive Measures Lead to Violence, Corruption, and Crime

According to legalization advocates, the law enforcement approach and the use of punitive and repressive measures have led to violence, corruption of public officials, and a significant increase in general crime.

It is true that levels of violence, general crime, and, to a lesser extent, corruption of public officials have increased over the past 20 years. These trends can be tied directly or indirectly to legal or illegal drug abuse. However, to suggest that the increase in crime levels is caused by the illegality of some substances, or marketing practices, stretches logic to the breaking point. It requires acceptance of the implausible claim that individuals who choose to use or distribute drugs, and subsequently become involved in additional unlawful activities, somehow bear no responsibility. The government is blamed because it has made the ingested substance illegal, difficult to obtain, or expensive.

This argument is naive. One reason people use mind-altering drugs is that they want to feel good. Individuals who continue drug use do so because they want to, or until they reach a point where they lose individual control over their lives. Up to this point, use of drugs is strictly voluntary. Thus, the inexorable drift to addiction on the part of some drug users is the result of a multitude of individual choices made over time.

The violence and criminal behaviors exhibited by people under the influence of drugs are not motivated by legal sanctions. The law, *per se,* does not cause their behavior. Individuals choose their behavior. If that behavior violates a law, harms another person or corrupts a public official, it is not reasonable to blame the law. We have not yet blamed the law in the case of the bank robber, wife beater, or shoplifter. In reality, most individuals involved in criminal activity are either oblivious to or contemptuous of the law. Social rules are for other people, not for them. In our experience, there are few drug addicts, drug dealers, or drug-induced criminals who would argue that the law, or law enforcement, caused his behavior. More to the point of the argument is that few drug traffickers would 'go straight' if narcotics were legalized.

One final note on the corruption of public officials: It is true that present illegal drug activities have provided the wealth needed to corrupt police officers, judges or others involved in the criminal justice system. But this should not be viewed as part of the drug problem. It is the result of having public servants who are susceptible to corruption and hence not fit for public service. Whether the motivation is drugs, money, or power, the problem of corruption is, in reality, a problem of character. In the final analysis, the problem of public corruption can be solved if we first select men and women of good character to be public servants.

The proponents of 'individual rights' have made the individual's freedom of choice the centerpiece of their argument for the legalization of drugs. While the law enforcement community acknowledges the importance of individual rights and liberty, it considers the probable common good to be endangered by the legalization of drugs. We hold that it is destructive of the common good to legitimize patterns of behavior with drugs by which individuals become a threat to others and an enormous community liability. Thus, we reject the argument that current drug laws have made the drug problem worse. What has made the problem worse are individuals who have made some very poor choices.

Supply Reduction Policies Have Failed

Proponents of legalization insist that despite law enforcement's best efforts, the supply and substance purity of drugs have increased while price has decreased. Thus, they argue, law enforcement has failed. This is far from true, and it misleads reflections about wise social policy. Of all illicit drugs, only cocaine has increased in availability and purity at decreased prices. Marijuana, heroin, and hashish have remained relatively stable and high priced, which is the objective of supply reduction. The principal reason cocaine has become more widely available is that the cocaine cartels have a huge supply of the easily stored drug, which they have been dumping on the North American market in order to increase demand. Despite recent events in Afghanistan, Iran, and Lebanon that have wiped out previously supportive law enforcement activities in those nations, our interdiction efforts have kept the supplies of other drugs fairly stable.

On the other hand, to claim that law enforcement has been completely successful with its reduction efforts is not justified. The law enforcement community now recognizes that it will not be able to eliminate the flow of illicit drugs into North America. The demand for drugs is too high and the ease of smuggling drugs over the borders is too well known for our efforts to be totally successful. However, capitulation in this area means a significant increase in drugs or—in the case of several countries that have *de facto* capitulation—the possible loss of the entire country. The recognition of this fact has led law enforcement to open a second front by devoting more resources to demand reduction programs. The Drug Enforcement Administration, and the Los Angeles police and sheriff's departments have been leaders in the development of demand reduction programs. As these programs have spread throughout the United States, they have been acclaimed by educators and parents as very effective. These modest programs will not, in and of themselves, solve the drug problem, but they do vividly point out that drug demand reduction efforts need to be greatly expanded, with more institutions directly involved in addressing the problem.

To claim that law enforcement supply reduction efforts have 'failed' is also to deny the fact that arrests, seizures, and forfeitures have significantly increased each year. The legalization argument does not address the issue of what the magnitude of the supply problem would be if *no* effort had been made. Considering the complex problems involved in supply reduction efforts, law enforcement would argue that our efforts have neither failed nor succeeded as well as we had hoped. Each year as we learn more about the problem, we make adjustments in our tactics and strategies. Each year, it becomes more difficult to smuggle all types of contraband into North America. Each year, it becomes more difficult to grow and conceal marijuana and tougher to transport the product from point to point. As we continue to improve our reduction efforts, seizures will continue to show modest increases. We would argue that we should stay the course on the supply reduction issue and not give in to a problem just because we have had only partial success.

Drug Prohibition Laws Cause Crime

Advocates of legalization argue that if we repealed laws presently making the production, distribution, purchase, and consumption of drugs illegal, we would reduce the number of crimes. This is not only misleading but untrue. The issue is whether, as advocates claim, repeal would take the profit out of drug dealing and thus result in less drug-marketing violence. We believe the answer is no. Unless the legalization proponents intend to sell any drug, to any person, at any time, in any amount desired, then a black market for drugs—and the attendant problems of crime and violence—will continue to exist. If drugs are freely available in the legal market and present addiction rates are maintained, it is reasonable to expect that the number of persons and the amount of drugs dispensed in the illegal market will increase. Thus, any short-term reduction of crime, however unlikely, would be rapidly negated. In the long term, the problems would probably be worse.

The argument that legalization would reduce the costs of drugs rests on the assumption that government can manufacture and distribute drugs more efficiently than the present illegal system, thus making drugs cheaper. Cheap drugs should, the argument states, reduce the necessity to commit crimes to finance drug purchases. Both of these assumptions are questionable. First, it is doubtful that the government could compete against the present illegal system of distribution, particularly if the illegal system chose to compete with the government. The current cost of the production of a kilogram of cocaine is approximately $300. This amount of cocaine presently sells on the streets of Canada or the United States for anywhere from $15,000 to $30,000. Today, the price of cocaine is set by the cocaine cartel and not subject to usual market forces. Firmly in control of supplies, enjoying a huge profit margin and not burdened by the bureaucracy that would be required by government market participation, the cartels would make competitive pricing by government difficult and might well require government subsidies—themselves a drain on economic resources—if implemented.

Furthermore, drug users not only have to buy drugs but also have the usual expenses of food and housing. Most heavy users are not able, or willing, to hold full-time employment after they pass a certain stage of addiction, yet they still need money. Since most addicts have found crime to be the easiest way to fund their lifestyles, it is reasonable to conclude that they will continue their predatory habits.

Finally, if the number of abusers increased as a result of legalization, then the amount of crime committed would also increase. Any reduction of violent crime achieved by the availability of inexpensive narcotics through government distribution would be negated by an increase in the number of drug users. The number of crimes such as assault, child abuse, and violence committed routinely by drug users would tend to increase as the drugs became more readily available. This is a lesson we have learned from our experience with alcohol abuse. It need not be repeated.

High Cost of Law Enforcement

Proponents of legalization estimate the cost of law enforcement in regard to the drug problem at about $10 billion annually and suggest that this money could be better spent on drug rehabilitation programs. While $10 billion is a lot of money, it is only a tiny fraction of the funds spent annually to promote the public good. It is not even a great deal of money in comparison to private expenditures for personal comfort. In July 1988, as reported by CBS News, Americans spent $4.3 billion on electricity to run air conditioners. Put another way, the $10 billion amounts to $40 per year per person. When viewed in this context, the amount we spend on drug enforcement is modest. One other mitigating factor is the dollar value of seizures of assets from drug organizations. In 1987, for example, DEA seizures amounted to more than their annual budget allocation.

The law enforcement community would certainly endorse building more drug treatment centers and is already working to build community support for such projects. Considering the gravity of the drug problem, the law enforcement community believes that an informed public would support allocation of funds to build adequate drug treatment centers without sacrificing our enforcement efforts. Since this is presently occurring throughout the United States and Canada, it would tend to support our contention that the public is quite willing to help with drug treatment, without yielding on the illegality of drug use or the cost of law enforcement. Protection of the public by law enforcement is not in competition with drug education and treatment; these purposes are not a zero-sum game.

Legalization Will Not Result in High Drug Use

Most proponents of legalization suggest that it would not lead to a dramatic rise in drug abuse. But even Nadelmann suggested this might be risky when he stated: "It is thus impossible to predict whether legalization would lead to greater levels of drug abuse, and exact costs comparable to most of alcohol and tobacco abuse."

Faced with the evidence of what has happened in terms of alcohol and tobacco abuse after sanctions were lifted on those substances, it is difficult to understand why it is impossible to predict the consequences of legalization of illicit drugs. Other historical examples show what happens when dangerous substances are not controlled. China's experience with opium from 1830 to 1930 is revealing. The Moslem Empire of the 11th century, the Inca Indians, Japan, and Egypt all experienced significant drug dependency problems in their histories. The recent British attempt to control heroin abuse through the medical process has been a significant failure. We should also remember that morphine and cocaine were readily available in the form of patent medicines after the Civil War. The result was that America experienced a drug abuse problem similar in scope to what we see today. In general terms, most societies throughout history have had problems with drugs or drug abuse. Those societies that solved the problem did so in the same fashion we are trying today.

Relevant information can also be drawn from levels of abuse of currently legal drugs such as valium. Our experience with methaqualone (Quaaludes), oxycondone (Percodan), and hydromorphone (Dilaudid) gives sufficient evidence that the control of legal drugs is difficult, expensive, and not always successful. In each case, the drug has been widely abused, despite the prescription process. These substances have found their way into the black market, having been illegally diverted or manufactured. All these facts indicate that if presently illicit drugs were legalized, whether they were distributed by the private or the public sector under specific controls, people disposed to drug use would in fact use them. Generalized use could rise, and illegal means of meeting demand would continue.

Consideration must be given to the claim that illicit drugs are not, and would not, become as popular as tobacco and alcohol. This is a hazardous assumption. The most dangerous drugs might not become widely popular, but use of debilitating narcotics that adversely affect behavior could. The drug traffickers have shown themselves to be extremely shrewd at marketing strategies, and they will continue to promote demand. Much more important than legalization is the mobilizing of community pressure against illegal narcotics, as has been done with tobacco and alcohol.

Law enforcement officials do not predict that legalization would cause 'doomsday'. We argue that legalization promises no improvement and unnecessarily risks an increasing of drug abuse.

Illicit Drugs Are Not as Dangerous as Believed

Legalization arguments depend on two additional assumptions: first, that illicit drugs are not as dangerous as is commonly believed and, second, that since some illicit drugs are highly dangerous, they are not likely to be popular. With respect to the first assumption, it is enough to say the medical community disagrees, as does every police officer who comes into contact with people debilitated by drugs from marijuana to 'crack'. The claim that illicit drugs are not dangerous falls of its own weight in the face of experience. The medical research community admits that current progress of research is insufficient to say *exactly how dangerous* illicit drugs are to physical and mental health. Funding for additional medical research should be a high priority so that the full measure of risk can be grasped. For the present, we have enough information from emergency room and morgue records, accident statistics and overall costs of lost productivity from drug abuse to know that the dangers are real. As drug epidemics ebb and flow, and new substances are introduced into the marketplace, we tend to neglect such evidence. It was just a few years ago that cocaine was thought by many to be safe and nonaddicting. The early studies of marijuana indicated some potential long-term health hazards, but most studies were done with samples containing half the THC now present in the sinsemilla and hydroponic varieties of marijuana. Current research tends to support the hypothesis that marijuana is a significant health hazard with a debilitating effect on motor skills. These are important skills used in driving, flying or handling a locomotive. Results of impairment have become all too familiar.

The claim that illicit drugs are not as dangerous as believed is wrong, and those who make it diminish the realism of the debate about legalization.

Conclusion

In our view, the proponents of legalization have not made a case for the freedom of individuals to choose to use illicit drugs regardless of the consequences. We believe the threat of intemperate drug use, whether legal or illegal, is a significant threat to our common welfare. The problem incurred by removing current sanctions would only make the threat more pronounced. We should protect ourselves by legislation where sanctions meet the combined test of common sense and the constitutions of the United States and Canada.

It is interesting to note that those making an argument for the legalization of illicit drugs have not recently made similar arguments on behalf of the common drunk. The drunk has become the 'leper' in our society as a result of his behavior while intoxicated. The alcoholic is no longer considered in some quarters to be without responsibility for his conduct, but rather to be in violation of standards of common decency. Being drunk is not given any weight, in any quarter, as an excuse for violent or abusive behavior, and the drunk driver is being punished more severely than ever before in our history. Where are the defenders of the drunk? Where are the defenders of the smoker these days? Simply put, staunch defenders of the drunk and the smoker are gone because many have recognized that tolerance adversely affects the individual and the society. Laws have been strengthened and the sanctions of custom are being used to discourage consumption.

While some commentators would suggest the problem of drug abuse is made worse by repressive measures of the criminal justice system, it is more reasonable to assume that the underlying cause of our problems lies within ourselves. Whether the causes reflect an absence of high personal standards, greed, inability to cope with rapid change or involuntary confinement to poverty, we must come to grips with the fact that a large number of people in our culture turn to drugs for relief. Law enforcement cannot address these basic problems alone. Considering the nature and the complexities of the underlying problems, it is obvious to us that the institutions of the family, education, religion, business, industry, media, and government all have crucial stakes in the solution of the problem. Drug abuse is no longer the other fellow's problem!

Even though the problems of drug abuse are severe in both the United States and Canada, we should pause and consider the success we have had in reducing the number of people who are smoking cigarettes, and the steps that the Mothers Against Drunk Drivers (MADD), Students Against Drunk Driving (SADD), and Alcoholics Anonymous (AA) have taken to bring alcohol abuse problems under control. Some recent surveys indicate that our teenagers' drug use may have peaked and perhaps dropped a bit in recent years as a result of an effective demand reduction program. This is evidence that we have made some significant progress in curbing the problem.

We need not haggle over how much each of us should do to bring the problem under control. We should not vilify those who suggest a different approach, or pass additional legislation in a hysterical atmosphere. This is a time to determine our best means and remedies for facing the problems and to move forthrightly to the task of reducing the problem to tolerable levels. For the short term, the law enforcement community hopes to continue to maintain reasonable and prudent pressure on supply interdiction and vigorous enforcement of existing laws, while at the same time continuing the development of demand reduction programs. This will buy time so that additional solutions can be developed and more players brought into the contest. In this regard, we in the law enforcement community stand ready to share our knowledge, resources, and dedication to solving the problem with any institution, public or private, at any time.

We are sensitive to the fact that mistakes have been made in the attempt to control drug abuse. However, rather than dwell on finding a scapegoat, we really should be working together, as men and women of good faith, in an attempt to safeguard present and future generations. Controlling the problems of narcotics will take a long time, and it is not going to be as simple—or ostensibly as easy—as the mere legalization of drugs.

The Drug Problem: Is There an Answer?

Merrill A. Smith

Merrill A. Smith, a former U.S. Chief of Probation, argues for legalization by maintaining that the current war on drugs is "a no-win war" and that it does more harm than good. He claims that we are seizing only a small percentage of the illegal drugs crossing the borders, and that we cannot reasonably hope to improve the situation.

He believes that understanding our attitudes toward illegal drugs requires understanding the historical background of the drug laws, and that understanding that history and the consequences of the current laws should lead people to favor legalization.

He contends that about a hundred years ago the proportion of persons addicted to opiates in relation to the total population was virtually the same as it is now, yet most people in society did not define that situation as a "drug problem" and "drug laws and enforcement apparatus were non-existent." But as a result of a number of historical events (particularly after 1900), temperance groups came increasingly to view addiction to opium less as a medical concern and more as a criminal concern.

[T]he Congress accepted that view. In 1914 the Harrison Narcotics Act was passed, ostensibly as a revenue measure. The following year the Supreme Court upheld a conviction under the Act and made clear its view that the Act's intent

'The Drug Problem: Is There An Answer?' by Merrill A. Smith (*Federal Probation: A Journal of Correctional Philosophy and Practice*, vol. 52, no. 1, March 1988, pp. 3–6). Used by permission. This article was adapted from an address given before the University Club of Claremont, California, on January 13th, 1987.

was not to produce revenue but control drugs. Thus drug suppression became Federal policy.

He relates that by 1922 narcotic clinics across the country had to be shut down, leading quickly to the development of a black market and the branding of addicts as criminals.

Like many other proponents of legalization, Mr. Smith contends that addicts commit a disproportionately large number of crimes because they cannot otherwise afford to pay for drugs whose prices have been artificially inflated by the black market. He also argues that illegal drugs account for a small percentage of drug-use-related deaths (about 5 percent), whereas alcohol and tobacco do much more harm.

He wants people to acknowledge recreational drug use and even drug addiction as ineradicable facts of life, with which we must cope. The way to cope with it, according to Smith, is to "develop massive educational programs —backed by equally massive funding—directed primarily at children and young people but reaching all levels of society." He thinks, however, that an educational program can be most effective only if drugs are legalized and their purity and potency subject to the same governmental standards as those that apply to other pharmaceuticals. In short, he wants us to do everything we can to reduce if not eliminate the black market in drugs, while we treat the misuse of drugs as social and medical rather than as criminal problems.

The purpose of this article is to challenge current public policy on drugs and drug abuse, a policy which prohibits and criminalizes with respect to certain drugs, while it freely permits—even encourages—the use of others. Our national policy sees these prohibited drugs as evil and their users as depraved. Our policy and laws declare war on the importation, production, possession, and use of many substances, the most common being opium, heroin, morphine, cocaine, and marijuana. We aim to discourage their growth and production throughout the world, to interdict them at our borders, to search out and destroy the drugs that find their way in, and to convict and imprison all persons who traffic in them. But this is a no-win war.

The War Can't Be Won

Consider these headlines and highlights from daily papers of the past 15 years:

1972   SEIZURES UP BUT IMPORTS RISE

HEROIN IMPORTS REACH $1.2 BILLION IN 5 YEARS

1973   DOPE EPIDEMIC CONTINUES

VETERAN DRUG AGENT ESTIMATES SEIZURES AT 5 TO 15 PERCENT

1979   U.S. SAYS BANKS, LAWYERS HANDLE DRUG TRADE CASH

GOOD GUYS LOSING NARC WAR TO ORGANIZED CRIME

ILLICIT UNTAXED PROCEEDS FROM DRUGS REACH ESTIMATED $40 BILLION A YEAR

1981 $10 THOUSAND A DAY HEROIN RING SMASHED

ILLICIT DRUGS GENERATE $54 BILLION RETAIL SALES

1982   FBI ENTERS DRUG FIGHT

1986   SUSPECT ABANDONS $6 MILLION CASH TO AVOID ARREST

$226 MILLION COCAINE CACHE NETTED

U.S. SENDS TROOPS TO HIT COCAINE SOURCES IN BOLIVIA

LAST CONTINGENT OF U.S. TROOPS RETURNS FROM BOLIVIA (four months later)

1987   BOLIVIA DRUG LORDS AGAIN RULE JUNGLE

$44 MILLION IN COKE SEIZED

And on and on—and we are seizing less than 15 percent of what crosses our borders.

Laws and law enforcement cannot win the drug war. Stephen Morse, professor of law, psychiatry, and behavioral sciences at the University of Southern California, wrote in 1986:

> Although the level of use fluctuates because of variables beyond our control, the never-ending war is inexorably being lost. Despite the cycles of alarm, action, and reassurance, current estimates of the yearly value of the illicit drug trade range as high as $110 billion . . . Criminal laws and enforcement cannot reduce the supply of, or the demand for, illicit drugs at an acceptable cost.[1]

A speaker, observed on TV news, addressing a graduating class of Illinois police officers at the Los Angeles Police Academy in December 1986, said flatly, "We are totally losing the war on drugs." John Lawn, chief of the Federal Drug Enforcement Administration, declared, "I no longer believe law enforcement can win the war on drugs."[2]

Morse said further:

> There is nothing new about the most recent proposals to wage a war against drugs. For once we should ask—What possible reason is there to believe that spending more money now, even lots of it, on the usual programs is likely to have any more than temporary limited success, if any?

The Curious History of the Drug War

Why do we have our present mind-set? How did we come by our present attitudes and policy? They have developed in *this* century, yet a hundred years ago when there was no 'drug problem' the proportion of persons addicted to opiates in relation to the total population was virtually the same as it is now.[3]

---

[1]Stephen J. Morse, 'We Can't Win A Drug War: Law Enforcement Won't Cut Supply or Demand', *Los Angeles Times,* 14th August, 1986, p. 7.
[2]Bill Farr and Carol McGraw, 'Drug Enforcers Losing Nation's Cocaine War', *Los Angeles Times,* 21st September, 1986, p. 1.
[3]Joseph D. McNamara, 'The History of United States Anti-Opium Policy', *Federal Probation,* June 1973, pp. 15–21.

At the turn of the century discussions of addiction, limited as they were, were found for the most part only in medical journals. The public was unaware of a drug problem, the police were unaware of a drug problem, and drug laws and enforcement apparatus were non-existent. Discovering what brought about the change requires a brief review of some interesting history. The following sketch is synthesized from an article by Captain Joseph D. McNamara, New York City Police Department, now retired.[4]

In the late 1890s an uprising by secret societies in China, nicknamed the 'Boxers', and the slaughter of hundreds of foreigners triggered an invasion by joint United States, British, German, French, Russian, and Japanese military forces and capture of Peking. In the aftermath two former missionaries, Mary and Margaret Leitch, saw an opportunity to generate pressure on Britain to renegotiate treaties with China which had required China to allow imports of Indian-grown opium shipped by the British.

The Leitches succeeded in getting before the President of the United States a petition signed by 21 missionary boards requesting the President to use his influence to change the British position. The International Reform Bureau shortly thereafter asked the Secretary of State for a hearing and informed him that it represented 33 missionary societies whose congregations made up more than one-half the population of the nation. Government response came quickly. The scope of the national and international conferences that followed broadened to include concern about the evils of opium throughout the world. Religious groups, the WCTU, the National Temperance Society, and the Anti-Saloon League all rallied to the cause. It had become apparent that the possibility of arousing public opinion in the United States was much greater if the public believed that opium was also an American problem. An international opium conference was held in 1909, and in the same year, with considerable pressure from the President and the Secretary of State, Congress passed the Opium Exclusion Act.

Two years later the Secretary of State asked Congress to amend the

[4]Ibid.

Act because of the "enormous misuse of opium in the United States", and, as we shall see, the request bore fruit in another three years.

The zeal of the temperance groups seems rather curious. Before 1900 none of the reform literature ever mentioned drugs. The 'problem'—if there was a problem—had always been there. A study done by two medical researchers in the 1920s traced narcotics use to colonial times. It is clear that the type of drug use targeted by the anti-opium group had existed long before they took up the cause, but it had been regarded as a *medical* and not a *criminal* problem.

The heat stayed on. Legislative efforts were based, not on firm statistics as a measure of the problem, but on estimates made by reform groups. These groups succeeded in defining the problem in criminal terms, and the Congress accepted that view. In 1914 the Harrison Narcotics Act was passed, ostensibly as a revenue measure. The following year the Supreme Court upheld a conviction under the Act and made clear its view that the Act's intent was not to produce revenue but control drugs. Thus drug suppression became Federal policy.

Addicts Become Criminals

Medical doctors were not barred by the Act from dispensing narcotics to persons under their care. Subsequent court decisions however gradually moved toward a position forbidding doctors to prescribe drugs to addicts for any reason. By 1922, enforcement agents, under the notion that addiction is a willful act deserving of punishment, were exercising such vigorous control over the medical profession that narcotic clinics across the country had to be shut down. Thousands of addicts who had been receiving treatment had the door slammed in their faces. There was no way that they could avoid breaking the law. A black market quickly developed, and addicts became branded as criminals.

The punitive legislation did not eradicate drug use. It simply made it a crime—and spawned the tremendously costly problem we face today.

Aside from the narcotics enforcement problem, what is the impact of our policy of suppression? A news item in December 1986 quoted Chief Daryl Gates, Los Angeles Police Department, as saying: "Major crimes reported in Los Angeles rose more than four percent this past year, much of it attributable to increases in narcotics trade and street gang violence."[5] A Temple University study on the link between heroin addiction and crime found that 237 addicts committed more than 500,000 crimes during an eleven-year period (192 per addict per year). It concluded: "It is opiate use itself which is the principal cause of high crime rates among addicts."[6] Only through crime can a habit be supported.

James Vorenberg, Harvard University professor of law, and executive director of the President's Crime Commission under a former administration, wrote several years ago:

> We also know that each year there are thousands of new drug addicts, most of whom are driven by their addiction and the nation's drug policy to prey on their fellow citizens in order to get money to buy heroin.
>
> The present drug enforcement policy . . . by requiring addicts to get their supply illicitly, puts tremendous pressure on them to rob, steal, prostitute themselves, or sell drugs to raise money.[7]

To sell, each new user must find new buyers, and the incidence of use is constantly increasing.

National drug policy has skewed our perspective. Our view has become distorted with respect to other pressing social problems. Our attention has been diverted. National policy outlaws some drugs and encourages the use of others. Consider nicotine. Our government supports tobacco growers, but the gross effects of tobacco use annually take 500,000 lives. Thus the mass effect is far more deadly than the use of cocaine. The number of deaths resulting from illicit drug use approximate 6 percent of those attributable to tobacco.[8] And what about alcohol?

---

[5]David Freed, 'Gates Blames Drugs, Gangs for 4 percent Rise in L.A. Crime', *Los Angeles Times*, 25th December, 1986, p. 1.
[6]Ronald J. Ostrow, 'Drug Use Is Cause of Crime, Study Finds', *Los Angeles Times*, 21st March, 1981, p. 1.
[7]James Vorenberg, 'The War on Crime: The First Five Years', *The Atlantic Monthly*, May 1972, pp. 64 and 68.
[8]R. T. Ravenholt, 'Addiction Mortality in the United States, 1980: Tobacco, Alcohol, and Other Substances', report of hearing entitled 'Beer and Wine Advertising: Impact of Electronic Media', Committee on Energy and Commerce, U. S. House of Representatives, 99th Congress, 1st Session—Subcommittee on Telecommunications, Consumer Protection, and Finance, 21st May, 1985, p. 328.

Between Christmas Eve 1986 and the following Sunday morning, 44 people died on California highways alone because of drunk driving. One hundred thousand deaths a year may be traced to alcohol abuse.[9] Chicago's medical examiner has said that every day he examines the remains of some bodies overdosed on drugs. But every day he examines many more bodies of dead pedestrians, dead motorists, dead swimmers, and fire casualties where alcohol is to blame.[10] We are waging an irrational and unconscionably costly war against the addictive substances that cause fewer than 5 percent of all drug-related deaths.

Another aspect of our policy is its impact on Third World nations. A recent news story reported that in Colombia, *narcoficantes*, as they are called, have become so wealthy and powerful that they offered to pay off the government's foreign debt of $13.5 billion, transfer their assets from foreign banks to Colombia, and surrender their processing laboratories in exchange for a guarantee of prosecution in Colombia where they could expect more lenient treatment than in the United States.[11] In countries that become our suppliers such as Colombia, Peru, and Bolivia, addiction reportedly is soaring. And now Thailand has become a major marijuana producer to meet U.S. demands.

What is the impact on American youth, given the hypocritical stance that some drugs are OK and others are not? We are sending mixed signals which are an invitation to distrust and rebellion. Also consider the impact on families—children watching as parents flaunt the law, and some even reporting parents to police. Is this really the kind of society we want?

The War is Based on a Myth

Why have we lost the war? It is not the fault of the hard-working law enforcement personnel. The answer is simple. Our efforts for the past 70 years have been based on a myth—the myth that human behavior can be

---

[9]Ibid.
[10]Paul Harvey, 'Alcohol Is a Big Menace', *Pomona (Ca) Progress Bulletin*, 11th November, 1986, p. B–2.
[11]Cecelia Rodriguez, 'Colombia Suffers a Narcotics Overdose', *Los Angeles Times*, 28th December, 1986, Opinion Section, p. 2.

changed by legislation. Dr. J. D. Reichard, former medical director of the Federal Narcotics Hospital at Lexington, Kentucky, said:

> There are a great many unhappy, maladjusted people in the world. As far back as there are records, we find that human beings have been attempting to make life less unendurable, or if you wish, more comfortable, by the use of chemical substances.[12]

Passing more repressive laws or throwing more billions of dollars into enforcement will not solve the problem. So what is the answer?

First, we have to learn to live with a problem—a health problem called drug abuse—just as we must live with alcoholism and venereal diseases and other health problems we don't like. Next, we need to develop massive educational programs—backed by equally massive funding—directed primarily at children and young people but reaching all levels and segments of society.

Third, we need to make drastic changes in our laws. It has been suggested that perhaps we should model after the British, with a system under which certified addicts could get their drugs from clinics, hospitals, or doctors at minimal cost. This is not the answer. Suppose we had terminated prohibition in 1933 only to the extent of dispensing liquor to alcoholics through clinics and doctors. Preposterous!

We need to repeal all laws that impinge on the free flow of opium and coca derivatives and marijuana. Cocaine, heroin, morphine, opium, and marijuana should be produced or processed by recognized, legitimate pharmaceutical companies and should be available without prescription to all adults. Purity and potency should be subject to the same governmental standards as apply to other pharmaceuticals, and prices should be controlled to assure that no one need seek illicit sources.

Would such a course produce an increase in drug use? Not likely. *The nation is now awash in illicit drugs.* Anyone who wants them can get them. Conceivably there could be an initial increase, but for those who first try drugs for the thrill of doing something extra-legal or for the kicks they

---

[12]J. D. Reichard, M.D., Address to U. S. Probation Officers Training Conference, August 1944.

find in taking a chance, those incentives will be gone. For those who get started because a pusher needs another new buyer (a substantial proportion), that incentive will be gone. For those who are addicted and want medical help, they will be able to turn to doctors who are free to provide treatment without fear of harassment or prosecution. Parenthetically it is interesting to note here that despite the ready availability of cocaine, its use among high school students actually decreased in 1987.[13]

The main effect will be that the rug is pulled from under the big-time syndicates by completely cutting off the demand for illicit drugs, and the thousands involved in the gigantic distribution system will no longer have a market.

Consider what could be done with the billions of dollars now wasted in a futile game of cops and robbers. Only a fraction of that amount would support vital educational programs, and treatment facilities could be provided on a massive scale.

The Tide Will Turn

Change cannot come easily even when the need is recognized. Pressure to maintain the status quo will come from three principal sources. First is the large segment of those who will hold to the view that such a change is morally wrong. Second are those who make up the vast drug-law enforcement network. Their jobs are on the line. Third are those who comprise the syndicates and organizations who dominate and control the importation and distribution of illicit drugs. They will stop at nothing and will spare no expense. They will be the first to lock-step with moral and religious groups and will finance any effort that will protect their turf.

In the long term change will come. Perhaps not in this century, but the tide is bound to turn.

A letter to the *Los Angeles Times* written by a Los Angeles County deputy district attorney concluded with these words:

---

[13]Jerry Estill (Associated Press), 'Cocaine Use Down for High School Seniors', *Pomona Progress Bulletin*, 14th January, 1988, p. A-3.

It's time to give fresh thought to the drug problem. The fact that cocaine is illegal is destroying Colombia. Drug laws are also corrupting public officials in our own country, clogging our courts, and encouraging the growth of new organized crime enterprises that begin with illegal drug distribution but quickly spread to other illegal activities.

Also, an enormous number of robberies, burglaries, and other crimes are committed by persons seeking funds to buy high-priced illegal drugs. The solution is legalization.[14]

Maybe you and I see it differently, but we will never find an answer to our present dilemma until we are willing to question the truth of beliefs we have absorbed and unless we constantly re-examine why we believe what we believe. This is what I hope every thoughtful American will do.

---

[14]Richard J. Chrystie, 'Letters to the Editor', *Los Angeles Times,* 10th January, 1987, Metro Section.

5

PROHIBITION
COMPARISONS

INTRODUCTION

Both legalizers and anti-legalizers have cited the U.S. prohibition of alcohol from 1920 to 1933 in support of their cases. In this chapter, we look at Prohibition from opposite perspectives, first from an article by Hodding Carter III, and then from an article by Dr. Mark H. Moore.

We're Losing the Drug War Because Prohibition Never Works

Hodding Carter III

Political commentator Hodding Carter III favors legalization, on the ground that prohibition "can't work, won't work, and has never worked, but it can and does have monumentally costly effects on the criminal justice system and on the integrity of government at every level."

He claims that the integrity of our government is threatened because the large profits made by drug traffickers are used to buy up "sheriffs, other policemen, and now judges." Further, many of the drug traffickers, says Carter, are also "buying up banks, legitimate businesses, and, to the south of us, entire governments."

While he grants the possibility that cases of addiction might increase, at least temporarily, if legal sanctions were removed, he thinks that a rise in addiction is less undesirable than "the costs of continued prohibition."

There is clearly no point in beating a dead horse, whether you are a politician or a columnist, but sometimes you have to do it just the same, if only for the record. So, for the record, here's another attempt to argue that a majority of the American people and their elected representatives can be and are wrong about the way they have chosen to wage the 'war against drugs'. Prohibition can't work, won't work, and has never

'We're Losing the Drug War Because Prohibition Never Works' by Hodding Carter III (*Wall Street Journal*, July 13th, 1989, p. A15). Used by permission.

worked, but it can and does have monumentally costly effects on the criminal justice system and on the integrity of government at every level.

Experience should be the best teacher, and my experience with prohibition is a little more recent than most Americans for whom the 'noble experiment' ended with repeal in 1933. In my home state of Mississippi, it lasted for an additional 33 years, and for all those years it was a truism that the drinkers had their liquor, the preachers had their prohibition and the sheriffs made the money. Al Capone would have been proud of the latitude that bootleggers were able to buy with their payoffs of constables, deputies, police chiefs, and sheriffs across the state.

Prohibition Creates Corruption

But as a first-rate series in the *New York Times* made clear early last year, Mississippi's prohibition-era corruption (and Chicago's before that) was penny ante stuff compared with what is happening in the U.S. today. From Brooklyn police precincts to Miami's police stations to rural Georgia courthouses, big drug money is purchasing major breakdowns in law enforcement. Sheriffs, other policemen, and now judges are being bought up by the gross. But that money, with the net profits for the drug traffickers estimated at anywhere from $40 billion to $100 billion a year, is also buying up banks, legitimate businesses, and, to the south of us, entire governments. That becomes an increasingly likely outcome in a number of cities and states in this country as well. Cicero, Illinois, during Prohibition is an instructive case in point.

The money to be made from an illegal product that has about 23 million current users in this country also explains why its sale is so attractive on the mean streets of America's big cities. A street salesman can gross about $2,500 a day in Washington, which puts him in the pay category of a local television anchor, and this in a neighborhood of dead-end job chances.

Since the courts and jails are already swamped beyond capacity by the arrests that are routinely made (44,000 drug dealers and users over a two-year period in Washington alone, for instance) and since those arrests barely skim the top of the pond, arguing that stricter enforcement is the answer begs a larger question: Who is going to pay the billions of dollars required to build the prisons, hire the judges, train the policemen and employ the prosecutors needed for the load already on hand, let alone the huge one yet to come if we ever get serious about arresting dealers and users?

Much is made of the cost of drug addiction, and it should be, but the current breakdown in the criminal justice system is not one of them. That breakdown is the result of prohibition, not addiction. Drug addiction, after all, does not come close to the far vaster problems of alcohol and tobacco addiction (as former Surgeon General Koop correctly noted, tobacco is at least as addictive as heroin). Hard drugs are estimated to kill 4,000 people a year directly and several tens of thousands a year indirectly. Alcohol kills at least 100,000 a year, addicts millions more and costs the marketplace billions of dollars. Tobacco kills over 300,000 a year, addicts tens of millions and fouls the atmosphere as well. But neither alcohol nor tobacco threatens to subvert our system of law and order, because they are treated as personal and societal problems rather than as criminal ones.

Indeed, every argument that is made for prohibiting the use of currently illegal drugs can be made even more convincingly about tobacco and alcohol. The effects on the unborn? Staggeringly direct. The effects on adolescents? Alcoholism is the addiction of choice for young Americans on a ratio of about 100 to 1. Lethal effect? Tobacco's murderous results are not a matter of debate anywhere outside the Tobacco Institute.

Drug Use May Increase

Which leaves the lingering and legitimate fear that legalization might produce a surge in use. It probably would, although not nearly as dramatic a one as opponents usually estimate. The fact is that personal use of marijuana, whatever the local laws may say, has been virtually decriminalized for some time now, but there has been a stabilization or slight decline in use, rather than an increase, for several years. Heroin addiction has held steady at about 500,000 people for some time, though the street price of heroin is far lower now than it used to be. Use of cocaine in its old form also seems to have stopped climbing and begun to drop off among young and old alike, though there is an abundantly available supply.

That leaves crack cocaine, stalker of the inner city and terror of the suburbs. Instant and addictive in effect, easy to use and relatively cheap to buy, it is a personality-destroying substance that is a clear menace to its users. But it is hard to imagine its being any more accessible under legalization than it is in most cities today under prohibition, while the financial incentives for promoting its use would virtually disappear with legalization.

Proponents of legalization should not try to fuzz the issue, nonetheless. Addiction levels might increase, at least temporarily, if legal sanctions were removed. That happened after the repeal of Prohibition, or so at least some studies have suggested. But while that would be a personal disaster for the addicts and their families, and would involve larger costs to society as a whole, those costs would be minuscule compared with the costs of continued prohibition.

The young Capones of today own the inner cities, and the wholesalers behind these young retailers are rapidly buying up the larger system which is supposed to control them. Prohibition gave us the Mafia and organized crime on a scale that has been with us ever since. The new prohibition is writing a new chapter on that old text. Hell-bent on learning nothing from history, we are witnessing its repetition, predictably enough, as tragedy.

Actually, Prohibition was a Success

Mark H. Moore

Mark H. Moore, professor of criminal justice at Harvard University, argues against advocates of legalization, employing one of the historical examples often favored by them, namely, Prohibition. He argues that many people, especially advocates of legalization, are ignorant of the historical facts.

He claims, for example, that the consumption of alcohol dropped "dramatically" during Prohibition, and that with the drop in consumption came a drop in alcohol-related medical problems.

He submits that his goal is to dispel what he regards as a misconception, namely, that morally motivated political movements cannot reduce drug use. He does not, however, argue in favor of returning to the prohibition of alcohol, since he believes that members of a democratic society may decide that recreational drinking is worth the medical, economic, and social costs that attend the misuse of alcohol.

Dr. Moore favors retaining laws against the use of "drugs such as heroin and cocaine", which he regards as dangerous enough to warrant the enforcement of laws to prevent new users and more "casualties".

History has valuable lessons to teach policy-makers but it reveals its lessons only grudgingly. Close analysis of the facts and their relevance is required lest policy-makers fall victim to the persuasive power of false analogies and are misled into imprudent judgments. Just such a danger is

'Actually, Prohibition was a Success' by Mark H. Moore (*New York Times,* October 16th, 1989). Used by permission.

posed by those who casually invoke the "lessons of Prohibition" to argue for the legalization of drugs.

What everyone 'knows' about Prohibition is that it was a failure. It did not eliminate drinking; it did create a black market. That in turn spawned criminal syndicates and random violence. Corruption and widespread disrespect for law were incubated and, most tellingly, Prohibition was repealed only 14 years after it was enshrined in the Constitution.

The lesson drawn by commentators is that it is fruitless to allow moralists to use criminal law to control intoxicating substances. Many now say it is equally unwise to rely on the law to solve the nation's drug problem.

But the conventional view of Prohibition is not supported by the facts.

First, the regime created in 1919 by the 18th Amendment and the Volstead Act, which charged the Treasury Department with enforcement of the new restrictions, was far from all-embracing. The amendment prohibited the commercial manufacture and distribution of alcoholic beverages; it did not prohibit use, nor production for one's own consumption. Moreover, the provisions did not take effect until a year after passage—plenty of time for people to stockpile supplies.

Benefits of Prohibition

Second, alcohol consumption declined dramatically during Prohibition. Cirrhosis death rates for men were 29.5 per 100,000 in 1911 and 10.7 in 1929. Admissions to state mental hospitals for alcoholic psychosis declined from 10.1 per 100,000 in 1919 to 4.7 in 1928.

Arrests for public drunkenness and disorderly conduct declined 50 percent between 1916 and 1922. For the population as a whole, the best estimates are that consumption of alcohol declined by 30 to 50 percent.

Third, violent crime did not increase dramatically during Prohibition. Homicide rates rose dramatically from 1900 to 1910 but remained roughly constant during Prohibition's 14-year rule. Organized crime may have become more visible and lurid during Prohibition, but it existed before and after.

Fourth, following the repeal of Prohibition, alcohol consumption increased. Today, alcohol is estimated to be the cause of more than 23,000 motor vehicle deaths and is implicated in more than half of the nation's 20,000 homicides. In contrast, drugs have not yet been persuasively linked to highway fatalities and are believed to account for 10 to 20 percent of homicides.

Prohibition did not end alcohol use. What is remarkable, however, is that a relatively narrow political movement, relying on a relatively weak set of statutes, succeeded in reducing, by one-third, the consumption of a drug that had wide historical and popular sanction.

This is not to say that society was wrong to repeal Prohibition. A democratic society may decide that recreational drinking is worth the price in traffic fatalities and other consequences. But the common claim that laws backed by morally motivated political movements cannot reduce drug use is wrong.

Hold the Line Now

Not only are the facts of Prohibition misunderstood, but the lessons are misapplied to the current situation.

The U.S. is in the early to middle stages of a potentially widespread cocaine epidemic. If the line is held now, we can prevent new users and increasing casualties. So this is exactly *not* the time to be considering a liberalization of our laws on cocaine. We need a firm stand by society against cocaine use to extend and reinforce the messages that are being learned through painful personal experience and testimony.

The real lesson of Prohibition is that the society can, indeed, make a dent in the consumption of drugs through laws. There is a price to be paid for such restrictions, of course. But for drugs such as heroin and cocaine, which are dangerous but currently largely unpopular, that price is small relative to the benefits.

6

LEGAL AND
PHILOSOPHICAL
ARGUMENTS: IS
THERE A RIGHT TO
USE DRUGS?

INTRODUCTION

The arguments over drug legalization often appeal to 'the facts', but also frequently appeal to fundamental moral, legal, and philosophical principles. For example, do individuals possess rights which it is wrong for the government to invade? If so, how far do those rights extend? And would the government be justified in overriding any individual rights if the social consequences of individuals exercising their rights freely were sufficiently grave? In the drug legalization debate, 'rights' considerations often have to be weighed against 'utilitarian' considerations. (In this connection, 'utilitarian' means 'having to do with repercussions for the welfare of everyone, or of a large number of people indirectly affected by individual acts'.) In most, though not all, cases, participants in the debate take the view that both rights and utilitarian considerations combine to support their own side.

The Zone of Privacy and the Right to Use Drugs: A Jurisprudential Critique

by John Lawrence Hill

One of the major principles upon which legal and philosophical arguments are based is the "zone of privacy". In the following essay written specifically for this book, law professor John Lawrence Hill, J.D., Ph.D. (Philosophy) presents a "jurisprudential critique" of the privacy principle. Dr. Hill argues that under certain circumstances (which he spells out) drug laws could be morally justified.

It is a commonplace nowadays, perhaps even a platitude, to maintain that certain activities are 'none of the law's business'. This view holds that a specified genre of behavior falls within the scope of a 'zone of privacy' that serves to prevent government intrusion into areas of human endeavor which are, in some morally relevant sense, 'personal'. The rise of the constitutional right of privacy is a recent, though limited, manifestation of this basic sentiment. The constitutional right extends to such activities as the rights to parental discretion in childrearing decisions, abortion, the use of contraception and the private possession of pornography in the home, among others. To this list we add the question whether the personal possession and use of drugs is also similarly 'private' and, as such, 'none of the law's business'.

The debate concerning the decriminalization of drugs raises a plethora of difficult issues—some philosophical, some political, and

---

This is an original essay, not previously published.

many, no doubt, empirical. Will decriminalization reduce the rate of criminal activity associated with drug use by making drugs more available and, as a result, less expensive? Will legalizing drugs increase the total number of users or will it reduce consumption by eliminating the allure of illicit and even dangerous use—the so-called "criminogenic" effect? Is education a more effective means of social control than state coercion? And, perhaps most fundamentally, is drug use intrinsically wrong or have many of the negative concomitants of drug use been the effect, rather than the cause, of criminalization and stigmatization?

These are all difficult questions. And yet they are, in one sense, philosophically secondary—at least for purposes of a discussion of whether the private possession and use of drugs should be decriminalized. The more basic question that must be asked and answered is whether the state may permissibly make the personal possession and use of drugs a crime in the first place. If the state may not rightfully use the coercive sanction of the criminal law to prohibit the ingestion of any of a variety of psychoactive substances, then these other considerations are rendered moot. If there truly is a 'zone of privacy' beyond which the state may not intrude, and if the private use of drugs falls within this protected sphere, then considerations of the social utility of criminalization are irrelevant.

My purpose here is to attempt to clarify the various philosophical considerations relevant to the 'zone of privacy' hypothesis as applied to the personal possession and consumption of drugs. It is not my intention here to argue in favor of, or in opposition to, the legalization of drugs. Nor do I endorse any particular view of government's role in regulating behaviors that are arguably self-regarding (actions which affect the agent but not others). Rather, I propose to examine the logical consequences of various philosophical positions with respect to the concept of a zone of privacy. I argue that the prohibition of drug use is not necessarily inconsistent with even a liberal construction of the zone of privacy, given certain empirical conditions and our view of the private zone.

In Part I, I first maintain that the concept of the right of privacy is now so ingrained in modern Western social thought that proponents of various versions of the zone of privacy sometimes do not fully understand the philosophical implications and presuppositions underlying the concept. I then discuss a number of moral and political orientations according to which a zone of privacy is ruled out or, minimally, heavily circumscribed. Next, in Part II, I discuss some of the systematic ambiguities inherent in the notion of privacy by contrasting John Stuart Mill's 'harm principle'—one of the most popular and liberal constructions of the private zone of choice—with the rather more pallid constitutional right of privacy. Finally, in Part III, I contend that, even under a liberal system such as one predicated upon Mill's principle, the government may be justified in regulating or prohibiting drug use provided that certain identifiable harms are determined to exist.

Part I: The Private Sphere and Some Objections

A. THE USE OF PRIVATE/PUBLIC LANGUAGE

The conviction that the state cannot rightfully regulate every aspect of human thought and activity may be firmly ingrained in the ethos of modern Anglo-American culture, but it is, nonetheless, recent and novel. Current debates concerning the decriminalization or constitutional protection of such activities as the use of contraception, abortion, pornography, or drugs typically focus on where to draw the line between matters of 'private' and 'public' concern. Few, however, dispute that there does (or should) exist a realm into which the government may not proceed. The rhetorical strategy of the advocate of government intervention is to concede the existence of the private realm but to argue that the behavior at issue is, for any of a variety of reasons, sufficiently 'public' to warrant regulation.

To understand the jurisprudential arguments regarding the decriminalization of drugs, it is necessary to distinguish varying notions of the public/private dichotomy. To that end, let us first present a description of the zone of privacy.

B. WHAT IS THE ZONE OF PRIVACY?

Before describing what the zone of privacy is, it is well to clarify what 'privacy', as used here, is *not*. Privacy, or what is private in the jurisprudential sense relevant here, is not necessarily the same as that which is 'private' in the everyday sense, as in that which is personal, intimate, or closed to public view.

'Privacy' in the jurisprudential sense is that which is beyond the legitimate concern of government and its laws. 'Public' activities, on the other hand, are those acts which the government may rightfully regulate. Accordingly, what one does 'in private' (for instance, in the bedroom) may not necessarily be private in the jurisprudential sense, but may in fact be a concern of the government and, thus, 'public'. Thus, the fact that a particular act of child molestation occurred in a bedroom does not make the act 'private' in the relevant sense here.

The fundamental principle which animates the zone of privacy is the notion that a person possesses the *right* not to be interfered with in making decisions that fall within a zone of personal autonomy even if these decisions may be socially inefficient. Indeed, this individual 'trump' against countervailing social interests is characteristic of rights in general.[1] Where the state possesses the power to expand or contract the individual sphere at will, there is no individual right, only governmental discretion. In the absence of a guarantee that the zone will not be violated, there is no 'right' to privacy at all. In sum, to posit the existence of a rightful domain of individual autonomy is to recognize an immutable and invariable barrier to state coercion—a domain possessed by right and not by privilege and a sphere that remains inviolate in the face of varying external dictates and social demands.

Further, such a zone is based upon the idea that, where conduct is self-regarding, the choice of the actor is the final word. (A more moderate, though still potent, version of the privacy right might temper this broad pronouncement by requiring that the actor's choice will be protected only if certain minimal requirements of rational capacity are met.) To put it another way, the *right* of an individual to do as he pleases takes precedence over the *good* of the individual, where 'good' is measured by some standard external to the agent's own wishes. In short, that the action of an agent is not in the agent's own 'self-interest',

------

[1]Ronald Dworkin, *Taking Rights Seriously* (Cambridge, Ma: Harvard University Press, 1977), pp. 90–94.

however this may be defined, is not a sufficient reason for over-ruling the agent's decision to perform that act.

In essence, the term 'privacy' is something of a misnomer. Rather than 'privacy', it is probably best to view the right as protecting a zone of autonomous choice.

C. SYSTEMS WHICH REJECT THE ZONE OF PRIVACY

We should begin by noting that the belief in theoretical limits to governmental authority (the belief in the existence of a zone of privacy) is a relatively recent innovation. Plato[2] and Aristotle[3] unquestionably advocated unlimited government. For Aristotle, because the function of the state was to promote a happy and virtuous citizenry, there was no private sphere into which the state could not rightfully proceed in achieving this end.[4] For a number of other reasons, various political philosophers (such as Hobbes) reached a similar conclusion.[5] Government is absolute and, though the state may choose not to regulate a particular activity, this is a matter of governmental discretion, not individual right. Only with the rise of modern liberalism and the thought of such philosophers as Locke, Kant, and Mill did the concept of human rights develop, and along with it the notion of limited government.

In general, two significant philosophical factors serve to predispose a culture toward the view that a zone of privacy should be maintained as a buffer against the state. First, the rise of moral pluralism is conducive to the recognition of a zone of privacy. (And such recognition, in turn, promotes moral pluralism.) As long as there is only one right way to live,

---

[2]Plato, *The Collected Dialogues of Plato,* 'The Republic', bk. III (edited by Edith Hamilton and Huntington Cairns. Princeton: Princeton University Press, 1961).
[3]Aristotle, *The Basic Works of Aristotle,* 'Politica', bk. I (edited by Richard McKeon. New York: Random House, 1941).
[4]In book II of the Politica, Aristotle chastises Plato for wishing to abolish private property and the family. Thus, his conception of the ideal state is not as extreme as is Plato's. Nevertheless, the proper function of the state is to promote virtue and happiness. To this end, the power of the state is unlimited. This is indicated by his claim that the State precedes the individual in priority. Ibid., bk. I, ch. 2.
[5]For Hobbes, the State is founded upon a social contract which gives the sovereign unlimited power. Thomas Hobbes, *The Leviathan* (edited by Michael Oakeshott. New York: Collier, 1962), p. 161.

it is natural to view the function of the state as that of preserving and fostering this proper lifestyle. Consequently, political and moral absolutism are familiar bedfellows. But once it is conceded that there is more than one permissible way of life, the individual must be accorded the right to choose and, with this development, the democratic state forfeits the function of moral arbiter in matters of individual choice. Those who maintain that there is some objective standard of individual moral behavior—the standards themselves may vary greatly—will be correspondingly disinclined to abdicate this moral function of the state.

Whether one is a moral pluralist or a moral absolutist, however, the degree to which one respects a zone of privacy may ultimately be dependent upon the second major philosophical factor: the view held regarding the proper function and derivation of government itself. If the function of government is simply to provide for the common defense along with other minimal duties, as the modern libertarian holds, then obviously there is no legitimate basis for regulating private conduct. Note that this view of government may in turn be derived from antecedent moral considerations such as the notion of the priority of liberty or human rights.

Those from a variety of differing philosophical standpoints will reject, or at least minimize, this notion that there is a private zone into which government may not intrude. In each case, however, this rejection of the zone of privacy is related to, or derived from, either some form of moral absolutism—where 'moral absolutism' is appropriately defined—or notions concerning the nature and function of government.

The first group likely to object to the moral priority of the zone of privacy are the 'perfectionists' of various stripes. Perfectionism is the doctrine which holds that the moral permissibility or acceptability of actions (or, as in this discussion, policies) is to be determined by the extent to which these activities or policies are conducive to the achievement of excellence.[6] Perfectionists vary as to the criterion for

------

[6]Edmond Pincoffs, 'A Defense of Perfectionism', in *Conduct and Character: Readings in Moral Theory* (edited by Mark Timmons. Belmont, Ca: Wadsworth, 1990), p. 229.

determining excellence. Aristotle, for example, focused on excellence of character. Other varieties of perfectionism may posit other ends for attainment.[7] As a general theory, however, perfectionism may be distinguished from a host of other moral theories by the fact that the locus of moral assessment for the perfectionist is the actor, not the action. For the perfectionist state, the function of the law is to develop those attributes in the individual that exemplify excellence. Not all members of society need reach the upper limits of excellence; rather, it is sufficient that policies advance individuals in that general direction.

Because perfectionism posits an objective moral standard by which to measure all legislative policies, to the extent that divergent life choices detract from attainment of this standard, the law will foreclose such choices. An individual will not be permitted to make choices—even in 'personal' matters—that do not conduce to this general standard. Of course, it is possible to imagine a perfectionistic regime where the standard of excellence is measured by personal fulfillment, the unfolding of the individual's native capacities and talents and the satisfaction of the individual's greatest life aspirations. Here, it might be thought that the best way to promote this development of excellence is to permit persons to make their own decisions regarding fundamental life choices. Thus, it might be argued, perfectionism is not incompatible with the existence of the private sphere. A form of 'liberal perfectionism' represents the possibility of reconciling moral objectivity with individual choice.

Yet even in a 'liberal perfectionist' state, the existence of a zone of privacy is a contingent and not a necessary part of such a regime. It does not, therefore, fulfill the description of a true zone of privacy. For even if the state has determined that it will not intrude into certain areas of personal decision-making, it does not follow from this that it cannot do so if it chooses to do so. (Even a totalitarian regime may decide, for any of a number of prudential reasons, not to overregulate.) In the example just cited, if it turned out, as an empirical matter, that permitting free expression of choice was not conducive to promoting the full flowering of human potential after all, then the perfectionist state would retain the

---

[7]For example, a theological conception might focus upon spiritual perfection.

option of changing the law in this respect. Where there is no guarantee that government will not interfere in the zone of privacy, the right is, at best, only a 'paper' right.

Classical utilitarians constitute the second group who appear to be committed, on theoretical grounds, to the view that government may permissibly intervene in certain aspects of private life if necessary. If the maximization of good, whether defined hedonistically, pluralistically or by preferences, is the *summum bonum* [highest good], then the state must have recourse to regulation in any sphere of activity which promises to reward regulation with an increase in the greatest good for the greatest number. This includes the possibility that the maximization of the good must come, in some instances, at the cost of personal liberty. Mill, the libertarian, struggled with Mill, the utilitarian, in an attempt to reconcile these two disparate moral schemes. He did so by fiat in *On Liberty* by arguing that happiness is maximized precisely by respecting a sphere of autonomous choice.[8] Mill maintained that individuals are usually the best judges of their own interests and, by maximizing freedom, we simultaneously maximize social utility.

This happy coincidence has been too much for many philosophers to countenance and criticism of Mill's position is well-known.[9] Basically, Mill has reconciled his utilitarianism with his libertarianism by merely asserting the missing empirical premise necessary to any utilitarian assessment and generalizing it to all behavior that falls within the scope of the private sphere. It is quite possible—and, indeed, quite likely in some instances—that net utility might be maximized only by incursions into the private domain. The present debate concerning the decriminalization of drug use provides a ready example. Though the private use of drugs may fall squarely within the ambit of this protected sphere of autonomous choice, private drug use may simultaneously serve to reduce the net social utility because of lost productivity, associated crime and a variety of other factors. Thus, a commitment to utilitarianism—even the more modern notions of preference and pluralistic utilitarianism—

---

[8]John Stuart Mill, *On Liberty* (edited by Currin V. Shields. Indianapolis: Bobbs-Merrill, 1956), p. 100.
[9]Martin P. Golding, *Philosophy of Law* (Englewood Cliffs: Prentice Hall, 1975) p. 58.

precludes an absolute commitment to the existence of a private sphere of autonomous choice beyond which the law may not proceed. As with liberal perfectionism, while utilitarianism does not necessarily preclude the recognition of a permissible zone of private activity, neither does it preclude the elimination of this sphere where the pursuit of net utility so demands. In the end, whether a utilitarian social scheme is, in reality, compatible with the existence of a private domain of autonomous choice is a matter of empirical contingency, not principle.

A third group that must stand opposed to the notion of a private sphere of individual choice are the legal paternalists. Legal paternalism provides that the choices of the individual may be over-ridden when another—in this case, the state—has decided that the decision is not in the best interests of the actor. Thus, while utilitarianism provides for the sacrifice of the individual choice for the good of others, legal paternalism permits a similar sacrifice for the sake of the individual whose liberty is restricted.[10] For example, where the state tells a motorcyclist that she must wear a helmet because it is *for her own good*, it violates the sphere of autonomous choice by replacing the decision of the individual with that of the state. Commitment to legal paternalism on the part of the state precludes recognition of a private zone of autonomous choice because the paternalistic state retains the right to second-guess the actor.

The concept of a private sphere of autonomous choice must also be repugnant to those manifesting an assortment of other philosophical predilections and predispositions. Legal moralists such as Lord Devlin maintain that society has the power, through use of the coercive force of the criminal law, to punish private activity that society deems to be immoral.[11] Political absolutists of various kinds hold that the state possesses the rightful capacity to preserve itself, even at the cost of individual liberty. Similarly, monarchists, Marxists, and fascists of various brands reject the notion of a private realm of individual choice as a chimera of modern liberalism. While many of these various theoretical orientations diverge in numerous ways, they share one essential characteristic—a characteristic inimical to the concept of a sphere beyond

---

[10]Gerald Dworkin, 'Paternalism', *The Monist*, vol. 56 (January, 1972), pp. 64–84.
[11]Patrick Devlin, *The Enforcement of Morals* (New York: Oxford University Press, 1965).

government intrusion: All of these theories give the state moral priority. Defenders of a zone of privacy, on the other hand, recognize the logical and moral primacy of the individual over the state. The individual is not, as it was for Aristotle, a part of the state.[12] Rather, the state is the creation of the individual and, as such, the servant of individual ends.

Part II: Moral Autonomy and the Constitutional Right of Privacy

To this point, I have elaborated the general contours of the notion of a private domain of autonomous choice; it is now time to offer a specific principle that will serve to wall off the public from the private sphere of decisions and acts. In *On Liberty*, John Stuart Mill proposed a principle which has influenced legal and philosophical thought on this issue for over a century:

> [T]he sole end for which mankind are warranted, individually or collectively, in interfering with the liberty of actions of any of their number, is self-protection. That the only purpose for which power can be rightfully exercised over any member of a civilized community, against his will, is *to prevent harm to others*. His own good, either physical or moral, is not a sufficient warrant . . . Over himself, over his body and mind, the individual is sovereign.[13]

While the scope of Mill's principle evinces its power and simplicity, some recent authors have maintained that the principle, in itself, is substantively empty and solves very little.[14] While we will encounter this problem in considering the difficulties inherent in applying Mill's principle to the issue of the use and possession of drugs in the following section, the remainder of the present section will be devoted to a consideration of the development of the closest constitutional analogue to Mill's principle: the right of privacy.

The ambiguities inherent in the concept of a 'privacy right' are clearly demonstrated in the recent development of the similarly-named constitu-

---

[12]Aristotle, *Politica*, bk. I, ch. 2.
[13]Mill, *On Liberty*, p. 13.
[14]Joel Feinberg, *Harm to Others* (New York: Oxford University Press, 1984), p. 12.

tional right. In 1965, the United States Supreme Court decided *Griswold v. Connecticut*.[15] This case involved a Connecticut statute that prohibited, under penalty of fine and imprisonment, the use of contraception and the counseling or assistance in such matters by a physician. The majority struck down the law, maintaining that it did so in the name of "a right of privacy older than the Bill of Rights."[16]

While the jurisprudential debate continues concerning the creation of a right for which there is no specific textual basis, an equally engaging controversy surrounds the scope of the privacy right. Most generally, the courts cannot agree about what 'privacy' means exactly. At least four distinct meanings have been attributed to the right with four correspondingly different applications. First, privacy has been employed to mean what might be called the right of repose—the "right to be let alone."[17] This appears to be at least part of the animating rationale in cases such as *Pierce v. Society of Sisters*,[18] a case upholding the right of parents to educate children in the manner in which they deem fit.

Second, privacy has been interpreted rather more literally in a number of decisions that focus on the *place* where a particular activity occurs. Thus, in *Stanley v. Georgia*,[19] the court upheld the right of the person to possess pornography, although this right was subsequently limited to possession *in the home*. In *Paris Adult Theatre I v. Slayton*,[20] a civil proceeding to enjoin the showing of two allegedly obscene films withstood constitutional scrutiny. *Paris* was distinguished from *Stanley* in large part because the films were being exhibited in a public theater. This interpretation of privacy as a function of the location of the activity in question is further supported by *dicta* in other decisions—most notably, *Griswold v. Connecticut*, where the Court invoked the "sacred precincts of marital bedrooms" as part of its justification for invalidating the anti-contraception law.[21]

---

[15]381 U.S., 479 (1965).
[16]381 U.S., 486.
[17]*Olmstead v. United States*, 277 U.S. 438, 478 (1928) (Brandeis, J. dissenting).
[18]268 U.S. 510 (1925).
[19]394 U.S. 557 (1969).
[20]413 U.S. 49 (1973).
[21]381 U.S., 485.

A third and even more literal interpretation of the privacy right occurred in *Lovisi v. Slayton*.[22] Here, the Fourth Circuit Court of Appeals upheld the conviction of a married woman who performed fellatio upon her husband and a third party. The law under which she was prosecuted rendered "sodomy" (of which oral sex is one variety) a felony. The Court, however, suggested that the privacy right would have provided a constitutional defense to the charge if the act had taken place between husband and wife. By introducing a third party into the relationship, however, the privacy right was lost. Thus, privacy, under this interpretation, appears to require a 'private association,' perhaps legally sanctioned by the matrimonial bond. This general line of reasoning is supported by decisions by the Supreme Court in *Moore v. East Cleveland*[23] and *Belle Terre v. Borass*.[24] The former case upheld the constitutional right of distantly-related family members to live together as against a zoning ordinance that permitted only more closely related family units. The latter case denied the same right to unrelated persons living together.

The fourth and final line of privacy cases affords an interpretation of the right of privacy that comes closest—though still not very close—to Mill's principle. Under this interpretation of the right, constitutional protection is extended to a number of *personal decisions* that intimately affect a person's life. In *Roe v. Wade*, the case that granted women the right to an abortion up to the point of fetal viability, the court predicated its rationale upon considerations of the diminished life chances, psychological distress and psychosocial stigmatization of the pregnant woman, along with a concern for the bodily integrity of women.[25] Similarly, in *Carey v. Populations Services Int'l*,[26] a case in which the Court struck down a statute that restricted the distribution of contraceptives to minors, the Court speaks at length about the fundamental right to decide whether to bear or beget a child.

This fourth interpretation of 'privacy' encompasses the notion that certain intimate decisions so affect a person's life that they must be left to

---

[22]539 F.2d 349 (1976).
[23]431 U.S. 494 (1977).
[24]416 U.S. 1 (1974).
[25]410 U.S. 113 (1973).
[26]431 U.S. 678 (1977).

the person and cannot be the object of state regulation. Even this construction of the right, however, falls far short of any reasonable application of Mill's principle. Indeed, this should have been evident from the outset. In *Griswold*, where the privacy right was first clearly enunciated, a concurring opinion states that the constitutionality of laws prohibiting adultery and fornication is "beyond doubt."[27] Further, in *Roe*, the Court explicitly rejects a Millian formulation of the privacy right:

> In fact, it is not clear to us that the claim asserted . . . that one has an unlimited right to do with one's body as one pleases bears a close relationship to the right of privacy previously articulated in the Court's decisions. The Court has refused to recognize an unlimited right of this kind in the past.[28]

Despite the hopes of liberals that the right of privacy would come to embody something like Mill's principle, this was simply not to be. Recent Court opinions have made it increasingly clear that the right of privacy does not extend to a range of consensual activities between adults (e.g. homosexual relations).[29]

The original use of the term 'privacy' may be viewed as an unfortunate misnomer which has, very likely, influenced the course of development of the constitutional right. Along with the diversity of meanings implicit in the privacy concept—diverse meanings that may have prevented the development of a univocal analytic principle—the privacy line has also precluded more potent, alternative interpretations of the right. As we suggested earlier, if the word 'autonomy' rather than 'privacy' had been used in the first place, some of these difficulties may have been avoided.

Before closing this section, it should be noted that there has been one major case decided that held unconstitutional, on privacy-right grounds, a law prohibiting the use and possession of marijuana as applied to private use in the home. In *Ravin v State*, the Alaska Supreme Court held that the United States and Alaska constitutions protect the noncommercial use of

---

[27]381 U.S., 498 (Goldberg, J. concurring).
[28]410 U.S., 154.
[29]*Bowers v. Hardwick*, 478 U.S. 186 (1986).

marijuana in the home.[30] The Court refused to extend constitutional protection to the purchase or sale of marijuana or to its use or possession in public places. The reasoning in *Ravin* was strongly predicated upon the location-dependent interpretation of privacy, thereby limiting constitutional protection to noncommercial use in the home.

Part III: The Principle of Autonomy and the Right to Use Drugs

Most generally, Mill's 'harm principle' provides that human society may not employ the coercive power of the state to prevent any activities that do not harm persons other than the actor himself. Any activity that reasonably comes within the ambit of this principle must similarly stand beyond the realm of the criminal law. Thus, the 'zone of privacy' or 'sphere of autonomous choice' is to be contrasted with the public domain not by some arbitrary distinction between essential and nonessential life choices, private and public locales or intimate versus nonintimate forms of association. Rather, the public realm is to be distinguished from the personal sphere by the *effect* activities have upon others in society.

More explicitly, in order to justify government intrusion into an area of autonomous individual endeavor, three requirements must be met. First, another individual must be affirmatively affected by the act. Second, the effect must be a direct result of the act. Third, the effect must be 'harmful'. In addition, in his discussion of paternalistic laws protecting children, the mentally handicapped and others, Mill suggests that lack of mental capacity is also a sufficient condition for government intervention to protect the individual from his own actions.[31] Thus, if it can be established that the acts of the person are not voluntary and autonomous, governmental intervention is warranted. This second, independent basis for state intervention distinguishes 'soft paternalists' from nonpaternalists.[32] While Mill himself apparently embraced soft paternalism only

---

[30]537 P.2d 494 (Ala. 1975).
[31]Mill, *On Liberty*, p. 117.
[32]Joel Feinberg, *Harm to Self* (New York: Oxford University Press, 1986), pp. 12–16.

with respect to certain discrete classes of vulnerable individuals (such as children), application of this requirement to all persons is theoretically consistent with the harm principle.

It is evident from the outset that the harm principle exhibits a certain 'open texture', owing to the ambiguities in applying the principle. For purposes of our discussion, there are three such ambiguities. First, what exactly counts for 'harm' under the principle? Second, how direct must the harm be to warrant intrusion by the state? Finally, what does it mean for a decision to be 'autonomous'?

As a preliminary matter, Mill knows about the potential link between private vice and public behavior. He states:

> [W]hen a person disables himself, by conduct purely self-regarding, from the performance of some definite duty incumbent on him to the public, he is guilty of a social offence. No person ought to be punished simply for being drunk; but a soldier or a policeman should be punished for being drunk on duty. Whenever, in short, there is a definite damage, or a definite risk of damage either to an individual or to the public, the case is taken out of the province of liberty, and placed in that of morality of law.[33]

Thus, while the private use of drugs would fall squarely within the ambit of Mill's principle, if and where this use leads to public crime, the *crime* may be punished but the drug use that produced it would remain unsanctionable. This distinction between private (unsanctionable) acts and public (sanctionable) acts leads to a consideration of one inherent difficulty in adopting Mill's principle as a guide to legislative or constitutional lawmaking. In cases where there is a well-established causal relationship between the performance of certain private acts and the occurrence of other public behavior, adoption of the harm principle renders the law helpless to attack the problem at the *cause*. The law can 'treat' but cannot prevent the onerous public manifestations of personal preferences.

For example, if drug use could be causally linked, as opponents of decriminalization maintain, to a variety of public concerns such as the

---

[33]Mill, *On Liberty*, pp. 99–100.

skyrocketing crime rate, the law would remain unable to address the problem at its cause where drug use is beyond the scope of government intervention. We can arrest and incarcerate those who steal for drug money but we cannot rightfully prevent the use of drugs itself. (I do not consider here whether decriminalization may make crime unnecessary by reducing the cost of drug use.) Application of this principle renders the law a reactive social institution only; it denies what might be called the 'preventive' function of the criminal law—the function the law plays in eradicating the causal antecedents of criminal behavior.

The ambiguity implicit in the concept of 'harm' also becomes apparent in the decriminalization debate. Under Mill's principle, it is clear that whatever harm the drug user does to himself is no basis for legal intervention. Similarly, the indignation and intolerance felt by members of 'straight' society at the knowledge that others are using drugs does not constitute 'harm' in the morally relevant sense. The remorse, disgust or resentment experienced by others—even when elevated to the status of 'moral outrage'—simply is not sufficient to place drug use in the category of proscribable behavior.

It is with respect to two other varieties of influence, however, that the application of the 'harm' principle becomes less clear. Is there not a real sense in which the drug abuser or the addict 'harms' her family, her friends, and those who love her? Perhaps more palpably, when the excesses of her lifestyle prevent her from fulfilling her duties to these others—educating her children, providing for her family, and so forth—is this not a sufficient basis for government intervention?

Mill appears to hold that such behavior is harmful in the relevant sense. Nevertheless, he distinguishes the failure to discharge one's duties from the act of drug use itself. He argues that the person may rightfully be punished for this failure that results from the drug use, but not for the use of drugs *per se*.[34] Nevertheless, it may be asked whether it makes much sense to treat such intimately related behavior so atomistically. Where two nominally different acts are part of the same general behavior pattern, why not prevent the effect by preventing its cause? (Once again, I

---

[34]*Ibid.*

do not presume to have established that the use of the criminal sanction does, as an empirical matter, prevent drug use. The point here is simply that, *if* it does, the best way to prevent the attendant evils of drug use may well be to prevent the drug use itself.)

There is a subtle philosophical difficulty with any response similar to that which Mill makes in distinguishing private behavior from public consequence. Distinguishing individually discrete acts in this manner prevents one from confronting *patterns* of activity where such private acts and public consequences may be intimately interrelated. Not only may drug use lead to secondary crime, but the converse may be true as well. The social alienation and stigmatization associated with a life of crime may reciprocally reinforce an entire lifestyle that includes the use of drugs. If one (private) form of behavior leads, with some regularity, to another (public) form of behavior, it makes sense from neither a social nor a humanitarian standpoint to continually punish the latter while leaving the former unregulated.

As for the emotional effect that the use of drugs might have on the family members of the user, this would not itself provide sufficient warrant for criminalization under Mill's principle. Indeed, libertarian proponents of decriminalization could point to a variety of legal activities that might similarly distress the family of the actor. If the criminal sanction is not warranted by virtue of such interests when an agent engages in dangerous sporting activities, hazardous occupation or dubious lifestyle choices, it similarly will not be sufficient in the case of the drug user.

A second and more controversial form of harm is presented by the claim that drug use contributes to a decline in economic productivity. Social scientists have pointed to the prevalence of an "amotivational syndrome", characterized by a decrease in task-oriented and other "productive" behavior, in regular drug users.[35] This syndrome presumably manifests itself by an increase in the number of days absent from work, a decrease in productive labor while on duty, and an increase in health costs necessary to treat chronic abusers, along with a

---

[35]David A. J. Richards, *Sex, Drugs, Death and the Law*, (Totowa, N.J.: Rowman and Littlefield, 1982), pp. 178–180.

variety of other ancillary social costs. If this is accurate and if this syndrome in turn contributes to a decline in general economic efficiency, thereby affecting the standard of living of the nation at large, is this a palpable harm sufficient to warrant government prohibition?

Mill responds by arguing that general economic loss to society at large does not constitute 'harm':

> But with regard to the merely contingent or, as it may be called, constructive injury which a person causes to society, by conduct which neither violates any specific duty to the public, nor occasions perceptible hurt to any assignable individual except himself, the inconvenience is one which society can afford to bear, for the sake of the greater good of human freedom.[36]

It is reasonably argued, however, that general economic loss is a variety of harm worthy of consideration in the legislative calculus. Mill does not contend that economic loss as such is not a form of harm. Rather, he maintains that this form of harm is not sufficiently direct to warrant the sanction of the criminal law. It is not that there is no harm but that, to be sanctionable, the harm must be localized to particular individuals and must constitute more than a *de minimus* loss to specified individuals.

In attempting to develop the implications of a scheme similar in kind to that which Mill proposes, a recent philosopher has argued that the relative gravity and distribution of aggregate harm may be considered by the legislature.[37] In essence, the law may make a trade-off between the *directness* of the harm and the gravity and widespread nature of this harm. Indeed, this seems to be the basis for the decision to criminalize actions that are destructive of the environment (such as oil spills). Though particular individuals may not be directly affected by such activities, nevertheless there is a *diffuse* and *cumulative* effect. To interpret Mill's principle in such a way as to rule out government intervention where the harm is 'indirect' is to preclude the use of the criminal sanction for polluting the air, fraud on the (stock) market, insider trading, govern-

---

[36]Mill, *On Liberty*, p. 100.
[37]Feinberg, *Harm to Others*, p. 216.

ment corruption and any other activity of an indirect but aggregate nature.

It is time now to turn to the third of the three previously-mentioned ambiguities inherent in the meaning and application of the harm principle: the problem of autonomous choice. While the harm principle denies the legitimate power of the government to intervene in fundamentally self-regarding activities, paternalistic government intervention may be warranted where there is a reasonably strong probability that such action is not the result of autonomous choice. Whether government is viewed as having the legitimate function of *ensuring* that self-regarding behavior is autonomous will depend upon whether the harm principle is augmented by another mediating principle embracing a 'soft paternalistic' justification. If a soft paternalistic rationale is justified, laws that protect the agent from undue influence or ensure that the action is truly autonomous will be permitted despite their liberty-limiting effect. Soft paternalistic laws include those laws that require a terminally ill patient to repeatedly manifest her desire and intent to die before euthanasia will be permitted (as in the Netherlands), laws that prohibit the sale of bodily organs for excessive amounts of money and laws that impose mandatory 'cooling off' periods for certain transactions.

If it is a legitimate function of government to ensure that potentially dangerous self-regarding behavior is autonomous in a manner consistent with the harm principle, it must next be determined what is meant exactly by the term 'autonomous'. The concept of autonomy has been susceptible to a variety of conflicting interpretations down through the history of philosophic thought. For example, Kant's rigorous notion of autonomy as action determined by pure reason alone, independent of heteronomous desires, preferences and social influences, is disparate indeed from our everyday conception of autonomy as action in accordance with choice. Because of the practical difficulties in implementing a Kantian notion of autonomy—a prospect that would most likely preclude nearly all everyday decisions from being considered autonomous—we will use the term here in something like the everyday sense. An action will be considered autonomous here if it is voluntary, performed in accordance with the agent's desires and if it is not the product of any compelling influences.

The concept of autonomy is implicated in two ways in the context of a consideration of the behavior of drug users. First, given the social pressures, the psychological influences and the hereditary factors responsible for drug use, is the initial decision to experiment with drugs typically autonomous? Second, even if the original decision to use drugs was an autonomous choice, is there a sense in which continued drug use may cease being autonomous because of the habituating effect of drug use? If, as a general matter, the use of drugs precludes autonomous choice in either of these two respects, it is possible even for a governmental regime that embraces the harm principle to justify regulation of private drug use. Of course, government policy may vary with respect to different drugs depending upon whether the autonomy-negating effects vary among diverse drugs.

With respect to the initial decision to experiment with drugs, it is undoubtedly true that people make this choice for many different reasons. From recent evidence indicating the existence of a genetic predisposition to use drugs on the part of some individuals to a range of psychological motivations to a variety of social influences, there are probably as many combinations of motivating factors as there are users. Though these various factors may exhibit a causal influence on the agent's behavior, this may not in itself entail that the behavior is not autonomous.[38] Indeed, all behavior is the result of similar influences. To hold that the original decision to experiment with drugs is not autonomous because it is causally precipitated by biological, psychological, or social influences is to be committed to maintaining that all behavior similarly influenced is not autonomous. In short, the claim that the initial decision to use drugs is not autonomous, as a *prima facie* matter, is philosophically untenable.

The question of autonomy becomes less clear when considering the habituating effect of continued drug use. If, as an empirical matter, it can

---

[38]Thus, according to the soft determinist, causation does not preclude freedom. Rather, it is compulsion or constraint which negates freedom. A. J. Ayer, 'Freedom and Necessity', *Polemic* (September–October 1946) p. 36. I have chronicled my reservations concerning this attempted compromise elsewhere. John Hill, 'Freedom, Determinism, and the Externalization of Responsibility in the Law: A Philosophical Analysis', *Georgetown Law Journal*, vol. 76, pp. 2059–63.

be demonstrated that the agent eventually loses her ability to 'just say "No"', a stronger claim can be made that government intervention is justified. Whether or not this is the case will depend upon two factors: First, how habituating are the drugs in question? Second, a definitional and normative issue, at what point does the desire to do drugs become so overwhelming that the decision is no longer autonomous? These are both vexing issues that have been the subject of a great deal of controversy over the last three decades. Moreover, particular responses to these questions have often been politically motivated. I do not presume to provide an answer to this question here. Nevertheless, designating exactly when regular drug use becomes a habit and, finally, an addiction is precisely the kind of empirical and philosophical line-drawing which the liberal legislature, following the harm principle, must undertake.

The problem of the drug user who eventually loses control over his own autonomous behavior is similar in principle to the question, considered by Mill, of decisions which tend to negate future liberty. Mill maintained that certain freedoms may be limited for the sake of preserving greater future freedom. He considers the problem of whether the state may legitimately refuse to enforce a contract under which one party sells himself into slavery:

> But by selling himself for a slave, he abdicates his liberty; he foregoes any future use of it beyond that single act . . . The principle of freedom cannot require that he should be free not to be free. It is not freedom to be allowed to alienate his freedom.[39]

It is not clear whether Mill completely understood the implications for the harm principle of this limiting consideration. If self-regarding behavior may be regulated because of the prospect that such behavior might lead to a future diminution of freedom, the class of activities that might be similarly regulated is enormous; riding a motorcycle without a helmet might lead to the death of the rider—a radical reduction in freedom, indeed. At any rate, to the extent that the use of an addictive drug poses an example not unlike the slave contract example, in principle

---

[39]Mill, *On Liberty*, p. 125.

at least, government intervention could be justified consistent with recognition of the harm principle. Because the drug user may lose the capacity to change his mind concerning future decisions to use the drug, and because freedom to pursue other opportunities may similarly be precluded because of an addictive habit, the state may be warranted in passing restrictive legislation even where harm to society at large is not present.

Conclusion

Acceptance and legal recognition of the harm principle or less potent forms of an individual zone of privacy entails a basic commitment to individual liberty as a primary value in the social system. In Part I, we examined a number of general philosophical orientations that do not permit, at least in principle, an unwavering guarantee of a sphere of individual liberty. In Part II, we discussed the constitutional right of privacy as a weak analogue of the sphere of autonomous choice. Finally, in Part III, we considered a number of ways in which even an 'extreme liberal' system could justify government intervention or prohibition of drug use. Regulation would be warranted if habitual private drug use and associated public harms were viewed not as discrete acts but as a coherent pattern of activity. Alternatively, prohibition would be justifiable if diffuse and indirect harm could reasonably be expected to result from decriminalization. Finally, prohibition might also be warranted in the case of certain specified drugs that pose a threat to the continued autonomy of the individual user.

Drugs: Getting a Fix on the Problem and the Solution

Mark H. Moore

Mark H. Moore, professor of criminal justice at Harvard University, argues against legalization because he believes that our "current regulatory scheme", though imperfect, is superior to any "legalization options".

Dr. Moore views the legalizers as relying on two distinct arguments. The first is based on the claim that drug use involves a personal decision that is none of the law's business; the second is based on utilitarian claims, such as the claim that legalization will achieve desirable social objectives, including reducing crime and promoting the welfare of the population. Although he disagrees with the first style of argument, since he believes that laws can be justified if they promote the general welfare, he is concerned principally with attacking the utilitarian argument.

His tack is to evaluate different legalization options ("regimes") and to compare and contrast their probable hypothetical consequences with the actual consequences of our current policy. Dr. Moore specifies six of the numerous legalization regimes, the most liberal of which would call for "total legalization", under which all restrictions on the production, sale, and use of drugs would be eliminated. The least liberal (or most conservative) regime would call for "decriminalization of use", which would continue to criminalize the production and distribution of currently illegal drugs but would eliminate criminal penalties for possession and use.

He submits that in general the more liberal we would treat the sale and use of drugs, the more we would reduce the black market and the more we would, most likely, increase the number of users. Correlatively, the "more

'Drugs: Getting a Fix on the Problem and the Solution' by Mark H. Moore (*Yale Law and Policy Review*, vol. 8, 1990, pp. 701–728). Used by permission.

limited legalization regimes provide some protection against the threat of explosive increases in narcotics use fueled by newly created legitimate markets, but only at the price of maintaining conditions that are favorable to a continuation of the black market."

Much of Dr. Moore's article is devoted to arguing against the claim that drug laws are rooted in moralistic and paternalistic concerns and not part of a rational scheme for regulating the uses of psychoactive drugs.

He submits that society has a legitimate interest in trying to regulate the use of drugs, since their use can, in his eyes, have important undesirable social consequences. Moreover, he submits that many if not most of the arguments in favor of legalization rely on controversial if not dubious empirical claims about the consequences of legalization.

While granting that different legal regimes will produce different consequences, he rejects the claim that there will most likely be a "large reduction in criminal violence" if drugs are legalized or decriminalized. Against that prediction he argues that, in the absence of total legalization, there will always be a black market in drugs. Further, many members of organized crime will very likely exercise their capacity for "sustained and disciplined violence" in other enterprises such as extortion, labor racketeering, loan sharking, and gambling. Still further, he sees little reason for believing "that today's drug gangs, now schooled in violence, will fade away."

Moore also attacks the claim that the number of crimes committed by drug users will probably sharply decline with legalization. He argues that there is evidence indicating that criminal activity often precedes drug use and is sustained after drug use declines. Further, he argues that some drugs (for example, cocaine) might cause some people to be more violent than they would be without the drugs. He maintains that while we cannot know for certain that drug use would increase after some form of legalization, we can reasonably believe that it would because of the increased availability of drugs and the decreased stigma attached to their use.

Dr. Moore argues for a many-sided approach to the growing use of cocaine, in which he calls for education as well as attempts to reduce the supply of and demand for cocaine. Because he believes that the social costs of drug legalization will be higher—possibly much higher—than they are under a "rational regulatory scheme for controlling the availability of psychoactive drugs according to reasoned estimates of their potential for abuse and their

124

value in legitimate medical use", he favors retaining the current laws against drugs.

Everyone agrees that the nation confronts an urgent drug problem. But the problem wears various faces.

Most threatening is drug-related violence. Daily, vicious murders are attributed to drug feuds.[1] More rarely, but more frighteningly, innocent citizens are caught in the cross-fire between warring gangs, or murdered for their opposition to drug dealing.[2] Statistics show dramatic increases in drug-related homicides in New York, Los Angeles, Detroit, and Washington.[3]

Closely related is a second face of the problem: the fear and demoralization spread by flagrant drug dealing. In open drug markets where drug dealers congregate and attract unsavory users, ordinary pedestrian traffic dries up.[4] Shopowners, who anchor these streets, relocate or retire. City sanitation workers hurry through their work. Teachers seek new assignments.

As neighborhoods yield to the drug culture, a third concern arises. Local children become exposed to and then involved in drug use, drug sales, or both.[5] While children from both middle class and poor families are affected, the stakes for society as a whole are particularly great when the youth who are most threatened are among those already most disadvantaged.[6]

---

[1]*See, e.g.,* 'Brutal Drug Gangs Wage War of Terror in Upper Manhattan', *New York Times,* March 15, 1988, B1, col. 5.
[2]*See, e.g.,* 'A Crack Plague in Queens Brings Violence and Fear', *New York Times,* October 19th, 1987, p. A1, col. 4.
[3]*E.g.,* 'Cities Move to curb Summer Crime Increase', *New York Times,* May 21st, 1989, § 1, p. 14, col. 3; 'Homicides in District Push Past 300 Mark', *Washington Post,* Aug. 30th, 1989, p. A1, col. 1; 'Murders in Queens Rise 25 Percent; Crack is Key Factor', *New York Times,* April 20th, 1988, p. A1, col. 1.
[4]*E.g.,* 'Drug-related Violence Erodes a Neighborhood', *New York Times,* April 4th, 1988, p. A10, col. 1.
[5]For social science evidence that this fear is justified, see Kandel, Treiman, Faust, and Single, 'Adolescent Involvement in Legal and Illegal Drug Use: Multiple Classification Analysis', *Social Forces* 438 (1976).
[6]*Cf.* J. Rawls, *A Theory of Justice* (1971) (public concern for justice should be greatest when the least advantaged are affected).

Widening drug use also poses increased threats to public health and economic productivity. It facilitates the spread of AIDS by occasioning shared intravenous injections and unsafe sexual practices.[7] Inattentiveness or recklessness caused by drug-induced intoxication results in serious accidents not only on the road, but also at work and at home.[8] Even when accidents do not result, employers worry that drug use among workers lowers productivity, at a time when American firms are struggling to compete more effectively against foreign firms as yet untouched by drugs.[9]

Finally, drug use and society's response to it help undermine key social institutions. Families are destroyed by the disabling effects of drugs on parents, and by the conflicts created in families of drug-using or drugdealing children.[10] Schools become less able to teach when there is widespread drug use in the student population, and when they are enlisted in ill-conceived efforts to institute punitive control regimes. The criminal justice system, which has been assigned a prominent role in the war against drugs, may well be overwhelmed and transformed by that effort.[11] The crush of cases may prove so great that it destroys what residual commitment these institutions now have to individualized justice or the hope of rehabilitation. The urgency of the job may lead officials to cut corners in investigating drug dealers. The enormous wealth created through the drug trade may tempt public officials into corruption.

These are society's current concerns about the drug problem—the way it is represented in newspapers, analyzed in legislative hearings, and

---

[7]Des Jarlais and Hunt, 'AIDS and Intravenous Drug Use', *National Institute of Justice AIDS Bulletin*, February 1988.

[8]A notorious example was the Amtrak-Conrail train crash which occurred in 1987. 'Drug Traces Found in Two Conrail Workers After Fatal Crash', *New York Times*, January 15th, 1987, p. A1, col. 4. Cocaine use was recently linked to traffic accidents. *New York Times*, January 12th, 1990, p. A1, col. 6.

[9]Dupont, 'Never Trust Anyone Under 40: What Employers Should Know About Drugs in the Workplace', *Policy Review*, Spring 1989, p. 52-53; Goetz, 'High on the Job: A Growing Problem?', *Psychology Today*, May 1987, p. 16.

[10]See 'The Crack Legacy: Children in Distress', *Washington Post*, September 10th, 1989, p. 1 A1, col. 2; *Los Angeles Times*, September 14th, 1986, § 5, p. 3, col. 1.

[11]See 'New Tactics in the War on Drugs Tilts Scales of Justice Off Balance', *New York Times*, December 29th, 1989, A1, col. 1.

discussed in radio talk shows. Without doubt, the concerns are some-what exaggerated. More is being attributed to the drug problem than drug use alone causes. If drug use ceased, crime would not disappear, nor would fear, urban decay, or the AIDS epidemic. Some of our worst fears actually are linked more closely to efforts to control drugs than to drug use *per se*.[12] Still, these alarming manifestations signal an important increase in levels of drug use and suggest that drug use and efforts to control it are producing significant adverse social consequences. The world of drug use has changed over the last 15 years, and it has changed for the worse.

In this Article, I note that the 'drug problem' is primarily a cocaine epidemic and suggest what we might learn from this fact. I then examine the current legalization debate, and conclude that the current regulatory scheme is more likely to be satisfactory than any of the legalization options. Next I evaluate current supply and demand reduction strategies. I conclude by exploring the tension between our need to mobilize to meet the epidemic in speedy fashion and our need to learn about which policies work and which do not.

I. The Epidemic of Cocaine Use

Today's drug problem is different from the one society faced in the late 1960s and early 1970s. Then, we worried about heroin addiction and street crime in urban ghettos, psychedelic drugs on (and off) university campuses, and marijuana use in the suburbs.[13] Now, we worry about crack-induced violence on city streets and the dangers of drug use on the job.

It is not so much that the old problems have disappeared. It is simply that they have been surpassed. Marijuana and heroin use has been fairly stable over the past decade. There have been some movements: for

---

[12]For an argument that virtually all of the worst aspects of the drug problem are consequences of current control efforts, see Wisotsky, 'Exposing the War on Cocaine: The Futility and Destructiveness of Prohibition,' 1983 *Wisconsin Law Review* 1305.
[13]*See* generally *Strategy Council On Drug Abuse, Federal Strategy for Drug Abuse and Drug Traffic Prevention—1973* 6–10 (1973) (describes possible causes of the 1960s drug epidemic).

example, marijuana use peaked in 1979 and then declined, while heroin use has climbed slightly over the last peak reached in 1974.[14] But there have been no dramatic changes. Abuse of these drugs, along with alcohol, might now be viewed as the nation's endemic drug problems. Cocaine use, on the other hand, has increased dramatically—by more than a factor of 10 over the last decade.[15] These statistics make it evident that the United States is not experiencing the growth of a generalized 'drug problem'. What gives the drug problem urgency today is a far more specific event: the United States is beset by a serious epidemic of cocaine use, including crack.

To a surprising degree, the cocaine epidemic crept up on us. Its first indications probably were reports by enforcement agents in the mid-1970s that they were encountering determined, violent cocaine traffickers from South and Central America.[16] Shortly thereafter, reported levels of cocaine use began to rise in household surveys used to gauge drug

---

[14]The United States currently relies on four basic statistical systems to monitor levels of drug use in the United States population: 1. National Institute on Drug Abuse, *The National Household Survey on Drug Abuse: Population Estimates* (a survey of the general population that has been conducted every two or three years since 1972); 2. University of Michigan Institute for Social Research, Monitoring the Future: A Continuing Study of the Lifestyles and Values of Youth (a survey of graduating high school seniors that has been conducted annually since 1975); 3. National Institute on Drug Abuse, *Data from the Drug Abuse Early Warning Network* (reports from a selected national sample of emergency rooms and medical examiners on drug involvement by patients); 4. National Institute on Drug Abuse, *Client Oriented Data Acquisition Process, Annual Summary Report* (reports from federally supported treatment programs regarding new clients admitted to treatment).

Each system has weaknesses as an accurate indicator of levels of drug use in the general population; thus, they are often used in conjunction with one another. One should keep in mind that descriptions of drug use levels in the general population are based on interpretations of these data—they cannot simply be read. I rely on an interpretation produced by David Boyum, who constructed indices of drug use levels based on combinations of data from the population surveys, the emergency room reports, and the federal treatment program reports.

These indexes suggest that marijuana use peaked in 1979 and then declined; heroin use reached an epidemic high in 1975, then declined precipitously until 1978, then increased gradually to end slightly higher than the epidemic level in 1987; cocaine use rose slowly from a small base from 1974 to 1982, and then increased dramatically from 1982 to 1987 with the fastest growth occurring from 1985 to 1986. D. Boyum, *A Second Look at Supply Reduction Effectiveness: New Methods and Applications*, pp. 15–17 (June, 1989) (Working Paper No. 89-01-17, Program in Clinical Justice Policy and Management, Kennedy School of Government, Harvard University).

For a simpler account of trends in drug use, see National Institute on Drug Abuse, *National Household Survey on Drug Abuse: Summary of Selected Findings—1982* (1983).

[15]D. Boyum, note 14, p. 16.

[16]This is based on personal experience. I was then the Chief Planning Officer of the United States Department of Justice's Drug Enforcement Administration.

abuse trends.[17] Newspaper articles began to appear describing cocaine use by entertainers, sports figures, and other celebrities.

These indicators should have set off alarm bells. But other indicators were not so discouraging. Until the early 1980s, the systems that monitored the adverse consequences of drug use (such as deaths, visits to emergency rooms, entrances into treatment programs, and arrests for street crimes) did not reveal a substantial cocaine problem.[18] The price of cocaine remained high—well out of reach for casual use by poor urbanites or teenagers.[19] Cocaine use seemed to be confined to America's upper and middle classes.

Suddenly, in the early 1980s, the cocaine problem mushroomed. The epidemic spread from upper and middle classes to the lower classes.[20] The indicators that registered the adverse social consequences of cocaine use began to escalate rapidly.[21]

In retrospect, the indicators probably were reflecting two distinct trends. Upper and middle class users who had begun using cocaine in the late 1970s had by 1983 become dependent on it and had been involved with cocaine long enough for its financial and social demands to have depleted their economic and social capital. Bank accounts had been emptied, the tolerance of employers exhausted, and the support of family and friends withdrawn. For the first time, the troubles of upper and middle class users registered not only in intimate private circles, but in public institutions and thus national statistics.

At the same time, cocaine moved into poorer neighborhoods, where the publicly visible effects of cocaine use appeared much more quickly. The financial, psychological, and social demands of cocaine use collapsed

---

[17]National Institute on Drug Abuse, *Highlights—1985 National Household Survey on Drug Abuse 2* (Press Release, 1986).

[18]*See* National Institute on Drug Abuse, *Dawn Semiannual Report Trend Data* (Statistical Series G, No. 17, 1986).

[19]*See* D. Boyum, note 14, pp. 6, 16.

[20]Interestingly, I believe this is the first drug epidemic thought to have spread this way. Other drug epidemics that have crossed class boundaries have moved up the socio-economic ladder rather than down it.

[21]National Institute on Drug Abuse, *Use and Consequences of Cocaine: Trends in Past Year and Past Month Use of Cocaine by Age Category, 1972–1985* (Press Release, October 1986). *See also* National Institute on Drug Abuse, *Dawn Semiannual Report Trend Data* (Statistical Series G, No. 23, 1989); National Institute on Drug Abuse, *Dawn Semiannual Report Trend Data* (Statistical Series G, No. 17, 1986).

the fragile supports of poor families, and the consequences spilled out into public institutions. The combined effect was to thrust the disastrous consequences of cocaine use into the public record and social consciousness.

Shortly thereafter, crack appeared.[22] This cheap form of cocaine facilitated cocaine's spread to poorer and younger consumers. This, in turn, created new marketing opportunities that led to conflicts among those competing to exploit them. Because the cocaine markets were on city streets rather than in hotels or houses, dealer violence spilled over to the general population.

In short, it is cocaine and crack rather than heroin, marijuana, and hallucinogens that are now shaping both our conception and the underlying reality of the drug problem. Our long-standing concerns about drug-related crime have changed: drug-related crime in the 1970s was mostly restricted to robberies and burglaries committed by heroin junkies desperate for a fix, but now it includes street violence committed by warring cocaine-dealing gangs. Similarly, we have long worried that drugs could trap our children, but the availability and low price of crack now make this an even more serious threat. But for cocaine, the drug problem might have remained what it had previously been.

Understanding that we are dealing with a cocaine epidemic makes it somewhat easier to analyze future prospects for growth or control of the problem. As David Musto reminds us, this is only the most recent cocaine epidemic the country has faced. We endured a previous cocaine epidemic around the turn of the century.[23] That experience provides a bench mark we might use to set expectations for the future.

---

[22]It is difficult to date the appearance of 'crack' as a commonly abused drug. The difficulty is conceptual as well as empirical. The conceptual problem is that smokeable crack has always been present to some degree among the population of cocaine users—it is therefore not clear how we should define 'commonly abused'. Empirically, it is difficult to get accurate information about when crack abuse crossed this conceptual threshold. It appears that by the summer of 1985 it had become recognized nationally. By the late fall of 1985, crack was apparently being commonly produced and consumed in the United States. Personal Communication with Nicholas Kozell, Chief of the Epidemiology Branch, National Institute on Drug Abuse (January 19th, 1990).

For a description of the impact of crack on the inner cities, see Johnson, Williams, Dei, and Sanabria, 'Drug Abuse in the Inner City: Impact on Hard Drug Users and the Community', in *Drugs and Crime* (M. Tonry and J. Wilson, eds.) (forthcoming) (*Crime and Justice: An Annual Review of the Research*, vol. 13, 1990).

[23]Musto, 'America's First Cocaine Epidemic', *Wilson Quarterly*, Summer 1989, pp. 59–64.

The last epidemic also was widespread. Indeed, cocaine was greeted warmly and enthusiastically, and prescribed for curing many ills, including addiction to opiates. At the outset, few adverse consequences of the growing consumption of cocaine appeared. It was not until about a decade into the epidemic that hints of bad effects began to appear. Careers of prominent people were ruined. The drug began to be linked to crime. As the negative consequences emerged, society's attitudes toward cocaine began to change. As a result, cocaine use began to decline, public policies regulating drugs became more restrictive, and penalties for violation became harsher. Society eventually learned that cocaine was dangerous, and its use gradually declined.

Unfortunately, as society's experience with cocaine receded into the distant past, the institutionalized opposition to cocaine use became more abstract. Opposition was no longer fueled by hard personal experience. Society became ready, once again, to be tempted by the appeal of what is initially an attractive drug.

In some respect, the last epidemic gives us reason to be optimistic. It indicates that society eventually learns through its collective experience that cocaine is dangerous, and this leads to decreased use. The problems, however, with viewing society's last bout with cocaine as a success story are first, that too many casualties resulted from the epidemic before society learned about the problem, and second, that the public policy measures at the end of the epidemic probably were harsher than they needed to be given that society was learning its lesson the hard way.

There are limits to analogizing the current epidemic to the last one. Features of today's society make it likely that the casualties taken in the upswing of the epidemic may be greater than they were at the turn of the century. By all accounts, crack appears to be a more dangerous drug than powder cocaine.[24] Society as a whole, or in pockets, may be more vulnerable to drug addiction than was American society at the end of the century. AIDS is a far greater threat to drug users than previous diseases spread through drug epidemics.

On the other hand, there are some signs that the scenario is repeating

---

[24]Vereby and Gold, 'From Coca Leaves to Crack: The Effects of Dose and Routes of Administration in Abuse Liability', 18 *Psychiatric Annals* 513 (1988).

itself. Middle class cocaine use seems to be diminishing.[25] Attitudes toward cocaine use are becoming more hostile.[26] Use may very well be declining—at least among society's better off.

Perhaps the most important lesson to be drawn from the past is that cocaine use is epidemic in the society rather than endemic; a sharp increase in use probably will be followed by a sharp decrease. As we wait for society to again learn through hard experience that this drug—cocaine—is a bad one, however, we can make long-term gains by acting aggressively now to stem the reach of the cocaine epidemic. This is the battle we must fight now.

II. Drugs and the Law

A cornerstone of America's drug policy is the law that prohibits the use of some psychoactive drugs and regulates the use of others. Recently, an old debate about whether it is wise social policy to regulate the use of drugs has been re-opened.[27] The issue is whether those psychoactive drugs now legally proscribed, such as heroin, marijuana, and hallucinogens, should be 'legalized' in the interests of ending moralistic state paternalism, reducing the criminal violence associated with black markets and criminalized users, and encouraging the development of informal social controls to keep drug use within safe bounds.

A. ANALYZING LEGALIZATION OPTIONS

The legalization debate really proceeds at two different levels of analysis. One level focuses on the justice or propriety of using the power of the criminal law to control what is arguably a personal decision to 'choose one's own road to hell'. The other level focuses on the practical effect of legalization on important social objectives such as minimizing crime and promoting the welfare of the population.

The first level of analysis is an exercise in political philosophy.

---

[25]*See* 'Rich Versus Poor: Drug Patterns are Diverging', New York Times, August 30th, 1987, p. A1, col. 2.
[26]*See* generally *The Media-Advertising Partnership for a Drug-Free America, Changing Attitudes Towards Drug Use* (1988) [hereinafter Changing Attitudes].
[27]*See* generally Nadelmann, 'The Case for Legalization', 92 *Public Interest* 3 (1988).

Indeed, much of the force of the argument for legalization comes from the sense that it is morally improper—or at least illiberal—for the state to impose its view of personal virtue on the citizenry. It is particularly inappropriate to do this with the moralistic fervor that is associated with the passage and enforcement of criminal laws. Thus it is wrong in *principle* for the state to criminalize drug use. This position is little affected by arguments about the societal effects of such laws.

The second level of analysis is more empirical and consequentialist; it is concerned with the effects of prohibition or legalization on society. To engage in the second level of analysis, it is necessary to take three distinct analytic steps.

1. Imagining alternatives. The first step is to specify the nature of the legal regime that is to be substituted for the current one. There are, after all, many possibilities. They include:

> 1. 'total legalization', under which all restrictions on the production, sale, and use of the drugs would be eliminated;
> 2. 'legal for all except minors', under which dealers would be prohibited from selling to minors, and minors would be prohibited from purchasing or using specified drugs on pain of minor civil penalties for violations;
> 3. 'legal under medical prescription', under which distributors would be allowed to sell only to those who had medical prescriptions, and only those with medical prescriptions would be allowed to possess and use specified drugs;
> 4. 'legal under limited medical prescription', under which physicians would be authorized to prescribe specific drugs only for a limited number of medical indications;
> 5. 'legal under the supervision of governmental clinics', under which the government would assume monopolistic responsibility for distributing the drugs through government-sponsored clinics, and only those enrolled in the clinics would be allowed to possess or use the drugs; or
> 6. 'decriminalization of use', under which the production and distribution of the drugs would remain illegal, but criminal penalties for possession and use would be eliminated.

While all these regimes might be considered 'legalization' regimes, they differ enough in their operations and likely social consequences to require us carefully to identify which particular form of legalization we are considering before making predictions about the likely social outcomes of 'legalizing drugs.'[28] Otherwise, the analysis becomes distorted.

For example, in estimating the impact of 'legalization' on the size and nature of the black market in drugs, and on the level of drug use, it matters enormously whether one is discussing the most liberal legalization regimes (those toward the top of the list presented above) or the more restrictive forms of legalization (such as those toward the bottom of the list). Only the most liberal legal regimes can be expected to eliminate the black market entirely, and these are the ones that have the greatest potential for leading to dramatic increases in levels of use. The more limited legalization regimes provide some protection against the threat of explosive increases in narcotics use fueled by newly created legitimate markets, but only at the price of maintaining conditions that are favorable to a continuation of the black market.

2. Estimating probabilities of consequence. The second analytic step is to predict how adopting one of these legalization regimes would affect the social dimensions of the drug problem. In general, these predictions cannot be precise 'point estimates'—for example, one cannot responsibly say that violent crime would be reduced by 10 percent below current levels by adopting a given regime. There is simply not enough empirical evidence or actual experience with previous epidemics to justify such precise predictions. At best, one can estimate the likely directions and magnitudes of the changes that would occur under a particular legalization regime for each of the relevant dimensions of the problem (such as crime, neighborhood decay, effect on children, public health and safety, and the proper functioning of major social institutions). Even these broad estimates must be regarded only as the most likely ones.[29]

For example, in estimating the impact of legalization on future levels of drug use, one can tell a plausible story that consumption would

---

[28]*See* generally Kleiman and Saiger, 'Drug Legalization: The Importance of Asking the Right Question' (forthcoming in *Hofstra Law Review*).
[29]For an analytic framework for making decisions under uncertainty, see H. Raiffa, *Decision Analysis* (1968).

decrease under a legalization regime because, for example, the profit motive now animating illegal drug dealers to recruit new users would weaken,[30] and some of the allure associated with 'forbidden fruit' would disappear. But one can also envision that under the same legalization regime consumption would increase, perhaps even dramatically: drugs would become cheaper and more available across wider elements of the society, thereby making drug use more convenient; the stigma associated with drug use would disappear, thereby encouraging more common use; and legitimate suppliers would have as much reason to encourage wider drug use as the illegal dealers would.

Similarly, one can point to evidence that indicates that tight legal restrictions on drugs have been ineffective. In countries such as Singapore even the most stringent regimes have failed to eliminate drug use,[31] and drug use in the United States has increased despite the existence of the current legal regime.[32] But one can also point to evidence indicating that tightening controls has succeeded in reducing drug consumption: when England restricted the prescription of heroin to a small number of physicians in 1968, the rate at which new addicts appeared in England diminished,[33] and when the United States succeeded in breaking up the traffic in heroin from Turkey and France in the early 1970s, creating a heroin shortage on the east coast, the rate at which people began using heroin slowed.[34]

Faced with such divergent reasoning and evidence, one cannot be certain about the impact of legalization on levels of drug use. Uncertainty, however, is not the same as ignorance. Some outcomes are more probable than others. We should let the weight of our observations shift our sense of what is more or less likely in one direction or another.[35]

---

[30]Nadelmann, note 27, pp. 23–24.
[31]D. Lipton, 'Drug Control Abroad' (Spring 1989) (unpublished manuscript on file with the author).
[32]Nadelmann, note 27, p. 3.
[33]*See* H. Judson, *Heroin Addiction in Britain: What Americans Can Learn From the English Experience,* pp. 63–64 (1974).
[34]*See* Statement of John R. Bartels and Dr. Robert L. DuPont before the Subcommittee on Future Foreign Policy Research and Development (April 23rd, 1975).
[35]H. Raiffa, note 29.

What makes one estimate better than another is that it is more consistent with what is really known about the problem. Often that means that the good estimates include a wide range of possibilities.

In addition, in calculating the consequences of legalization one must recognize that a shift in the legal regime could produce unanticipated consequences in areas outside the current focus of consideration. For example, it is possible that any of the legalization strategies would undermine the effectiveness of many current treatment programs that seem to depend in part for their effectiveness on legal compulsion and difficult conditions in drug markets.[36] Perhaps a legalization regime would be good for most of the nation's communities, but have particularly bad consequences for the nation's poorest communities. Or, perhaps a legalization policy would salvage the criminal justice system, but break the back of the nation's medical and educational institutions. Obviously, one cannot anticipate or calculate every consequence. The point is that one must guard against the tendency to analyze the strengths of a given policy in dealing with only a few aspects of today's problems, while ignoring the proposed policy's weaknesses in dealing with the new problems that may arise once the legalization policy has been introduced.

3. Valuing uncertain consequences. The third analytic step is to consider what social values we most want to advance through drug policy. It is unlikely that a legalization strategy would be better than the current regulatory strategy for all relevant social concerns. In all likelihood, a legalization strategy would be better in some areas of performance, and worse in others.[37] For example, legalization might reduce criminal violence, but at the expense of reducing the health and social functioning of drug users and their children. Similarly, though legalization might reduce the state's reliance on coercion to achieve its purposes, and protect the criminal justice system from corruption, it might also

---

[36]*See* 'Special Issue: A Social Policy Analysis of Compulsory Treatment for Opiate Dependence,' 18 *Journal of Drug Issues*, fall 1988.
[37]For a discussion of the role of values in policy analysis, see Moore, *'Social Science and Policy Analysis: Some Fundamental Differences'*, in *Ethics, the Social Sciences, and Policy Analysis*, pp. 271–291 (1983).

increase public expenditures for treatment and prevention, and produce unfortunate results for the schools and medical institutions forced to contend with more widespread drug use. Which of these worlds one prefers is a matter of values as well as estimated consequences.

A complete analysis of the legalization question is beyond the scope of this paper. Before leaving the subject, however, it is worth casting some doubt on the optimistic predictions of those who favor legalization.

B. THE CURRENT LEGAL REGIME:
MORAL PROHIBITION OR RATIONAL REGULATION?

One of the most frustrating aspects of the current debate about legalization is that the debaters often seem ignorant about the current legal regime. The system of laws regulating drug use is often painted as a moralistic and paternalistic scheme rather than as a rational one for regulating the uses of psychoactive drugs.[38] It is true that much of the spirit of drug policy could be characterized as moralistic and paternalistic. It is also true that there are some important prohibitionist features of the current law. There are some drugs, for example, whose use is entirely prohibited in the United States. In addition, there are severe criminal penalties attached to illegal trafficking and use.

Still, the actual federal statute controlling the production, distribution and use of psychoactive drugs in the United States owes much to the spirit of regulation. It does not seek to eliminate all psychoactive drugs from society; it seeks to strike a reasonable balance between society's worries about the potential for drug abuse and its interest in being able to use the drugs for legitimate medical purposes.

The federal statute pursues these aims by establishing five levels of controls on drugs.[39] The most stringent level—Schedule I—is reserved for drugs that have no recognized legitimate medical uses. Heroin, marijuana, LSD, and other psychedelic drugs are included in Schedule I. Schedules II through V are used for drugs that have legitimate medical uses, but also some potential for abuse. The higher the estimated

---

[38]*See* generally Wisotsky, note 12.
[39]For a general description of the Controlled Substances Act, see Quinn and McLaughlin, 'The Evolution of Federal Drug Control Legislation', 1972–73 *Drug Abuse Law Review* 144–185.

potential for abuse, the higher the schedule and the more extensive the controls that are placed on the drug.

Cocaine, for example, is in Schedule II. It is legally manufactured and distributed in the United States as a topical anesthesia. In this sense, cocaine already is legalized, though it is very tightly regulated. Production is restricted to the amount estimated to be necessary to meet the very limited demand for its specialized medical uses. Only licensed physicians distribute it, and only to patients with well-established needs. Manufacturers, drugstores, physicians, and patients are all subjected to close governmental scrutiny.

Benzodiazepams, such as Valium, are in Schedule IV. This reflects the view that these drugs are less vulnerable to abuse than cocaine and that they have far wider medical applications. These drugs may be produced and distributed only by those licensed to do so, but the restrictions are less strict than those regulating cocaine: there are no manufacturing quotas, no special requirements that vendors keep the drugs in safes to guard against theft, and slightly looser record-keeping requirements.

The logical coherence and operational administration of this regulatory scheme can be attacked on several fronts. First, neither alcohol nor tobacco—two of the most widely used and abused drugs in the society—are included within its scope. Second, the schedules do not give weight to the recreational uses of drugs—regardless of how harmless the drugs might be. Only psychoactive drugs with approved medical uses can be used in the society, and only for those approved uses. Third, the methods used to estimate the abuse potential of drugs are flawed, and government decisions are often influenced by commercial manufacturers of psychoactive drugs with legitimate medical uses.[40] Still, despite its weaknesses, this statute is an honest piece of legislation that simultaneously expresses our society's deep concerns about the potential hazards of psychoactive drugs and its desire to harness the medical benefits they can produce. It provides a coherent framework within which to regulate psychoactive drugs.

---

[40]For a description and critical evaluation of these methods, see M. Fischman and N. Mello, *Testing for Abuse Liability of Drugs in Humans* (National Institute on Drug Abuse Research Monograph No. 92, 1989).

C. LEGALIZATION AND DRUG-RELATED CRIMINAL VIOLENCE

The confidence with which proponents of legalization predict large reductions in criminal violence as a consequence of some form of legalization strategy is unwarranted and is based on a misconception of the connection between drug distribution, drug use, and criminal violence.[41] In analyzing the impact of legalization on criminal violence, we must distinguish between the violence associated with illegal trafficking and the violence associated with drug use.[42]

Advocates of legalization may be correct that violence associated with illegal trafficking would decrease under a legalization regime. Creating a legitimate sector of drug production, distribution and use would weaken the illegal distribution system by creating an alternative source of supply for drug users.[43] To the extent that legal competition would drive illegal dealers out of business, and to the extent that the illegal drug business constitutes the only motivation and economic outlet for the criminal violence of the dealers, legalization would reduce the criminal violence associated with drug trafficking. It might also be true that once illegal dealers lost their powerful economic position as the sole source of drugs and as the principal creators of wealth in some communities, these dealers would become much easier to identify and arrest. The community would no longer be dependent on them for drugs and money. Both effects would tend to reduce criminal violence.

But there are reasons to be worried that the pacifying effect of legalization would be smaller than many anticipate. Only the most liberal legalization regime, complete legalization, would entirely eliminate the black market in drugs. The other regimes create conditions for black

---

[41]For a detailed exploration of these relationships, see Fagan, *Intoxication and Aggression;* Chaiken and Chaiken, 'Drugs and Predatory Crime', and Hunt, 'Drugs and Consensual Crime: Drug Dealing and Prostitution', each in *Drugs and Crime*, note 22.

[42]This is easy to do conceptually, but difficult to do empirically. For a successful effort at making this distinction, and for showing that the distinction matters, see Goldstein, Brownstein, Ryan, and Bellucci, *'Crack and Homicide in New York City, 1988: A Conceptually-Based Event Analysis'*, in *Contemporary Drug Problems* (forthcoming) [hereinafter Goldstein].

[43]Moore, *'Supply Reduction and Drug Law Enforcement'*, in *Drugs and Crime*, note 22.

markets to arise precisely because they impose restrictions on use.[44] Granted, the markets that arise to meet the demand that lies outside the legally tolerated uses might be less violent than those that now exist. After all, depending on the legalization regime adopted, drugs might be supplied by small-scale diversion from legal markets, rather than by international criminal cartels.[45] But one should not be too sanguine about this prospect. The black market in amphetamines—a legalized but stringently regulated drug—has involved violent motorcycle gangs as well as patients who divert their prescribed drugs to others.[46] When a profitable undertaking lies outside the law, it always seems to attract some level of violence.

Similarly, it is by no means clear that people with a talent for violence will stop using that talent for economic gains simply because one important opportunity disappears. The Mafia has shown that organizations with a capacity for sustained and disciplined violence can make a great deal of money from enterprises such as extortion, labor racketeering, loan sharking, and gambling as well as drugs.[47] No small amount of violence is associated with struggles over the control and conduct of these enterprises.[48] Consequently, there is little reason to believe that today's drug gangs, now schooled in violence, will fade away, any more than there was reason to believe that the gangs that arose during Prohibition would fade away once Prohibition ended.

It may also be that the portion of criminal violence attributable to drug trafficking is smaller than it now appears to be.[49] The definition of a 'drug-related killing' is sufficiently loose that one cannot be sure that the apparent increase in drug-related homicide has not been inflated by attributing more homicides to this category than would have been

---

[44]H. Packer, *The Limits of Criminal Sanction*, pp. 277–282 (1968).
[45]Moore, *'Drug Policy and Organized Crime'*, in *America's Habit: Drug Abuse, Drug Trafficking, and Organized Crime*, Appendix G pp. 49–54 (1986).
[46]Office of Intelligence, Drug Enforcement Administration, *Project Crystal City: A Survey of Methamphetamine Trafficking and Abuse in the United States*, pp. 21–22 (1989).
[47]*See* Schelling, *'What Is the Business of Organized Crime?'*, 20 *Journal of Public Law*, pp. 73–75 (1971); *see generally* P. Reuter, *Disorganized Crime: The Economics of the Visible Hand* (1983).
[48]For a recent discussion of the role of violence in illegal drug markets, see M. Kleiman, *Marijuana: Costs of Abuse, Costs of Control*, pp. 122–133 (1989).
[49]*See* Goldstein, note 42, p. 22.

attributed several years ago.[50] If this were true, then the elimination of drug-related homicides would be less important than one might now assume. All these caveats make one less confident that legalization strategies would produce a marked and significant reduction in violent crimes associated with drug trafficking.

The prediction that legalization would reduce significantly violent crimes committed by drug users is even shakier. This prediction is based heavily on the idea that drug users commit crimes to earn money to pay for their habits.[51] In legalized markets, the argument goes, drugs would be cheaper so crime would decrease. If users do not commit crimes exclusively to pay for their habits, however, it is less clear that legalization would control crime.

If, for example, drug users commit crimes because criminal enterprise represents the best way that they know to get money, and if users would spend more on other commodities if they spent less on drugs because legalization made them cheaper, there is no reason to predict that legalization would reduce drug user crime. Or, if what links drugs to crime are physiological states caused by drug use that either stimulate excitability or aggression or dull the psychological inhibitions to violence, then crime by users will vary according to consumption and not price. Any increased level of drug consumption associated with legalization actually would produce an increase, rather than a decrease, in drug-related crime.[52]

The first possibility is supported empirically by evidence indicating that criminal activity often precedes drug use, and is sustained even after drug use declines.[53] The second argument seems implausible when discussing heroin, but more likely when considering cocaine.[54] More-

---

[50]For a methodological discussion of the problems in producing and applying an operational definition of drug-related homicide, see Goldstein, 'Drugs and Violent Crime', in *Pathways to Criminal Violence*, pp. 16–24 (1989).

[51]See *Drug Use and Crime: Report of the Panel on Drug Use and Criminal Behavior*, 3 (1976).

[52]For a discussion of these possibilities, see Fagan, 'Intoxication and Aggression', in *Drugs and Crime*, note 22.

[53]*See* Nurco, Hanlon, Kinlock, and Duszynski, 'Differential Criminal Patterns of Narcotic Addicts over an Addiction Career', 26 *Criminology* 418 (1988).

[54]National Institute on Drug Abuse, 'Cocaine Use in America', *Prevention Networks*, April 1986, pp. 6–8; National Commission for Injury Prevention and Control, *Injury Prevention: Meeting the Challenge*, pp. 206, 226 (1989).

over, alcohol's close relationship to violent crime reminds us that mere intoxication can be strongly associated with violence.[55]

Again, these observations do not prove that legalization would fail to reduce crime; they simply decrease one's estimate of the likelihood that crime would decrease. There is a real possibility that legalization will not produce a large reduction in crime.

D. LEGALIZATION AND LEVELS OF DRUG USE AND ABUSE

The most optimistic predictions made by proponents of legalization are first, that drug use would not increase significantly as a result of legalization, and second, that even if drug use increased, the social consequences would not be as severe as those we now face, because drugs would be available in more benign forms, and informal social controls would arise to minimize drug abuse.

The prediction that drug consumption would remain constant or decline under a legalization regime seems to be based on one of three hypotheses. The first is that only the illicitness of drugs makes them attractive to potential users. If the profit motive for illegal dealers were taken away, and the 'forbidden fruit' aspect of drugs eliminated, drugs would lose their appeal.[56]

A second theory is that the demand for drugs is perfectly inelastic. There are some people who are predisposed to use drugs who cannot be discouraged from using drugs by price or inconvenience. Others will not be tempted into use by ready access and social acceptability. Under this theory, legalizing drugs would not result in increased use.

The third hypothesis is that people would learn from experience which drugs are safe and which are not. Once it becomes clear that some

---

[55]Collins, 'Alcohol Use and Criminal Behavior: An Empirical, Theoretical, and Methodological Overview', in *Drinking and Crime: Perspectives on the Relationship between Alcohol Consumption and Criminal Behavior* (1981). For another discussion of this relationship, see Gerstein, 'Alcohol Use and Consequences', in Panel on Alternative Policies Affecting the Prevention of Alcohol Abuse and Alcoholism, *Alcohol and Public Policy: Beyond the Shadow of Prohibition*, pp. 203–07, 216–17 (1981) [hereinafter *Alcohol and Public Policy*].
[56]Nadelmann, note 27, p. 12.

drugs are dangerous, people will voluntarily choose not to use them. In this view, the laws give only redundant protection once society has learned about the different drugs.[57]

There is relatively little evidence to support any of these hypotheses, and, in some cases, the reasoning is quite flawed. The claim that illicitness alone makes drug dealers aggressive marketeers is almost certainly wrong—at least as a general proposition. We know from empirical studies that drug users are rarely recruited into drug use by drug dealers.[58] Indeed, new drug users are among the most dangerous consumers for illegal dealers to recruit.[59] Instead, neophytes are recruited by drug using peers who are themselves just starting drug use and show few of the negative consequences of drug use.[60]

Illicitness may increase the appeal of drugs for some potential users who seek 'forbidden fruit', but it may well discourage others. Further, it is only the most liberal form of legalization that eliminates the illicit aspect for children and teenagers. And it would be hard in any case to make drug use seem boring and conventional. Drug use is inherently risky and precocious behavior, regardless of its legal status, and thus inevitably appeals to some teenagers.

One must also acknowledge that while legalization weakens the black market in drugs, it establishes a legitimate market that has some of the same internal incentives for expansion as the illegal one. Our experience with legalizing alcohol and gambling shows that legitimated vice industries have a zeal for profits and market development. Remarkably, these motives remain strong even when, as in the case of gambling, the enterprises are run by governments.[61]

---

[57]*See* generally Maloff, Becker, Fonaroff, and Rodin, 'Informal Social Controls and Their Influence on Substance Use', in *Control Over Intoxicant Use Pharmacological, Psychological, and Social Considerations,* pp. 53–76 (1982) (informal controls, as opposed to formal mechanisms, may be more effective policy alternatives for controlling substance use and addiction).
[58]*See* Simons, Conger, and Whitbeck, 'A Multistage Social Learning Model of the Influences of Family and Peers Upon Adolescent Substance Abuse', 18 *Journal of Drug Issues,* pp. 293–315 (1988)
[59]M. Moore, *Buy and Bust,* pp. 18–19 (1977).
[60]Simons, Conger, and Whitbeck, note 58, p. 304.
[61]For a discussion of government-controlled gambling, see C. Clotfelter and P. Cook, *Selling Hope: State Lotteries in America* (1989).

The second claim, that there is a fixed number of drug users in society, flies in the face of both common sense and experience. After all, societal drug use has not remained constant. Cocaine use has increased dramatically in the past decade.[62] This increase has not been associated with a corresponding decline in alcohol use among similar age cohorts.[63] There is thus no reason to believe that the demand for drugs is invariant in the society.

In fact, experience tells us the opposite: behavior is influenced by opportunities. If the opportunities for drug use are distributed more widely through the population, with less stigma associated with use, more people will exploit the opportunity. It should not seem surprising that the most widely used psychoactive substances are tobacco and alcohol—drugs that are now legal. Moreover, it seems fairly clear that reducing accessibility to drugs has an impact on levels of consumption: when alcohol was prohibited, alcohol consumption fell by a third;[64] when states have raised taxes on alcohol, alcohol consumption has fallen, apparently even among chronic alcoholics;[65] when England restricted the prescription of heroin to a small number of government-supervised physicians in 1968, the rate at which new heroin addicts appeared in England slowed;[66] when Vietnam veterans who used drugs heavily in Vietnam under conditions of ready availability returned to the United

---

[62]National Institute on Drug Abuse, *Epidemiologic Trends in Drug Abuse* I-1 (1989).
[63]Surveys conducted by the National Institute on Drug Abuse over the past decade indicate a constant level of alcohol use by American citizens; it is neither increasing nor decreasing. *See* P. O'Malley, G. Bachman, and L. Johnston, 'Period, Age, and Cohort Effects on Substance Abuse Among American Youth, 1976–1982', 74 *American Journal of Public Health* pp. 682–688 (1984) (alcohol use by young adults ages 18–25 and adults over age 25 remained stable in survey years 1979, 1982, and 1985). On the other hand, these surveys also indicate a distinct upward trend in cocaine use by American citizens in general. Obviously, this indicates an increase in drug demand in this society. If the idea that drug demand remains constant were true, we would have to see alcohol users 'switching' to cocaine, and therefore a decrease in alcohol use, in order to account for the rising numbers of cocaine users. The idea that cocaine is somehow "replacing' alcohol as the drug of preference is simply not true. The simple fact is that the demand for drugs and the absolute number of drug users are rising.
[64]*See* generally N. Clark, *Deliver Us From Evil: An Interpretation of American Prohibition*, pp. 146–147 (1976).
[65]*See* Cook, 'The Effect of Liquor Taxes on Drinking, Cirrhosis, and Auto Accidents', in *Alcohol and Public Policy*, note 55, p. 256.
[66]H. Judson, note 33, p. 64.

States, where drugs were less readily available, many abandoned their use;[67] and when cocaine traffickers arrived in the United States with tons of cocaine, an epidemic of cocaine use was launched.

Such observations do not 'prove' that levels of drug use would increase if drugs were legalized, but they certainly influence the betting odds. The bet that drug consumption would decrease seems like a long shot. The bet that drug consumption would increase seems surer. One would even have to put reasonable odds on the chance that drug use would increase significantly.

Probably the shakiest prediction made by advocates of legalization is the third prediction: that informal controls would arise, rooted in personal experience, that then would guide individual users in the proper use of drugs and would shield the population as a whole from dramatic increases in levels of drug use and/or its adverse consequences. This prediction is based principally on a hopeful analogy to what now is occurring with respect to smoking.[68]

To some extent, this prediction seems plausible. If drugs were legal, one would see many more people using drugs in controlled and successful ways than one now sees under the current legal regime. Drug users in a legal regime would be psychologically and sociologically different—generally sturdier—than those who use drugs under a prohibitionist regime, and informal controls would, in fact, arise to give them guidance about safe drug use.

While the proportion of drug users who are in trouble with a drug will diminish as a fraction of all drug users, however, the absolute number of users in trouble would increase because the total number of users probably would have increased. Moreover, even those who use drugs relatively safely have accidents. And while the probability of such accidents may be low, due to the fact that they are using drugs safely, the absolute burden on the society would be large because there would be more people now using drugs.

---

[67]L. Robbins, *The Vietnam Drug User Returns*, pp. 78–79 (Special Action Office for Drug Abuse Prevention Monograph Series A, No. 2, 1973).
[68]*See* generally U.S. Department of Health and Human Services, *Report of the Surgeon General, Reducing the Health Consequences of Smoking: 25 Years of Progress* (1989).

In sketching these possibilities, I am drawing heavily on an analogy with alcohol.[69] Society now exhibits a very broad distribution of drinking practices. Many of these practices are reasonably safe in the sense that they are unlikely to produce a crime, an accident, or a collapse of a social institution. Because there is a great deal of 'safe drinking', one might say that society's informal social controls are working well.

On the other hand, a small fraction but huge absolute number of people are in serious trouble with alcohol—a number that dwarfs our estimates of the number in serious trouble with drugs.[70] Moreover, a significant portion of what society views as the alcohol problem— namely, traffic accidents, domestic fights, even lost jobs—is generated by the large group of drinkers whose consumption patterns are fairly benign, but who cannot entirely eliminate the risks associated with being intoxicated at the wrong place and the wrong time.[71] There is no reason to ignore this pattern in making predictions about patterns of drug consumption and consequences under a legal regime.

E. A CONTINGENT CONCLUSION

In sum, I am sympathetic to the notion that society should have a rational regulatory scheme for controlling the availability of psychoactive drugs according to reasoned estimates of their potential for abuse and their value in legitimate medical use. I believe that the current statutes create a workable framework for such a regime.

In answer to the question of whether society would be better off if it widened legitimate access to drugs such as heroin and cocaine, I would say no. My judgment is that consumption would increase substantially, and while that increased consumption would in many ways look more benign than the drug use we now see, this appearance would be an illusion because it would hide significant absolute increases in the damages associated with drug use. Indeed, widening access to cocaine

---

[69] *Alcohol and Public Policy*, note 55, pp. 16–47.
[70] Approximately ten million people are classified as problem drinkers. Gerstein, 'Alcohol Use and Consequences', in *Alcohol and Public Policy*, note 55, p. 208. There are less than a million daily users of heroin and cocaine, however.
[71] *Alcohol and Public Policy*, note 55, p. 44 ("[a]lcohol problems occur *throughout* the drinking population").

seems like a particularly reckless move at a time when society is trying to cope with dramatic increases in the use of a drug that has proven over the last decade its capacities to attract unwary users and to inflict significant losses on American communities.

III. Supply-Versus Demand-Reduction Strategies

If legalizing drugs does not solve the drug problem, what is the alternative? The current policy debate generally focuses on the wisdom of relying on supply-reduction versus demand-reduction strategies. Supply reduction strategies include crop eradication, drug interdiction at national borders, and the immobilization of trafficking networks.

Demand-reduction strategies are often divided between treatment programs designed to help experienced users abandon their drug use and prevention programs designed to dissuade non-users or novice users from drug experimentation. Specific efforts include broadcast media campaigns designed to alert citizens to the hazards of drug use; counselling programs that train high risk adolescents in methods of resisting peer group pressures to experiment with drugs; and treatment programs, therapeutic communities, and methadone maintenance programs designed to reduce users' reliance on drugs.

Each of these approaches has a certain logic. The logic of the supply reduction strategy is simple: if drugs aren't available, people won't use them. In addition, supply-reduction strategies have the political advantage of externalizing the problem by focusing public hostility on popular villains.

The logic of demand-reduction approaches is equally simple: so long as people want to use drugs, someone will find it profitable to supply them. Consequently, the only permanent solution is to reduce demand and the conditions that create demand. Demand-side strategies have the political advantages of focusing society's energies on opportunities for children and glorifying the efforts of parents' groups.

The question of which approach works best is more difficult to answer. In recent years, we seem to have witnessed some of the important limitations of supply-side approaches to the drug problem. We have more than doubled the resources on the supply-side efforts, focused them increasingly on cocaine, and yet seen violence rise as the price of cocaine has fallen to historically low levels.[72] One can argue, of course, that the situation would have been even worse but for the heroic supply-side interventions, but the argument rings a bit hollow.

Two pieces of empirical data suggest that supply-reduction efforts can be successful in reducing the supply of drugs. First, the price of drugs in illicit markets is much higher than the price of the same drugs in legal markets. Heroin is 60 times more expensive than equivalent doses of morphine; cocaine is 15 times more expensive in illicit markets than in legal markets.[73] The price elasticity of demand for these drugs does not have to be great for such huge price effects to significantly decrease the consumption of these drugs.[74]

Second, an examination of the prices and quantities of drugs consumed by the United States population over approximately the last two decades reveals three periods in which supply-reduction efforts seemed to have succeeded. Those were periods in which the measured price of drugs increased even as the indicators of the quantity consumed fell. In the early 1970s, crop control efforts in Turkey and enforcement actions against the 'French Connection' produced a shortage of heroin on the East Coast.[75] In the late 1970s, crop eradication programs in Mexico seemed to produce a nationwide reduction in the supply of heroin. Recently, expanded interdiction efforts seem to have produced a reduction in the supply of marijuana. These successes must be compared with a clear failure: for the last ten years, the price of cocaine has been falling as the quantity consumed has increased.[76]

Thus, it is unclear whether supply-reduction efforts are contributing to the solution of the drug problem. There have been some successes, and some failures. We can only engage in informed speculation as to why some efforts succeed and some fail. Current thinking suggests that the important long-run effects of supply-reduction efforts operate by making

---

[72]*See* generally Moore, 'Supply Reduction and Drug Law Enforcement', in *Drugs and Crime*, note 22.
[73]D. Boyum, note 14.
[74]Moore, 'Supply Reduction and Drug Law Enforcement', in *Drugs and Crime*, note 22 (numerical estimates of price elasticities).
[75]Statement of John R. Bartels and Dr. Robert L. DuPont, note 34.
[76]Moore, 'Supply Reduction and Drug Law Enforcement', in *Drugs and Crime*, note 22.

it extremely difficult for dealers to complete risky transactions.[77] This, more than control over raw materials, technology, capital, or labor, reduces the supply of drugs to illicit markets and forces the price well above the prices for equivalent drugs in legitimate markets.

On the demand side, we are accumulating evidence that treatment programs do succeed in reducing drug use and improving the behavior and condition of many drug users who participate—at least so long as the drug users remain in the programs.[78] Drug treatment programs rarely produce 'cures' in the sense that those treated reduce their drug use to zero and stay that way for the rest of their lives. Instead, they produce reductions in drug use and criminal conduct, and improvements in health and social functioning while the user remains in treatment.[79] Sometimes these effects last for a period after treatment. While such results are not necessarily cures, they are valuable in the way that successful efforts to manage chronic diseases are valuable: they improve the patient's quality of life and her social functioning.

The fact that drug treatment programs produce important changes in behavior only so long as the users remain in treatment heightens the significance of treatment programs' capacity to retain users. A significant finding now emerging is that legal compulsion—either through court diversion, formal probation, or civil commitment—helps to retain users in treatment without losing effectiveness.[80] This finding is important not only because it suggests ways of increasing the effectiveness of treatment, but also because it widens the range of users who usefully might be treated to include reluctant criminal offenders as well as those users who have simply decided they have had enough. In many ways, coerced treatment programs are superior to prisons and jails as a social response to crime-committing drug users; they seem to provide significant crime suppression results (to say nothing of other therapeutic benefits) at lower economic costs.[81]

---

[77] *Id.*
[78] *See* Anglin and Hser, 'Treatment of Drug Abuse', in *Drugs and Crime*, note 22.
[79] *Id.*
[80] *See* Anglin, 'The Efficacy of Civil Commitment in Treating Narcotics Addiction', in *Compulsory Treatment of Drug Abuse: Research and Clinical Practice* (National Institute on Drug Abuse Research Monograph 86, 1988).
[81] *Id.*

The evidence on prevention programs is much harder to come by. It is true that society's attitudes are turning against cocaine, and that this change follows a mass media campaign to alert people to the hazards of the drug.[82] But it is also true that society has been accumulating real, immediate experience with cocaine during the same period. We have seen attitudes toward smoking change dramatically, and this holds out hope that society's ideas about other drugs might change as it learns they are dangerous.[83] As noted above, if history repeated itself, attitudes about cocaine use will change as well. It is also clear, however, that society, and individual drug users, pay an enormous price in learning about tobacco and cocaine the hard way. Prevention programs should try to substitute for the hard learning that comes from widespread personal experiences.

With respect to the effectiveness of the more focused drug prevention programs targeted at high risk youth, the jury is still out.[84] It seems that school-based programs that focus intensively on teaching resistance skills either alone or in combination with general life skills do delay the onset of drug use.[85] Achieving greater and more durable preventive effects, however, appears to require programs combining focused efforts on children with mass media appeals and other measures that affect parents and other community institutions.[86] Apparently, the message must be communicated through the broader environment as well as in one's individual life, and individuals must learn how to behave consistently with the message as well as simply hear it.

The conclusion, then, is that there is room for optimism about demand-side approaches, but they do not offer certain success any more than do supply-reduction approaches.

If one analyzes trends in federal spending for supply and demand

---

[82]*Changing Attitudes,* note 26.
[83]*Reducing the Health Consequences of Smoking: 25 Years of Progress,* note 68.
[84]For an overview of the literature in this area, see Botvin, 'Substance Abuse Prevention: Theory, Practice and Effectiveness', in *Drugs and Crime,* note 22. For some experiments with prevention programs, see P. Ellickson, R. Bell, M. Thomas, A. Robyn, and G. Zellman, *Designing and Implementing Project ALERT: A Smoking and Drug Prevention Experiment* (Rand Corporation Publication No. R-3754-CHF, 1988); W. DeJong, *Arresting the Demand for Drugs: Police and School Partnerships to Prevent Drug Abuse,* 106–120 (National Institute of Justice, Issues and Practices Series, 1987).
[85]W. DeJong, note 84, pp. 106–120.
[86]*Id.,* pp. 129–130.

reduction over the last two decades, two facts stand out. First, overall spending has increased a great deal—by a factor of 10 since 1972, and by a factor of 40 since 1969![87] Second, the proportion of spending devoted to treatment has declined dramatically, while the proportion devoted to both supply reduction and preventive education have increased dramatically. In fact, the fastest growing component of federal drug abuse expenditures seems to be preventive education.

To a degree, one can see these trends as an appropriate response to the emerging cocaine epidemic. After all, when the epidemic is rising, it is most important that future growth be dampened, and both supply-reduction efforts and drug education serve this function. Recognizing that society's current capacity to treat cocaine dependence is quite limited makes the argument even stronger.[88] In theory, spending money on cocaine treatment is desirable; it is just that existing programs have not been particularly effective.

Still, one has the distinct sense that current drug strategy underinvests in treatment efforts. There are, by now, many casualties of the epidemic who need even the limited help that can now be provided but cannot afford it. Furthermore, society urgently must experiment with a wide variety of programs for treating cocaine use. Society, then, should shift its response to the drug problem in the direction of increased treatment. This need is made particularly urgent by the threat that AIDS now poses to intravenous drug users.

To this extent, then, categorizing policy into supply- and demand-reduction approaches is useful. But this categorization is also problematic. Instead of illuminating opportunities for effective joint action, the categories seem to foster a polemical debate about which approach should predominate. This debate, in turn, tends to obscure the important and

---

[87]The principal references on which I am relying in making these estimates are the following: *Strategy Council on Drug Abuse, Federal Strategy for Drug Abuse and Drug Traffic Prevention—1975* (1975); *Strategy Council on Drug Abuse, Federal Strategy for Drug Abuse and Drug Traffic Prevention—1979* (1979); and *The White House, National Drug Control Strategy—1989* (1989).

[88]For an overview of treatment effectiveness, see Kleber and Gawin, 'Cocaine Abuse: A Review of Current and Experimental Treatments', in *Cocaine: Pharmacology, Effects, and Treatment of Abuse*, (National Institute on Drug Abuse Research Monograph 50, 1984). For a discussion of the opportunities for treating cocaine use, see Rawson, 'Cut the Crack: The Policymaker's Guide to Cocaine Treatment', *Policy Review*, Winter 1990, pp. 10–19.

valuable interactions between supply-reduction efforts and demand-reduction efforts.

For example, drug policy should concentrate on supply reduction and drug law enforcement to create an environment in which it is difficult and inconvenient for potential users to acquire drugs, and in which life for experienced users is sufficiently uncomfortable that they are motivated to seek treatment.[89] In this way, supply-reduction and law-enforcement efforts support prevention and treatment programs.

Another point: the drug laws are an important educational statement that shapes the public's views of the various drugs. A law does more than create a liability for criminal prosecution; it is a powerful normative statement.[90] That statement may not be particularly influential to those who have already begun using drugs, or who define themselves in opposition to the broader society. Nonetheless, for those who have not yet started using drugs, or for those who have not settled into an oppositional stance, the fact that society has legislated against some drugs may have a useful educational impact.

Finally, at local levels, in the cities where drug use is now producing devastating effects, the opportunity exists for communities to combat drugs by combining law enforcement, preventive education, and treatment. Law enforcement at street levels is needed to help parents maintain control over the environments that their children encounter, and to reinforce the message produced in educational programs that drugs are dangerous, particularly for kids. Street-level law enforcement also helps to control drug-related crime and improve the condition of drug users by motivating the users directly or indirectly to seek treatment.[91] Treatment programs are valuable because they are more effective than jails in controlling crime and re-integrating offenders into the community (they are also less expensive and more available than jails). The opportunity to recognize and exploit the synergy of these approaches is obscured by a categorization that seems to reflect the organization and responsibilities

---

[89]*See Domestic Council Drug Abuse Task Force, White Paper on Drug Abuse,* pp. 2–4 (1975).
[90]*See generally* M. Golding, *Philosophy of Law,* pp. 39–43 (1975).
[91]*See* M. Kleiman, A. Barnett, A. Bouza and K. Burke, *Street Level Drug Enforcement* (National Institute of Justice Issues and Practices Series, 1988).

of the federal government rather than the opportunities available to state and local governments.

This categorization fosters a polemical debate because it is closely tied to broader political outlooks. Generally speaking, conservatives tend to favor law enforcement and supply reduction over demand reduction and treatment. Liberals tend to prefer demand reduction and treatment. Such broad political views count heavily in determining policy positions —especially in a world where little reliable information about effectiveness is available.

The categories of supply and demand reduction are also closely, though not perfectly, aligned with professional interests. Supply reduction and law enforcement are often seen as the same thing since it is assumed that enforcement efforts are properly directed at sources of supply rather than users. These measures tend to attract the support of police and criminal justice officials. Demand reduction and the social/ medical approach are assumed to be equivalent because they do not appear to rely on the coercive power of the state, and use volunteers, parents, and physicians more than enforcement personnel. Quite naturally, they attract the support of physicians and public health personnel. This alignment with professional interests tends to harden divisions in the war against drugs.

Insofar as the categorization of supply- and demand-reduction efforts provides a way to track federal priorities, it is a useful analytic device. Insofar as it fosters a continuing political stalemate, or divides the institutions that must deal with the problem, however, the categorization stands in the way of effective governmental action. We must keep clearly in mind that the war on drugs is being fought block by block in cities. We must defend those blocks by establishing effective working partnerships among parents, schools, police, courts and treatment agencies at local levels. That requires us to understand the complementary nature of supply- and demand-reduction strategies.

IV. Groping Toward an Effective Drug Policy

With respect to drugs, society is now trying to do two difficult tasks simultaneously. It is mobilizing itself to take action against an urgent problem that is probably going to get worse before it gets better, and that would respond to prompt and effective action, with substantial long term rewards for the society. As it takes action, however, it is searching for more certain and effective ways of responding to the problem.

This is not unusual, of course. Society often must simultaneously act to confront urgent social problems even as it develops the perspective and knowledge that it needs to address the problem effectively. Problems come upon us unannounced; not everything can be predicted or prepared for.

Moreover, it is not particularly bad that these things occur simultaneously. Necessity does produce inventions. The inventions, if reviewed and analyzed, provide an experimental basis for important social learning.

Unfortunately, our opportunities for learning are usually squandered because the forms of discourse appropriate to mobilization for action are inconsistent with the forms that are appropriate for learning. Mobilizing the society to take action seems to require a language of urgency about the problem and certainty about the solutions. Building commitment to the cause seems to require certainty about the direction. On the other hand, the forms of discourse that are appropriate for learning often seem inconsistent with the requirements for action. The social scientists who seek to develop society's perspective on social problems, and organize its learning about what works and what does not, often establish a discourse that seems to require that the world stand still and that first premises be re-examined before any action is taken. Otherwise, any intellectual inquiry is tainted by the rude requirements of the practical world and is not to be trusted.

The challenge before society is to see whether it can forge a form of discourse that allows society to learn and adapt even as it acts aggressively to deal with the urgent task of limiting the cocaine epidemic and with the longer term problem of reducing the endemic social consequences of using heroin, marijuana, alcohol, and tobacco. There is much need for more disciplined thought and fact gathering as society confronts these problems. In this dialogue, the question of the proper legal regime has a place. But it would be unwise to waste all our intellectual and political capacity for debate on this question. There are many other important questions, such as the proper role of community self-defense against drug use, the best form of treatment for cocaine use, and whether coerced treatment programs are more or less successful than jails in controlling crime in the short run, and rehabilitating users in the long run.

The question remains: Will we be able to create the institutional forms in which that intellectual work can be done even as we are trying to mobilize the society to act? It is an urgent question, for unless we succeed in this, we will be flying blind in fighting the war against drugs and failing to learn from our accumulating experience.

The Legalization of Drugs: Why Prolong the Inevitable?

Todd Austin Brenner

Todd Brenner, writing for the Capital University Law Review, argues for legalization by appealing both to a right to autonomy and to the value of utilitarianism. Developing ideas from John Stuart Mill's On Liberty, *Mr. Brenner argues that adults have a right to develop practices and habits in line with their values, provided that they do not harm other people. After elaborating on the idea of a right to moral autonomy, he develops utilitarian arguments in favor of legalization.*

He submits, for example, that although the vast majority of Americans would oppose laws against the consumption of nicotine and alcohol, both of those drugs proportionally kill more of their users than do illegal drugs.

Continuing to develop a utilitarian line of argument, Mr. Brenner argues that drug interdiction has largely been a failure, and that drug laws are ineffective deterrents because the vast majority of illegal drug users usually escape arrest. He contends that if much more severe punishments were more widely enforced, our prisons and courtrooms would be even more overcrowded than they are today and drug users would have more incentive to kill policemen to avoid punishment.

He does not believe that drug-related crime would probably increase because of legalization. In fact, he argues that our present policy of prohibition "forces drug users to steal for money and brings them into contact with 'real' criminals, the consequences of which are the commitment of incidental

'The Legalization of Drugs: Why Prolong the Inevitable?' by Todd Austin Brenner (*Capital University Law Review*, vol. 18, 1989 pp. 237–255). Used by permission.

crime." He argues that even if the use of certain drugs made some people more likely to commit crime, we would not be justified in criminalizing those drugs because we would then be punishing "factors for the will" rather than behavior that directly causes harm to others.

Mr. Brenner advocates legalizing marijuana first, and then completely legalizing the use of all narcotics. Some drugs, however, such as heroin and crack would be banned from sale but available "free of charge at clinics where addicts have registered." He is hopeful that with more education, more emphasis on the value of personal choice, and greater health-consciousness, "the drug problem" will be reduced.

I. Introduction

The controversy lives. Social and legal philosophers, law enforcement officers, and politicians continue to debate over the never-ending question: What should be done about drugs? Since the enactment of the Harrison Act of 1914,[1] society has answered that question by prohibiting certain forms of drug use. Despite the flaws resulting from drug criminalization, flaws which border on economic and social catastrophe, proponents of prohibition maintain that legalization of drugs would catapult this country into anarchy, social immorality, and national drug addiction.

This comment will examine the above-mentioned arguments in light of the effects of criminalization on both the autonomous individual and society. Certain seemingly social hypocrisies, such as the legalization and widespread use of tobacco and alcohol, will also be analyzed. An attempt to reveal the imminent social problems resulting from prohibition will be made in addition to the proposition that the individual is adversely affected by the restriction of his free choice to use drugs.

Thus, both a utilitarian perspective, that criminalization of drugs harms society and its aggregates more than it benefits it, and an

---

[1] 38 Stat. 785 (1914). This act is often referred to as the Anti-Narcotic Drug Act.

anti-utilitarian viewpoint,[2] which suggests that the individual can do with his body anything he chooses to do so long as no harm results to third persons, will be implemented in this essay. Both perspectives lay the groundwork for a much-needed, practical, and realistic solution to this country's drug crisis. This proposed solution, of course, is the legalization of drugs, a solution which perhaps will result in short-term confusion but which will eventually afford a long-term remedy.

II. Background

One of the strongest arguments against legalization has been posed by the pragmatic question: What drugs, specifically, should be legalized? The first step in answering this logical inquiry is to define what is meant by the word 'drug'.

The typical pharmacological definition is that a drug is a chemical agent which, when taken into the body, affects living processes or alters the structure or function of any part of the organism.[3] This broad definition obviously encompasses both 'legal' drugs, including nicotine, alcohol, and caffeine, and 'illegal' drugs, as both categories fit into the definition of chemical agents altering the function of the organism.[4]

Drugs may also be defined with regard to the impact on social utility. 'Hard' drugs, such as hallucinogens, are thought to have no social utility, primarily because these drugs can cause bodily harm.[5] Hence, society sees no valuable purpose in allowing the intake of these drugs. 'Soft' drugs, conversely, are those in which there is minimal social utility but minimal harm to the body.[6] Marijuana is an example. Although prescribed occasionally by doctors and used in the context of religious practices, 'pot' is criminalized, though the sanctions are casually

---

[2]*See* Richards, *Sex, Drugs, Death and the Law* (1982). The author, in implementing this anti-utilitarian view, suggests that the individual is afforded a human right founded in the U.S. Constitution as well as many fundamental religious beliefs to make an autonomous choice in matters of self-regarding conduct, such as drug use.
[3]*See* Sloan, *Drug and Alcohol Abuse and the Law* (1980).
[4]*Id.*, p. 33.
[5]*See* Sloan, note 3 p. 37.
[6]*Id.*

enforced, because of its relatively minor social utility.[7] The third category of drugs consists of those used for medicinal purposes. Drugs of this type are viewed as socially approved even if, outside of the medicinal purposes, no social utility is recognized.[8]

To further analyze societal classifications of drugs, a brief discussion of the history of drug use in the United States should be undertaken. The logical starting point is the 1880s, when, surprisingly enough, drugs in this country were legal and readily available.[9] Many 'drug stores' at the time, in fact, offered nothing but narcotic derivatives, such as "Mrs. Winslow's Soothing Syrup" and "Dr. Bull's Cough Syrup."[10] Cocaine was the drug of choice and was a key ingredient in Coca Cola until 1903.[11] Opium use was also widespread, predominantly by middle-class women who obtained it through a doctor's prescription.[12] Ironically, the intake of opium was deemed to be fashionable—to the point where one of every 400 Americans became addicted.[13]

By the turn of the century, attitudes toward drug use changed dramatically. A political stigma which attached to certain prescribed narcotics forced doctors to curtail dispensation of these drugs.[14] Public morality also played a role in the attitude shift. The danger to users and families was such that drug use became no longer morally acceptable.[15] The public demise of drugs was officially pronounced by the Harrison Act of 1914. Originally, this Act was designed simply to record all prescriptions and sales of drugs. However, the United States Supreme Court took a tougher stance when it interpreted the legislation.[16] The

---

[7]*See* Kaplan, 'The Role of the Law in Drug Control', 71 *Duke Law Journal*, 1065 (1971).
[8]*Id.*, p. 1069.
[9]*See* Bennett, *Crimewarps: The Future of Crime in America*, p. 219 (1987).
[10]*Id.*
[11]*Id.*
[12]*Id.*
[13]*Id.*
[14]*See* Branch, 'Let Koop Do It', *The New Republic*, October 24th, 1988, p. 22. For example, the two most widely-used illegal drugs, cocaine and heroin, each carried the stigma of a hated, lower-class minority, "from 'cocaine-crazed Negro rapists' to 'opium-addled Chinese' immigrants."
[15]*Id.*
[16]*See Nigro v. United States*, 276 U.S. 332 (1928). The Court, in interpreting the Act as amended February 24th, 1919, found that "the prohibition . . . against selling, bartering, exchanging, or giving away drugs, except in pursuance of an order form, is not limited to persons required to register, but applies to 'any person'." (p. 335)

Court prohibited persons, even addicts, from possessing drugs, the result of which left thousands of people without relief.[17]

Since the passage of the Harrison Act, the government has unrelentingly communicated its disapproval of drug use. "Reefer Madness", a campaign beginning in the late 1930s, was a constant reminder of the government's attitude.[18] The Bureau of Narcotics used the expression "Assassin of Youth" during this time to describe marijuana.[19] The progression of the government's disapproval eventually led to the enactment of the Comprehensive Drug Abuse Prevention and Control Act of 1970, popularly known as the Controlled Substances Act.[20]

Under this act, drugs are divided into five schedules, the first of which contains those drugs with the highest potential for abuse, for which no use is permitted.[21] Schedules II to V list those drugs for which medical use is permitted.[22] Interestingly, alcohol, caffeine, and nicotine are excluded as those unregulated by the Act.[23] The Act's regulatory effect became widespread with its adoption by 42 states.[24]

In spite of Congress's attempt to control the illicit use and sale of the drugs categorized, the prevalence of illegal drugs in this country remains staggering. The following statistics reveal this truth: There are 18 million regular users of marijuana; 6 million users of cocaine; 3 million stimulant users; and 1 million people who regularly take hallucinogens.[25] All told, it is estimated that 36 million Americans are regular users

---

[17]*See* Bennett, note 9, p. 220.
[18]*The New Republic*, note 14, p. 23.
[19]*Id.*
[20]84 Stat. 1236 (1970).
[21]*Id.* These drugs contain the following: heroin (an opiate); LSD, mescaline and psilocybin (hallucinogens); marijuana and hashish (cannabis).
[22]Schedule II drugs contain opium, methadone, demerol, and cocaine; Schedule III contains paregoric, barbituates, and amphetamines; Schedule V contains codeine compounds and valium.
[23]*See* Sloan, note 3, pp. 35–37.
[24]These states have adopted what is known as the Uniform Controlled Substance Act (U.C.S.A.), which is modeled after the federal act. These states are: Alabama, Arkansas, California, Connecticut, Delaware, Florida, Georgia, Hawaii, Idaho, Kansas, Kentucky, Louisiana, Maryland, Massachusetts, Michigan, Minnesota, Mississippi, Missouri, Montana, Nebraska, New Hampshire, New Jersey, New Mexico, New York, North Carolina, Oklahoma, Pennsylvania, South Carolina, South Dakota, Tennessee, Texas, Utah, Virginia, Washington, West Virginia, Wisconsin, and Wyoming.
[25]*See* '1985 Statistics', *Drug Abuse Update*, September, 1988, pp. 20–21.

of illegal drugs.[26] Thus it is not surprising that the untaxed annual revenues generated by such a demand are thought to be in the vicinity of $100 billion.[27]

In contrast, the number of Americans who use legal drugs, namely, alcohol and nicotine, is estimated to be 113 million and 60 million, respectively.[28] Other information reveals that the number of Americans who die from alcohol use may be 100,000 a year and those who die annually from nicotene, 500,000.[29] Conversely, only 30,000 people die from the use of illegal drugs per year.[30] Given these numbers and assuming their accuracy, proportional analysis discloses that one in every 288 users of legal drugs dies from the intake thereof, while only one of every 1,200 illegal drug users dies as a result of intake. Apparently, the chances of self-harm are much greater when ingesting either of the legal drugs.

The United States is not the only nation confronted with a drug crisis. Other countries, however, have employed different strategies in fighting drug proliferation. In the Netherlands, for example, the government has devised an interesting approach. In 1976, jail terms were tripled for anyone dealing in hard drugs but, simultaneously, the possession of less than 30 grams of marijuana or hashish was, to a great extent, decriminalized.[31] The result of this tactic has been decreased use in marijuana and heroin, most notably among young people.[32] Only 8% of all Dutch students have tried marijuana, compared with over 60% of American students. Moreover, less than 5% of heroin addicts in Holland are under 22 years old, down from 14% in 1981.[33] Other results are less favorable, however; street crime has increased, and Amsterdam, the capital city where marijuana and hashish are sold in cafés, has become known as a 'drug Mecca.'[34]

[26]*Id.*
[27]*See* Kraar, 'The Drug Trade', *Fortune*, June 20th, 1988, p. 27.
[28]*See Drug Abuse Update*, note 25, p. 20.
[29]*Id.*
[30]*Id.*
[31]*See* 'Institutional Tolerance of Marijuana in Holland', *Whole Earth Review*, March 22nd, 1987, p. 58.
[32]*Id.*
[33]*See* Kupler, 'What To Do About Drugs', *Fortune*, June 20th, 1988, p. 40.
[34]*See* 'Lax Dutch Attitude to Drugs Under Attack by Law Enforcers', *Reuter Library Report*, January 5th, 1988, p. 2.

The Netherlands provides free methadone drug rehabilitation programs for addicts.[35] Such programs, though, were originated in England. In 1968, clinics were established for the dispensation of heroin or cocaine to nearly 3,000 registered addicts.[36] This humane effort to rehabilitate addicts was a novel approach to curing addiction but nevertheless was met by unpleasant results. The number of addicts increased by 37% in a five year period, prompting the government to switch to methadone, a decision also resulting in unfortunate consequences.[37] There are 12,000 registered addicts on methadone maintenance, but since street heroin remains relatively inexpensive and is the drug of choice, most addicts remain on heroin.[38]

III. Personal Freedom

A. AUTONOMY-BASED ARGUMENTS

1. The Right to Personal Autonomy. There is a consensus that the underlying premise of the concept of human rights, as found in the U.S. Constitution and much religious philosophy, is that people, as individuals, have a range of capacities that enables them to develop higher-order plans for actions and to act upon them.[39] A number of legal scholars have devoted much attention to the concept of personal autonomy, one of whom is Immanuel Kant,[40] who theorized that the capacity of persons for rational autonomy is the capacity to be "free and rational sovereigns in the kingdom of ends."[41] Perhaps the most well-known and respected autonomy arguments, however, were posed by John Stuart Mill in his classic treatise, *On Liberty.*[42]

---

[35]*Id.*
[36]*See* 'High Times in America', *Heritage Foundation Policy Review,* Winter, 1987, p. 46.
[37]*Id.,* p. 51.
[38]*Id.*
[39]*See* Richards, note 2, p. 9.
[40]*See* Kant, *Foundations of the Metaphysics of Morals* (L.W. Beck translation, 1959). Kant theorized that the concern embodied in the idea of human rights is not with the maximizing the individual's pursuit of any particular "lower-order end" (e.g., pleasure, talent), but rather with respecting the higher-order capacity of the individual to exercise rational autonomy in choosing and revising his ends, whatever they may be.
[41]*Id.,* p. 52.
[42]J.S. Mill, *On Liberty,* (A. Castell edition, 1947).

Mill, a noted utilitarian, posed the theory that the only just purpose for forcing an individual to perform or refrain from performing a certain act was to prevent harm to others. "His own good, either physical or moral, is not a sufficient warrant."[43] Mill firmly believed that an "indirect harm" was not a "harm to others" and therefore intervention to prevent this harm was unjustified.[44]

Mill further argued for the intrinsic "good" of individuality, good achieved only through self-development free from governmental intrusion.[45] Self-fulfillment, Mill insisted, is the primary reason for existence and can be realized only if the affairs of the individual are self-directed, because, after all, a normal adult is much more likely to know his interests and talents than is any other party.[46] Hence, according to Mill, when an external conception of one's own good is imposed upon him, this imposition will almost always be self-defeating.[47]

Mill, in a utilitarian fashion, realized that the right of rational autonomy outweighed the possible consequences of extending that right, namely, "empty distractions, idle fantasies and wasted lives."[48] A philosophy of this type allows a person to achieve his own good by making his own decisions, even if his actions lead to personal catastrophe, autonomy is more important than personal well-being. Third party intervention is therefore inappropriate. Furthermore, Mill's philosophy suggests that, so long as no direct harm to others results, a person is granted a right to make foolish decisions, to err and to be mistaken.

When adopting the Millian-utilitarian philosophy and applying it to drug use, the only rational conclusion which could be extracted is that rational autonomy affords a person the freedom to do with his body as he wills, i.e., to ingest drugs if he so desires. So long as no direct harm is

---

[43] *Id.*, pp. 9–10.
[44] *Id.*, pp. 90–91.
[45] *Id.*, p. 99.
[46] *Id.*, pp. 101–102.
[47] *See* Feinberg, 'Sovereignty, Autonomy, and Privacy: Moral Ideals in the Constitution?', 58 *Notre Dame Law Review*, p. 459 (1983). The author interprets Mill's theory of external interference as not being absolute. In those "rare cases" when the intervening party *knows* that free exercise of a person's autonomy will be against his own interest, "there, Mill concedes, we are justified in interfering with his liberty in order to protect him from extreme harm."
[48] *Id.*

caused to third parties by that ingestion, and even if personal, bodily harm results, he is free to make that decision.

Utilitarian formulations have been attacked in this regard, however, because utilitarianism fails to give full weight to the idea of human rights; instead, utility arguments focus on individuals as serving aggregate functions in society. David Richards made this observation and developed an anti-utilitarian approach whereby human rights are of paramount importance.[49] From this perspective, Richards advocates decriminalization of drug use because the moral theories rooted in the Constitution and American tradition reflect the conception that human rights and autonomy are "fundamental."[50] Condemning drug use, then, is "moral slavery" and an arbitrary abridgement of personal freedom.[51]

Richards continues his anti-utilitarian argument by observing that the unwarranted conception of drug use has been caused by misidentification of selfhood as a perfectionist ideal of self-control:

> The view of drug use as producing a drunken anarchy . . . underestimates the distinctively human capacity for self-control and overestimates the force of drug experience as a kind of satanic possession, the demands of which inexplorably undermine the rational will.[52]

Richards condemns such a misconception by stating that drug use is "merely one means by which the already existing interests of the person may be explored or realized."[53]

2. Right of Privacy. Although from different perspectives, both Mill and Richards would vehemently argue against unwarranted intrusions into the personal lives of individuals. The concept of personal autonomy, as employed by these scholars, has been taken by many to mean 'the right of privacy'. This privacy right has been interpreted by the United States Supreme Court, the analysis of which needs now to be undertaken.

The landmark decision of *Griswold v. Connecticut*[54] laid the ground-

---

[49]*See* Richards, *supra*, note 2, pp. 168–195.
[50]*See* Richards, *supra*, note 2, p. 186.
[51]*See* Richards, *supra*, note 2, p. 169.
[52]*See* Richards, *supra*, note 2, p. 171.
[53]*See* Richards, *supra*, note 2, p. 173.
[54]381 U.S. 479 (1965).

work for establishing boundaries for the right of privacy. The rationale behind the Court's decision to strike down an anti-contraceptive statute as unconstitutional was that there exists penumbras, or zones, around each explicit right in the Constitution in which implied rights must be inferred.[55] The Constitution contains, according to Justice Douglas, various penumbras of privacy, whereby "zones of privacy" means "zones of individual discretion."[56]

What followed after *Griswold* were important cases interpreting the extensions of privacy. *Stanley v. Georgia*[57] extended the right to privacy to the right to witness pornographic movies in one's own home. The *Stanley* court recognized the fundamental right to freedom from unwarranted instrusions into a person's privacy.[58] In *Roe v. Wade*,[59] the Court granted the discretionary right to all pregnant women to decide whether to abort their pregnancies, at least in the first six months of pregnancy. The Court found this right to be derived from the right of privacy.[60]

Other courts have extended the right of privacy to other forms of self-regarding conduct. In *Superintendent of Belchertown State School v. Saikewicz*,[61] the court held that a terminally ill patient may voluntarily end her life or have it ended by an appointed guardian. Two other vitally important cases have also interpreted the right of privacy in perhaps a more relevant context, the use of marijuana and peyote.[62]

In *Ravin v. State of Alaska*,[63] the court struck down a statute as unconstitutional which prohibited the use of marijuana in the home. The court found that the *Stanley* holding guaranteed personal possession for purely private, non-commercial use.[64] The ingestion of marijuana, the court stated, was "relatively harmless" and thus the individual's right of privacy outweighed the state interest in regulation.[65]

The use of peyote for religious purposes was held to be constitution-

---

[55]*Griswold*, 381 U.S., p. 484.
[56]*Id*.
[57]394 U.S. 557 (1969).
[58]*Stanley*, 394 U.S., p. 565.
[59]410 U.S. 113 (1973).
[60]*Roe*, 410 U.S., p. 153.
[61]373 Mass. 728, 370 N.E.2d 417 (1977).
[62]Peyote is a hallucinogen.
[63]537 P.2d 494 (Alaska 1975).
[64]*Ravin*, 537 P.2d, p. 501.
[65]*Ravin*, 537 P.2d, p. 504.

ally protected in *People v. Woody.*[66] In balancing the interests of the parties involved against those of the state, the court reasoned that since the drug was used in a bona fide pursuit of a religious faith, thereby creating only a slight danger to the state, the burden of proving the right of privacy was relatively light and the scale, therefore, tipped in favor of the drug users' constitutional protection.[67]

The pattern of the preceding cases appears to establish a direction toward the absolute protection of self-regarding conduct in a Millian sense. The Court's collision course with Mill's principle of liberty, though, became dramatically apparent with the decisions holding that privacy does not extend to such things as the length of policemen's hair,[68] consensual viewing of pornographic movies in public places,[69] or homosexual intercourse in private.[70] The reasoning invoked for the Court's apparent zig-zagging inconsistency is that some individual rights have been deemed to be 'fundamental' (such as the right to privacy), subject to state interests, and others are thought to be 'basic' life choices.[71] Basic life choices are given the greatest protection possible by the courts when balancing individual freedoms against state interests. These basic life choices consist of "those liberties which are most fecund, those exercised in the pivotally central life decisions and thereby underlying and supporting all the others."[72]

The question becomes, then, whether or not drug use can be classified as a 'basic' life choice. Richards, and probably Mill, would answer this question in the affirmative. Richards recognizes that since some religious beliefs have centered themselves on drug use, whereby the exploration and realization of higher-order interests are sought, hence

---

[66]61 Cal.2d 716, 394 P.2d 813, 40 Cal. Rptr. 69 (1964).
[67]*Woody,* 61 Cal.2d, p. 722. When explaining the role of peyote in the Native American Church, the court stated that: "the theology of the church combines certain Christian teachings with the belief that peyote embodies the Holy Spirit and that those who partake of peyote enter into direct contact with God . . . peyote serves as a sacramental symbol similar to bread and wine in certain Christian churches."
[68]*See Kelley v. Johnson,* 425 U.S. 238 (1976).
[69]*See Paris Adult Theatre v. Slaton,* 413 U.S. 49 (1973).
[70]*See Bowers v. Hardwick,* 478 U.S. 186 (1986).
[71]*See* Feinberg, note 47, p. 489.
[72]*See* Feinberg, note 47 p. 490. The author comments on the difficulty of line-drawing in the context of basic life choices. The distinction between watching pornographic movies in one's home and taking drugs is a narrow one indeed, he argues. "As the Supreme Court has shown, it is difficult to apply a restricted concept in ways that do not seem arbitrary."

becoming a basic life choice, other forms of self-identifying drug experiences should be cast in the same light.[73] Society clearly denounces this view, however; it is dogmatic to assert that people cannot, through drug use, rationally advance their ends.[74] Thus the goal of protecting individuals (which is inarguably the purpose of the Constitution) has been subordinated to the protection of strongly structured groups, such as religious organizations.[75]

3. Legal Paternalism. The concept of legal paternalism suggests that a state may interfere with a person's liberty solely to prevent that individual from harming himself, even though no third party interests are threatened by such conduct. Generally, paternalistic interference comes into play in two types of scenarios: first, when the harms sought to be avoided are unknown to the person; second, when the harms are known by the person yet the values incorporated in the interference are ones that the person does not personally share.[76] There is general agreement that the interference of the first type is justified; indeed, society should prohibit access to nuclear power plants, for example, if there is a hint of radiation leakage. The second type of interference, however, has been met with justifiable criticism.

Richards argues that the largest fault of the unjustified interference is that it fails to treat persons as equals and simultaneously fails to take seriously the separateness of other individuals. It fails to treat persons as equals in that it allows certain types of dangerous behavior, such as mountain climbing, while prohibiting others, such as drug use. Thus where the criminal law imposes a duty on one to take better care of oneself, he will feel as if he is being unfairly treated as compared to those who are not forced to take similar precautions. The interference fails to take rights seriously because it rejects a person's right to realize his own self-fulfillment by preventing him from deciding the direction in life he wishes to take.[77]

A glaring inconsistency in our paternalistic society is that of alcohol use. Society disallows drug use because of its harm on the body and to

---

[73]*See* Richards, note 2, p. 186.
[74]*See* Richards, note 2, pp. 170, 176–77.
[75]*See* Richards, note 2, p. 187.
[76]*See* Richards, note 2, p. 183.
[77]*See* Richards, note 2, p. 184.

society, but it allows, almost encourages, the consumption of alcohol.[78] Drinking in today's world is the cultural norm, despite the numerous societal problems associated with it. The reason for its allowance is simple: since the repeal of Prohibition, the use of alcohol has become embedded in the cultural roots as acceptable, moral behavior. In short, alcohol is legal because it has 'been around' longer than most other drugs. Yet the longstanding popularity of alcohol is a weak reason for approving it while at the same time condemning other drugs. Statistics alone refute such hypocrisy.[79]

Another inconsistency is revealed in the form of certain laws, or lack thereof, which allow the type of personal harm proponents of criminalization try to curb. One such example is motorcycle helmet laws. In most states, the cyclist is no longer required to wear a helmet.[80] These repeals seemingly reveal the attitude that cyclists can protect themselves and can use rational judgments in determining whether, for their own benefit, wearing a helmet is a prudent idea. Moreover, utilitarian arguments suggesting that enforcement costs are too high with regard to helmet requirements are unsupportable; police can easily determine if the cyclist is wearing a helmet.[81]

4. Legislating Morality. From its inception, the American criminal justice system was designed as a mechanism by which Calvinistic religious ideals of morality could radically reform human nature. Thus criminal law has historically been a means of enforcing public morality. Prohibition of alcohol epitomized purity reform movements.[82] To say that the Prohibition experiment failed, however, is a gross understatement.[83]

---

[78]*See Drug Abuse Update,* note 25, p. 3, 38. In 1986, the advertising expenditures for alcohol in the U.S. were $1,400,000,000. Incidentally, expenditures in the tobacco industry totaled $2,400,000,000.

[79]*See Drug Abuse Update,* note 25, pp. 4–7. Besides the deaths caused by alcohol use, other direct and indirect consequences of alcohol use include the following damages to U.S. economy: $13,000,000,000 in treatment costs; $1,500,000,000 in health support services costs; $18,000,000,000 in mortality costs; $66,000,000,000 in reduced productivity and $5,000,000,000 in lost employment (1983 statistics).

[80]At present, there are 33 states that don't require, in certain situations, the wearing of a helmet.

[81]*See* Kaplan, note 7, p. 1074.

[82]*See* Richards, note 2, pp. 160–61.

[83]For a complete detailing of Prohibition's failure, from an economic, social, and criminal perspective, see Kobler, *Ardent Spirits: The Rise and Fall of Prohibition* (1973).

Learning from past mistakes is thought to be a basic tenet of human evolution, but the continuing criminalization of drugs demonstrates, to a degree, society's 'blind eye'.

Proponents of morality legislation argue that the chief purpose of curtailing immorality through the law is to reduce the amount of secondary harm resulting from the activity and to limit the frequency of the immorality itself.[84] The right to privacy cases previously discussed reveal that when no secondary harm results from an activity (such as watching pornographic movies in one's own home), morality laws are not justified. As for limiting the frequency of immorality itself, the criminal law system is now obsolete.[85]

Beneficiaries to the concept of legislated morality are politicians. Obviously, a candidate who is more 'in tune' with the moral attitude of society and who promises to 'do something about it' has a much better chance of winning an election than does an 'immoral' counterpart. Unfortunately for society, politicians sometimes fail to explore whether or not the conduct to be prohibited is sufficiently harmful in terms of secondary harms. Furthermore, they often forget the possibility that the proposed law is not enforceable. Marijuana laws present a good example of such a situation, where the chances of getting caught are approximately 1.5 percent.[86]

5. Tobacco. The sale and use of tobacco in the United States is another inconsistency in a criminal system attempting to legislate morality. Nicotine is a known, addictive drug which kills half of a million people a year and whose presence is offensive to millions more.[87] Yet society does not criminalize tobacco, mainly because of its utilitarian value in the economy and because of its prolonged existence in the American way of life. Congress thus continues to subsidize tobacco growing while simultaneously taxing it.

However, in spite of the legalized status of tobacco and its accessibili-

---

[84]*See* Kaplan, note 7, p. 1074.
[85]*See Drug Abuse Update*, note 25, pp. 20–21 which reveals the prevalence of drug use in the U.S.
[86]*See* p. 250, where the likelihood of being arrested for possession of marijuana is estimated to be 1 in 63.
[87]*See Drug Abuse Update*, note 25, p. 20.

ty, only 32 percent of Americans smoke today, as opposed to 43 percent twenty-three years ago.[88] Thus education, as well as societal disapproval, has acted as a valuable deterrent. Over time, this country's citizens have become enlightened as to the relative merits of tobacco use and have decided, absent paternalism or morality legislation,[89] that nicotine consumption is no longer as desirable. Perhaps a similar enlightenment is possible with other forms of drugs.

B. SOCIAL UTILITARIANISM

1. Generally. Each of the previous arguments has been based on the assumption that individuals are responsible and rational enough to decide for themselves whether or not the intake of drugs will cause personal harm or harm to others. That society fails to share this assumption is regrettable. However, even if society cannot accept the human rights arguments of personal autonomy and anti-paternalism, surely society must realize, in a utilitarian sense, how criminalization of drug use is adversely affecting, at the very least, the economic and criminal justice systems. The remainder of this essay will explore these harms.

2. Economic Concerns. The effects on the economy caused by drug criminalization are inarguably devastating. Americans spend at least $100 billion a year,[90] or twice as much as is spent for oil,[91] to purchase illegal drugs. This money is untaxed, of course, and is reputed to fall into the hands of organized crime, which is lured into the business by the incredible profit margin inherent to the industry.[92]

Hurting the economy much worse than untaxed revenues are the government's attempts to limit the supply of drugs entering the country and to seize this supply once it has crossed the borders. Since 1981, the U.S. government has spent over $10 billion to stop the importation of

---

[88]*See Heritage Foundation Policy Review*, note 36, p. 51.
[89]Although, of course, advertising has been restricted and warnings placed on packages.
[90]*See* Kraar, note 27, p. 29.
[91]*Id.*
[92]*Id.*, p. 32. For example, the street price of heroin in the U.S. is estimated to be $2,000,000 per kilogram, compared to $400,000 wholesale, for a 500 percent profit margin. Additionally, the street price of cocaine is estimated to be $200,000 per kilogram as opposed to $18,000 when bought at wholesale, a 1,100 percent margin.

drugs, with little or no success.[93] There are as many drugs in the country now as there ever have been, and the continual decline in price of most drugs suggests that competition is building year by year.[94] The truth of the matter is that sealing America's borders is a futile, unintelligent attempt at controlling supply. The United States has a 5,400 mile border with Canada and a 1,900 mile border with Mexico.[95] To 'seal' these borders, $14 billion for airplanes and another $6 billion for operations is necessary, a recent study revealed.[96] Such a proposal is not economically feasible. As it now stands, only 10% of all illegal narcotics are prevented from entering the country, while it is estimated that only another 10% would be blocked if further draconian, military measures are undertaken.[97]

Another sobering fact with regard to interdiction is that "hard drugs" such as cocaine are easy to conceal. In fact, one fully loaded cargo plane could supply the entire U.S. market for one year.[98] It is no surprise, then, that the estimated price per 'drug bust' in 1987 was between $350,000 and $400,000.[99] Yet, these 'busts' have little impact on buyers because of the voluminous supply; consequently, demand remains unaffected.[100]

A major benefit arising from legalization of drugs would be the revenues generated from the taxation of these drugs. The societal view of taxing "sinful" activities is not a favorable one, but the government nevertheless taxes cigarettes, alcohol and even *Hustler* magazine.[101] Perhaps if society were educated about the pragmatic results of taxation, views could change. For instance, taxing marijuana alone would produce $20 billion at the current rate of consumption.[102] Currently, $1.2 billion is spent annually on drug treatment, or one-eighteenth of the amount

---

[93]*See* 'Cost of Drug Warfare', *USA Today*, July, 1988, p. 21.
[94]*See* 'A War on Drugs With Real Troops?', *News and Comment*, July 1st, 1988, p. 13.
[95]*See* 'Facing Up to Drugs', *New York*, August 15th, 1988, p. 20.
[96]*See News and Comment*, note 94, p. 14.
[97]*See* 'Oh, What a Lovely War', *The Progressive*, July, 1988, p. 7.
[98]*See News and Comment*, note 94, p. 14.
[99]*Id.*
[100]See News and Comment, note 94, p. 15.
[101]*See Buckley, 'A View from the Inside: Drugs in Prisons', National Review*, October 4th, 1985, p. 54.
[102]*See* Branch, note 14, p. 26.

taxing marijuana would generate.[103] The problem, of course, is convincing the public that taxing drugs is no more sinful than taxing pornography.

3. Criminal Law Concerns: a. Deterrence. Proponents of drug criminalization insist that the threat of arrest acts as a valuable deterrent.[104] Simple logic refutes such a conclusion, however, in that the chances of getting caught with drugs are so slight that anyone taking the least of precautions will avoid arrest. In fact, the drug most easily detected, marijuana, is nearly undetectable. In 1987, there were 378,709 marijuana arrests and 25 million people who used the drug.[105] Thus the chance of getting caught for these users was about 1 in 63. For more potent drugs which are harder to detect, the risk is even smaller.

Criminalization does not provide a valuable deterrent because it doesn't take into account that choices people make are intrinsically determined; what people decide to do with their bodies is the result of individual choice. Therefore, deterrence of drug use should be achieved through education rather than the law. Once this process is in gear, other forces such as peer pressure and socially-felt stigmas attached to drug use will produce a domino educational effect, a force much more powerful than the law. Furthermore, the thrill of illegality will be removed from those who cherish it.

Criminalization proponents counter with the suggestion that if tougher, draconian measures were invoked, deterrence of drug use would be more effectively achieved.[106] While this may be true, the costs would simply be too high. Prisons and courtrooms would be excessively crowded, enforcement costs would increase, and subsequently taxes would be raised to fund such measures. Moreover, if prison sentences were inflated or capital punishment imposed on drug dealers, killing policemen would be worth it. Sentencing drug users, furthermore, to jail

---

[103]*See Drug Abuse Update*, note 25, p. 14.
[104]*See New York*, note 95, p. 25.
[105]*See* 'Highpoints', *National Organization for the Reform of Marijuana Laws* (NORML), September, 1988.
[106]*See New York*, note 95, p. 25.

or prison would not only expose them to 'real' criminals, but also crowd the prisons to the point where neither the drug user nor the hard criminal would have a realistic chance of reform.

b. Drug-Related Crime. Another concern of anti-legalizers is the level of crime that would result due to legalization. An initial consequence would be a reduction in junkie-related robberies and deaths. The significantly reduced prices of drugs[107] would alleviate the temptation to steal or rob for drug money and also curb the desire to attack drug dealers or gangs. Gang warfare would be reduced as would incidental murders.

Drug-related crime, though, would increase if drug users were permitted access to inexpensive drugs, criminalization proponents maintain. This criminogenetic philosophy, on the surface, seems logical. However, what advocates of this reasoning fail to realize is that criminalization forces drug users to steal for money and brings them into contact with 'real' criminals, resulting in the commission of incidental crime.[108] Furthermore, the stigma attached to engaging in an illegal activity may encourage chemical dependence because of the fear of coming forward for help, thus causing the temptation of incidental crime necessary to support the dependency. Also, the use of depressant drugs, such as heroin and marijuana, is thought to suppress violent behavior, whereas alcohol, the most popular drug, heightens violent tendencies.[109]

Where the criminogenesis argument is most weak, though, is in its underlying rationale: to prevent drug-related crime, society forbids the use of drugs themselves. Crimes are punishable because of the harm caused to society; culpability is assessed only upon the discovery of the

---

[107]Applying simple economic theory, assuming that the wholesale prices of cocaine, heroin and marijuana remain at a constant while also assuming that current demand remains constant for these drugs, government regulations would increase the supply of these drugs, causing a fall off in price due to the lowering of the equilibrium on the supply/demand curve. Furthermore, since the government would be regulating the industry, there would be no more astronomical profit margins in selling drugs. For a complete and detailed analysis of the effects drug legalization would have on supply and demand, see Wisotsky, 'Exposing the War on Cocaine: The Futility and Destructiveness of Prohibition', 1983 *Wisconsin Law Review*, 1305 (1983).
[108]*See* Bennett, note 9, pp. 212–220.
[109]*See* Bennett, note 9, p. 220.

intentional will of the actor. The intake of drugs may lead to temptation, but temptation is only a factor in a person's will. Therefore, punishing a person for drug use to stop him from committing a crime is to punish factors for the will, not the direct causes.[110]

4. Other Concerns: a. Children. Perhaps the greatest concern of those opposing legalization of drugs is its possible effects on children. Undoubtedly a wave of confusion will be felt by children if drugs are legalized. Confusion, though, may be a favorable alternative to what children are feeling today.

Children today are bombarded with news about the drug problem. They hear repeatedly about the 'Just Say No' campaign. They hear from adults about the evil of drugs. They hear about classmates who may happen to indulge in drugs. The problem with all this communication is that at the same time children hear it, they also know that drugs are illegal. The result is that children begin to feel a sense of disrespect for law and authority.[111]

Additionally, children already have the ability to obtain drugs, but in a very dangerous manner. They have to deal with drug dealers, who may very well manipulate these children into taking harder drugs or 'dealing' drugs to friends. Furthermore, the contents of the drugs these children buy are dangerously questionable. In the worst-case scenario, upon legalization only those persons who would be over the majority age would be permitted to purchase drugs and these drugs would be in pure form, free from dangerous substances.[112]

---

[110]*See* Weiss and Wizner, 'Pot, Prayer, Politics, and Policy: The Right To Cut Your Own Throat in Your Own Way', 54 *Iowa Law Review* 709 (1969). The authors suggest (p. 731) that: "To punish factors is to change the concept of guilt. Having a law of crime, not criminals, and acknowledging the tremendous range of factors that may lead to the commission of crimes, leads to the conclusion that even if drug use is associated with substantially higher crime commission, it may not be proscribed on those grounds."

[111]For a similar argument, see Kaplan, *Marijuana—The New Prohibition* (1970), p. 34. Reporting on a survey designed to elicit student attitudes toward the marijuana laws, Kaplan reveals that: "Their [the students'] 'reasoning' . . . runs something along the line, 'This law is stupid and unjust; probably a lot of other laws are stupid and unjust. I am not going to be too concerned about violating this law—or other laws that seem to interfere with my total freedom.'"

[112]"Pure form" suggests that the manufacture and distribution of drugs would be carefully regulated and controlled, as all legal drugs are today.

In the final analysis, it is parents who must exercise responsibility in educating and disciplining their offspring. Parents should give their children an honest description of the effects of drugs and help them understand that this is a society in which freedom of choice is considered extremely important and that wisdom and responsibility are vital.

b. Pronouncing Benediction. Another gargantuan roadblock for legalization advocates is society's view that to legalize is to advocate. This attitude is a fatal misconception. Society surely does not advocate watching pornography nor does it advocate riding a motorcycle without wearing a helmet, but those activities are not criminalized. One way to overcome the benediction concern is to use some of the enormous tax money for negative, or at the very least educational, advertising, while at the same time forbidding any form of promotional advertising. Such an approach would run contrary to the alcohol industry, which spends enormous amounts of money for promotional advertising,[113] and would run nearly parallel to the cigarette industry, where warnings are now placed on every pack of cigarettes. The nicotine warnings have had positive effects, such as lowering the rate of use.[114]

c. Increased Addiction. The possibility of increased addiction to drugs has been another argument against legalization. The simple rebuttal to this conjecture is that there is no evidence to support it. A popular belief is that drug use itself leads to addiction, a belief totally unfounded.[115] Studies have shown that psychological factors are more directly attributable to drug addiction than physical factors.[116] Hence, a person's desire to become addicted, whether obscure or overt, dictates whether or not he will indeed become addicted.

Another misconception about addiction is that productivity is sure to take a 'nosedive' once a person becomes dependent or that an addict cannot live a normal life. Interestingly, doctors have the highest addiction rate of any group, without leading abnormal or unproductive lives.[117]

Criminalizing drug use discourages addicts from coming forward

---

[113]*See Drug Abuse Update,* note 25, p. 4.
[114]*See Heritage Foundation Policy Review,* note 36, p. 27.
[115]*See* Bennett, note 9, p. 224.
[116]*Id.*
[117]*Id.*

with their problem. In the first place, addicts are afraid to come forward because of the criminal label associated with such an action. Secondly, in areas of the country where drug addiction is widespread, insufficient funding for treatment programs has created waiting lists up to several months long.[118] Legalization would cure both defects, taking the fear out of coming for help while also generating tax dollars to support treatment programs.

IV. A Realistic Proposal

A. STEP ONE

Criminalizing the use of marijuana amounts to what can be described as a half-law—it is on the 'books' but not enforced. Several states have realized the futility of enforcement as well as the exorbitant demand for the drug and, as a result, have decriminalized marijuana on that basis.[119] The time has come for federal recognition of those facts. A law which labels 18 million users as criminals is absurd.

B. STEP TWO

Following the inevitable success of the decriminalization experiment should be the complete legalization of marijuana. This stage would act as the real test. Distribution and taxation of the drug would be handled the same way alcohol is dispensed—through licensed sellers. Restrictions on time, place, and manner of sale would also apply, just as with alcohol. Public ingestion would be strictly prohibited, as would the sale of marijuana in places of public accommodation. Furthermore, stiff penalties for driving while under the influence of marijuana would be strictly enforced.

C. STEP THREE

The final step in the enactment, assuming that marijuana legalization proves successful, is the complete legalization of all narcotics. Legaliza-

---

[118]*See* Bennett, note 9, p. 226.
[119]There are 11 states that have decriminalized marijuana use. Alaska has gone so far as to allow citizens to grow marijuana in their backyard.

tion, however, does not mean commercial sale. Drugs causing permanent addiction, such as heroin and 'crack', would be banned from sale. Instead, these drugs would be offered free of charge at clinics where addicts have been registered. Simultaneously, these addicts would be helped in trying to overcome their illness and would hopefully be cured.

The initial results of this proposal will undoubtedly be disturbing. Confusion over national morality will certainly mount. It is vitally important that legalization be accompanied by education. The reasons why legalization of drugs has occurred should be communicated to all citizens. Everyone must know that as individuals, people ought to be afforded a choice to define their personal well-being and ultimate aspirations. Revenues from the taxes imposed on the drugs will be used in massive education of this type along with non-promotional advertisements. In the long run, not only will drug use decrease, but national strength will be re-established as a result of a country proud of individual freedom.

D. DRUG-TESTING

The compromise to such a proposal takes the form of drug-testing. The right to use drugs is absolute only to the extent that no direct harm is felt by others. Therefore, persons on whom many lives depend, such as airline pilots, must recognize the fact that their conduct has the potential to injure many persons. Thus the airline pilot is still afforded a freedom of choice: he can use drugs and not be an airline pilot or not use them and perform his assigned duty.

However, in jobs where lives do not depend on the assigned performance of the worker, testing would probably not be necessary because if the employee is unable to perform at the acceptable level, the employee is likely to lose his job anyway. In any event, employers should be given more discretion upon the legalization of drugs when deciding whether a drug test is in order.

V. Conclusion

America is becoming more and more health conscious. Americans are eating and sleeping better and exercising more. In this country's shifting attitude toward improved health, there has never been a legislative enactment requiring people to stay fit. Paternalism did not act as the guide; rather, individual instincts and personal pride were responsible. Drugs will not stand in the way of this fitness evolution. The citizenry simply knows better.

The drug problem has largely been caused by unnecessary over-criminalization. Since almost all damage caused by drugs is felt by the user himself, legislating moral behavior is no longer necessary. The problem cannot be effectively curtailed by the government's new 'shotgun' approach of 'zero tolerance'[120] and massive federal spending. The time has come for the government to look for the individual for help, not vice versa.

---

[120]*See* 'What Zero Tolerance Adds Up To', *U.S. News and World Report,* June 6th, 1988, p. 11. "Zero tolerance" is a governmental attitude created by the Reagan Administration whereby the 'get-tough' message has been sent to the U.S. Coast Guard and other military factions. This policy allows these forces to search any boat or automobile upon the slightest suspicion. One of the many unfortunate examples of this policy's implementation is the seizure of the *Oak Royal,* a $2,500,000 yacht in international waters between Mexico and Cuba after the U.S. Coast Guard found one-tenth of one ounce of marijuana on board. The owner, who was not on board and who knew nothing of the drug's presence, was forced to pay $1,600 in fines and fees.

Statement of Steven Wisotsky Before the Select Committee on Narcotics Abuse and Control

Steven Wisotsky

Steven Wisotsky, professor of law at the Nova University Law Center, also favors legalization, arguing that American drug policy has been "largely futile". He claims, for example, that although former President Ronald Reagan doubled and redoubled the federal anti-drug enforcement budget from $645 million in 1981 to over $4 billion in 1987, the quantity of drugs smuggled into the U.S. continued to grow. Argues Dr. Wisotsky: "The social 'return' on the extra billions spent during that time has been a drug abuse problem of historic magnitude, accompanied by a drug trafficking parasite of international dimensions."

He further maintains that, by criminalizing drugs, the U.S. government has created an underground economy in which at least $100 billion per year "finances or supplies the incentives for . . . homicide, street crime, public corruption and international narcoterrorism."

Wisotsky submits that, motivated by fear and frustration, we have let the government increasingly aggrandize its power at the expense of individual rights. He says, for example, that the desire to apprehend drug users is so strong that ordinary people are subject to intrusions of privacy, as in the drug testing of public or private employees. He further contends that the courts have

Prepared Statement of Steven Wisotsky, Professor of Law, Nova University Law Center, before the select committee on Narcotics Abuse and Control, House of Representatives, Concerning: A New Beginning in U.S. Drug Policy, Steven Wisotsky (September 29th, 1988, pp. 410–454).

increasingly come to permit police and other government officials to question citizens without probable cause, to make warrantless searches of automobiles, to obtain search warrants based on tips from undisclosed informants, and so on. He implies that our priorities are misplaced, on the ground, for example, that drug penalties are "more stringent in fact than sentences typically meted out to robbers or rapists."

Dr. Wisotsky maintains that we need 1. to admit that the current policy is a failure; 2. to reduce drug abuse; and 3. to reduce "the black market pathologies" resulting from the billions in drug money generated by drug law enforcement. After admitting that current drug policy is a failure, we should, according to him, 1. clearly define what is meant by 'drug problem'; 2. state our goals (with concern for important distinctions, as between problems arising from drugs and problems arising from drug money); and 3. "set realistic and principled priorities based on truth" (priorities that acknowledge that not all recreational drug use need be harmful).

He concludes by claiming that an acceptable revised drug policy will protect children, make cigarettes less available to minors, increase cigarette and alcohol taxes more consistently with their social costs, create policies to protect the public from accidents (as on the highway or in the workplace), and respect people's individual liberty.

[T]he history of the narcotics legislation in the country "reveals the determination of congress to turn the screw of the criminal machinery—detection, prosecution and punishment—tighter and tighter."

—The U.S. Supreme Court in
Albernaz v. United States,
450 U.S. 333, 343 (1981)

The chief cause of problems is solutions.

—Eric Sevareid

Mr. Chairman, I would like to express my appreciation to the Committee for inviting me to participate in this important hearing on U.S. Drug Policy. This hearing could be and should be the start of a new beginning in the conception and execution of our drug laws. Indeed, if there is one over-riding theme in my prepared statement, it is just that: more than anything else—more than revised laws or the commitment of new resources—we need a careful, comprehensive study of the costs and benefits of present drug policy, followed by a clear articulation of the fundamental goals sought to be achieved by our drug policy.

First, let me identify myself for the record. I am both a lawyer and a law professor. I have been a full-time member of the law faculty of the Nova University Law Center since 1975. One of my primary areas of specialization is the criminal justice system. Since the late 1970s, I have followed developments in U.S. drug law. With the aid of a grant from the Nova Law Center in 1982, I published what is to my knowledge the first critique of the U.S. War on Drugs, the substance of which is clearly indicated by its title, 'Exposing the War on Cocaine: The Futility and Destructiveness of Prohibition', 1983 *Wisconsin Law Review* 1305.[1]

My published work in this field has been cited widely by the press, being summarized, for example, in the *Atlantic Monthly* cover story on cocaine, of January 1986. I am most widely known as the author of *Breaking the Impasse in the War on Drugs,* reviewed in the *New York Times* Book Review Section in December 1986. I have spoken on drug law and policy at many panels and conferences in the United States and in Europe.

My prepared statement for this hearing addresses three fundamental questions. What is the state of the War on Drugs? How did we get there? Where should we go from here?

The current 'War on Drugs' began on October 2nd, 1982, with a radio address by President Reagan to the Nation: "The mood towards drugs is changing in this country and the momentum is with us. We are making no excuses for drugs—hard, soft, or otherwise. Drugs are bad and we are going after them".[2] Twelve days later, in a speech delivered at the Department of Justice, the President followed with an "unshakable" commitment "to do what is necessary to end the drug menace" and "to

---

[1]My more recent publications are: 'Crackdown: The Emerging "Drug Exception" to the Bill of Rights', 38 *Hastings Law Journal,* 889 (1987); Wisotsky (ed.), 'The War on Drugs: In Search of a Breakthrough' (Symposium), 11 *Nova Law Journal,* 891 (1987); Wisotsky, 'The Ideology of Drug Testing,' 11 *Nova Law Journal,* 763 (1987).
[2]President's Radio Address to the Nation, 18 Weekly Comp. Pres. Doc. 1249 (October 2, 1982) [hereinafter Radio Address].

cripple the power of the mob in America."[3] He cited the "unqualified success" of the Miami Task Force on Crime and Drugs as a model to build on.[4]

It is important to note that President Reagan was not the first to declare war on drugs. President Nixon had done the same in 1971. In a message to Congress he had described drug abuse as a "national emergency", denounced drugs as "public enemy number one" and called for a "total offensive".[5]

First Drug War or not, the President's statement about the mood of the country seemed accurate. At the time of his October 1982 speeches, some 3,000 parents groups had already organized nationwide under the umbrella of the National Federation of Parents for Drug Free Youth.[6] Within the government, the House Select Committee[7] and the attorney general's Task Force on Violent Crime[8] had urged the President to declare War on Drugs.

The President's October 14th speech called for and got more of nearly everything:[9] 1. more personnel—1,020 law enforcement agents for the Drug Enforcement Agency (DEA), Federal Bureau of Investigation (FBI), and other agencies, 200 Assistant United States Attorneys, and 340 clerical staff; 2. more aggressive law enforcement—creating 12 (later 13) regional prosecutorial task forces across the nation "to identify, investigate, and prosecute members of high-level drug trafficking enterprises, and to destroy the operations of those organizations"; 3. more money—$127.5 million in additional funding and a substantial realloca-

---

[3]President's Message Announcing Federal Initiatives Against Drug Trafficking and Organized Crime, 18 Weekly Comp. Pres. Doc. 1311, 1313–14 (October 14th, 1982).
[4]*New York Times,* October 15th, 1982, p. A20.
[5]E. Epstein, *Agency of Fear,* pp. 173, 179 (1977). Nixon consolidated agencies and created DEA as the lead agency in drug enforcement.
[6]Gonzales, 'The War on Drugs: A Special Report', *Playboy,* April 1982, p. 134.
[7]House Select Committee on Narcotics Abuse and Control, H.R. Rep. No. 418, pp. 1–2, 97th Cong., 2d Sess. 50 (1982).
[8]Attorney General's Task Force on Violent Crime, Final Report 28 (1981).
[9]The call for the buildup in the size and scope of the federal drug enforcement bureaucracy also occurred under the Nixon Administration. At the end of June 1968, the Bureau of Narcotics and Dangerous Drugs had 615 agents. By June 1970, this number had increased to over 900, with authorization for at least 300 more agents during 1971. See H.R. Rep. No. 1444, 91st Cong., 2d Sess. 18 reprinted in 1970 U.S. Code Cong. & Admin. News 4566, 4584.

tion of the existing budget from prevention, treatment, and research programs to law enforcement programs; 4. more prison bed space—the addition of 1,260 beds at eleven federal prisons to accommodate the increase in drug offenders to be incarcerated; 5. more stringent laws—a "legislative offensive designed to win approval of reforms" with respect to bail, sentencing, criminal forfeiture, and the exclusionary rule; 6. better interagency coordination—bringing together all federal law enforcement agencies in "a comprehensive attack on drug trafficking and organized crime" under a Cabinet-level committee chaired by the attorney general; and 7. improved federal-state co-ordination, including federal assistance to state agencies by training their agents.

Energized by the hardening attitude toward illegal drugs, the administration acted aggressively, mobilizing an impressive array of federal bureaucracies and resources in a co-ordinated, although largely futile, attack on the supply of illegal drugs—principally cocaine, marijuana, and heroin. The administration hired hundreds of drug agents and cut through bureaucratic rivalries with greater vigor than any administration before it. It acted to streamline operations and compel more co-operation among enforcement agencies. It placed the FBI in charge of DEA and gave it major drug enforcement responsibility for the first time in its history.[10] And, as the centerpiece of its prosecutorial strategy, it fielded a network of Organized Crime Drug Enforcement Task Forces in 13 'core' cities across the nation.[11]

To stop drugs from entering the country, the Administration attempted to erect a contemporary anti-drug version of the Maginot Line: the National Narcotics Border Interdiction System (NNBIS), an intelligence network designed to co-ordinate radar surveillance and interdiction efforts along the entire 96,000-mile border of the United States. As part

---

[10]*See* 28 C.F.R. §§ 0.85(a), 0.102 (1986). Authority for federal drug law enforcement is distributed among several agencies, including the DEA, the Customs Service, the Coast Guard, the FBI, and the IRS. Supporting roles are played by the Immigration and Naturalization Service, the CIA, and the Department of Defense. See National Drug Enforcement Policy Board, *National and International Drug Law Enforcement Strategy* (January 1987).

[11]*See* 'Organized Crime Drug Enforcement Task Forces: Goals and Objectives', 11 *Drug Enforcement*, 6 (1984); Maitland, 'President Gives Plan to Combat Drug Networks', *New York Times*, October 15th, 1982 § A, p. 1.

of that initiative, NNBIS floated radar balloons in the skies over Miami, the Florida Keys, and even the Bahamas to protect the nation's perimeter against drug-smuggling incursions.[12]

The CIA joined the war effort by supplying intelligence about foreign drug sources, and NASA assisted with satellite-based surveillance of coca and marijuana crops under cultivation.[13] The administration also initiated financial investigations, aided by computerized data banks and staffed by Treasury agents specially trained to trace money-laundering operations.[14] The State Department pressured foreign governments to eradicate illegal coca and marijuana plants and financed pilot programs to provide peasant farmers with alternative cash crops.[15] It also negotiated Mutual Assistance Treaties to expose 'dirty' money secreted in tax-haven nations and to extradite defendants accused of drug conspiracies against the laws of the United States.[16]

The government also literally militarized what had previously been only a rhetorical war, deploying the armed forces of the United States to "assist" drug enforcement operations. The Department of Defense provided pursuit planes, helicopters, and other equipment to federal civilian enforcement agencies, while Navy E-2C 'Hawkeye' radar planes patrolled the coastal skies in search of smuggling aircraft and ships.[17] The Coast Guard, receiving new cutters and more personnel, intensified its customary task of interdicting drug-carrying vessels at sea. 1981 amendments to the Posse Comitatus Act relaxed the century-old ban on military enforcement of criminal laws and permitted Coast Guard board-

---

[12]*See* Gibson, 'Anti-Smuggling System Would Have CIA Links', *Ft. Lauderdale News & Sun-Sentinel,* June 18th, 1983, § A, p. 1. See also Office of Technology Assessment, U.S. Congress, 'The Border War on Drugs', pp. 33–39 (1987) [hereinafter 'Border War'].

[13]*See* Coates and DeLama, 'Satellite Spying on Narcotics Operations Is a Promising Tool for Drug Task Force', *Miami Herald,* June 23rd, 1983, p. 11A.

[14]For a description of Operation Greenback, the prototype money-laundering investigation, see Financial Investigation of Drug Trafficking: Hearing Before the House Select Comm. on Narcotics Abuse and Control, 97th Cong., 1st Sess. 65 (1981).

[15]*See* International Narcotics Control: Hearings Before the House Committee on Foreign Affairs, 97th Cong., 2d Sess. 156 (1982); International Narcotics Trafficking: Hearings Before the Permanent Subcomm. on Investigations of the Senate Comm. on Governmental Affairs, 97th Cong., 1st Sess 201–02 (1981).

[16]*See* President's Commission on Organized Crime, 'America's Habit: Drug Abuse, Drug Trafficking and Organized Crime', pp. 412–419 (1986).

[17]Starita, 'Radar Planes to Hunt Drugs in S. Florida', *Miami Herald,* March 13th, 1982, p. 1B.

ing parties to sail on Naval warships serving as 'platforms' for Coast Guard interdictions.[18] Finally, for the first time in American history, Navy vessels, including a nuclear-powered aircraft carrier, began directly to interdict—and in one case fired upon—drug smuggling ships in international waters.[19] On a purely technical level, the Administration could rightly claim some success in focusing the resources of the federal government in a historically large and single-minded attack on the drug supply.

What were the results of this extraordinary enforcement program? It set new records in every category of measurement—drug seizures, investigations, indictments, arrests, convictions, and asset forfeitures. For example, DEA, FBI and Customs seized nearly one-half billion dollars in drug-related assets in 1986.[20] DEA arrested twice as many drug offenders in 1986 (12,819) as in 1982, and the percentage of arrestees constituting high-level traffickers also rose from roughly one-third to one-half.[21] DEA, FBI, and other federal agencies seized over 100,000 lbs. of cocaine in 1986.[22] From the end of 1980 to June 30, 1987, the prison population (counting felonies only) soared from 329,021 to 570,519. Roughly 40 percent of new prison inmates now go in for drug offenses. In recognition of this boom, the 1989 budget submission of the President seeks a 48 percent increase for the U.S. Bureau of Prisons in order to accommodate an anticipated increase in prisoners from 44,000 today to 72,000 by 1995.

Despite the Administration's accumulation of impressive statistics, domestic marijuana cultivation took off and the black market in cocaine grew to record size. In 1980, the supply of cocaine to the U.S. was

---

[18]Congress has likened the drug smugglers to an invading army, complete with generals, soldiers, and an armada that operates over the unpatrolled coastline and unmonitored airspace of the United States. See Note, 'Fourth Amendment and Posse Comitatus Act Restrictions on Military Involvement in Federal Law Enforcement', 54 Geo. Wash. L. Rev. 404, 417 & nn. 140–42 (1986).
[19]Stein, 'Naval Task Force Enlists in Drug War', *Miami Herald*, August 24th, 1983, p. 13A.; Balmaseda, 'Navy Bullets Riddle Pot-Smuggling Ship', *Miami Herald*, July 17th, 1983, p. 1A.
[20]National Drug Policy Board, 'Federal Drug Enforcement Progress Report, 1986' Exhibit II-2, pp. 19–20 [hereinafter "Progress Report"].
[21]*Id.*, Exhibit II-11, p. 35.
[22]*Id.*, Exhibit III-1, pp. 74–78.

estimated at 40 metric tons; by 1986 it had risen to 140 tons. As a result of this abundant supply and a more-or-less stable pool of buyers, prices fell dramatically. In 1980, a kilo of cocaine cost $50,000–$55,000 delivered in Miami; by 1986, it had fallen to the range of $12,000–$20,000; $14,000 was typical for much of 1988. In 1980–81, a gram of cocaine cost $100 and averaged 12 percent purity at street level. By 1986, the price had fallen to as low as $80 ($50 in Miami), and the purity had risen to more than 50 percent.[23] Around the nation, crack was marketed in $5 and $10 vials to reach the youth and low-income markets.[24] More than 22 million Americans report having tried cocaine; and roughly 5.8 million report having used it during the month preceding the 1985 National Household Survey.[25] Cocaine-related hospital emergencies rose from 4,277 in 1982 to 9,946 in 1985, and then to more than 26,000 in 1987.[26]

As if to mock the aggressive efforts of the War on Drugs, this rapid market growth occurred in the face of President Reagan's doubling and redoubling of the federal anti-drug enforcement budget from $645 million in fiscal year 1981 to over $4 billion in fiscal year 1987.[27] Resources specifically devoted to interdiction rose from $399 million to $1.3 billion, one third of the current budget; and military assistance rose from $5 million to $405 million,[28] including the provision of (the services of) Air Force AWACS and Navy E-2C radar planes; Army Black Hawk helicopters used in Customs pursuit missions; and the Customs Service's own purchases of P-3 radar planes, Citation jet interceptors, and Blue Thunder interceptor boats. DEA personnel rose from 1,940 in 1981 to 2,875 special agents in 1988, with more on request for 1989, along with a 47-position air wing for DEA.

This budgetary expansion seems all the more remarkable when

---

[23]Data on price, purity and supply are taken from the annual reports of the National Narcotics Intelligence Consumers Committee called 'The Supply of Illicit Drugs to the U.S. from Foreign and Domestic Sources'.
[24]'Progress Report', p. 7.
[25]*Id.*, p. 5.
[26]*Id.*, p. 6. 1987 data from 1987 NNIC Report.
[27]Congressional Research Service, Library of Congress, 'Drug Abuse Prevention and Control: Budget Authority for Federal Programs', FY 1986–FY 1988 [IP334D] (February 27th, 1987). The budget dropped to 3 plus billion in FY 88.
[28]Leen, 'Drug War Proving a Costly Failure', *Miami Herald*, September 11th, 1988, p. 18A.

compared to the 1969 anti-drug budget of $73.5 million.[29] Commenting specifically upon the interdiction budget, the Office of Technology Assessment concluded:

> Despite a doubling of Federal expenditures on interdiction over the past five years, the quantity of drugs smuggled into the United States is greater than ever. . . . There is no clear correlation between the level of expenditures or effort devoted to interdiction and the long-term availability of illegally-imported drugs in the domestic market.[30]

The social 'return' on the extra billions spent during that time has been a drug abuse problem of historic magnitude, accompanied by a drug trafficking parasite of international dimensions.

This latter point is crucial. It is not simply that the War on Drugs has failed to work; it has in many respects made things worse. It has spun a spider's web of black market pathologies, including roughly 25 percent of all urban homicides, widespread corruption of police and other public officials, street crime by addicts, and subversive 'narcoterrorist' alliances between Latin American guerrillas and drug traffickers.[31] In the streets of the nation's major cities, violent gangs of young drug thugs engage in turf wars and open shoot-outs with automatic rifles.[32] Innocent bystanders are often shot. Corruption pervades local police departments and foreign governments. Some Latin American and Caribbean nations have been effectively captured by drug traffickers.[33] Where capture is incomplete,

---

[29]Select Committee on Narcotics Abuse and Control, 95th Cong., 2d Sess., Congressional Resource Guide to the Federal Effort on Narcotics Abuse and Control 250 (Comm. Print 1976).

[30]'Border War', p. 3.

[31]These phenomena are described in some detail in *Breaking the Impasse in the War on Drugs*, Chs. 7–9.

[32]'The Drug Gangs', *Newsweek*, March 28th, 1988, p. 20.

[33]The leader of Panama, General Manuel Noriega, is currently under two separate federal indictments for drug trafficking offenses. The Chief Minister and the Commerce Minister of the Turks and Caicos were convicted in the U.S. of drug smuggling charges in 1985. Top officials in Haiti, Honduras, and Nicaragua are also under investigation in the U.S. 'Oppenheimer, U.S. urged to step up drug fight', *Miami Herald*, February 14th, 1988, p. 14A. George Baron, a U.S. government witness in the Carlos Lehder Rivas cocaine conspiracy trial, testified that he paid $3 to $5 million in bribes to Bahamian Prime Minister Lynden O. Pindling. Baron testified that he paid Pindling $15 for each pound of marijuana smuggled through the Bahamas to protect the boats from Bahamian police. AP, *Miami Herald*, February 17th, 1988, p. 10A.

intimidation reigns: one third of the Colombian supreme court was assassinated in a (suspected) narco-terrorist raid. An estimated 60 Colombian justices have been murdered in a recent five-year period.[34]

Of course, these pathologies were foreseeable. They are a function of money. Drug law yields to a higher law: the law of the marketplace, the law of supply and demand. The naive attack on the drug supply through an aggressive program of enforcement at each step—interdiction, arrest, prosecution, and punishment—results in what Stanford Law School Professor Herbert Packer has called a "crime tariff".[35] The crime tariff is what the seller must charge the buyer in order to monetize the risk he takes in breaking the law. It is in short a premium for taking risks. The criminal law thereby maintains hyper-inflated prices for illegal drugs in the black market.

For example, an ounce of pure pharmaceutical cocaine at roughly $80, just under $3.00 per gram, becomes worth about $4,480 if sold in the black market at $80 per diluted gram (at 50% purity). The crime tariff is thus $4,400 per ounce. This type of law enforcement succeeds to some unknown extent in making drugs less available—to the extent (probably slight) that demand is elastic or sensitive to price. But because the crime tariff is paid to lawbreakers rather than the Government, it pumps vast sums of money into the black market, more than $100 billion per year by government estimate.[36] The flow of these illegal billions through the underground economy finances or supplies the incentives for the pathologies described above: homicides, street crime, public corruption and international narcoterrorism. If these phenomena were properly costed out, one might well conclude that the War on Drugs makes a net negative contribution to the safety, well-being and national security interests of the American people.

Confronted by these threatening developments, both the public and the politicians predictably react in fear and anger. The specter of

---

[34]See Bin, 'Drug Lords and the Colombian Judiciary: A Story of Threats, Bribes and Bullets', 5 *Pacific Basin Law Journal*, p. 178 (1986).
[35]H. Packer, *The Limits of the Criminal Sanction*, pp. 277–282 (1968).
[36]House Select Committee on Narcotics Abuse and Control Annual Report for the Year 1984, H.R. Rep. No. 1199, 98th Cong., 2d Sess. 9 (1985).

uncontrolled and seemingly uncontrollable drug abuse and black marketeering leads to frustrated reaction against the drug trade. The zeal to "turn the screw of the criminal machinery—detection, prosecution, and punishment—tighter and tighter"[37] leads directly to the adoption of repressive and punitive measures that aggrandize governmental powers at the expense of individual rights.

This reactive, almost reflexive growth of governmental power and the correlative squelching of personal liberty occur as two closely related, if not inseparable, phenomena: 1. the government's sustained attack, motivated by the perceived imperatives of drug enforcement, on traditional protections afforded to criminal defendants under the Bill of Rights, and 2. the gradual but perceptible rise of 'Big Brotherism' against the public at large in the form of drug testing, investigative detention, eavesdropping, surveillance, monitoring, and other intrusive enforcement methods.

It may be difficult for those not familiar with criminal law and procedure to understand the degree to which the War on Drugs has disempowered the criminal defendant, especially in drug cases. Perhaps by focusing on a few of the most important of the many restrictions that have been imposed, one may begin to appreciate the severity of the crackdown on the rights of those accused of crime.

First, let us consider pre-trial detention. It is important to understand that in the U.S. the law has always favored pre-trial release to reinforce the presumption of innocence and to allow a defendant to aid counsel in his defense. The Eighth Amendment to the United States Constitution prohibits excessive bail; and while the cases do not establish a 'right' to bail, the law has evolved as if there were a presumptive right to pre-trial release on bail (or other conditions) except in capital cases where "the proof is evident or the presumption great". This was changed radically by the Comprehensive Crime Control Act of 1984,[38] which not only authorized pre-trial detention but created a statutory *presumption* in favor

---

[37]*Albernaz v. United States,* 450 U.S. 333, 343 (1981).
[38]Pub. L. No. 98-473, Tit. II, ch. 1, § 203(a), 98 Stat. 1976 (1984) (codified at 18 U.S.C. § 3142) (Supp. 1986).

of it in any case in which, *inter alia,* the defendant is charged with a drug offense punishable by ten years or more in prison.[39] Although the presumption is rebuttable, in the first seven months under the act, the government won 704 motions for pre-trial detention while defendants won only 185.[40] Pre-trial detention is a severe blow to the morale of a defendant and to his ability to assist in the preparation of his defense.[41]

Another major erosion in the rights of defendants is the more permissive use of illegally seized evidence. Since 1914, the Fourth Amendment to the U.S. Constitution has been interpreted to exclude from use in court evidence obtained by federal law enforcement authorities in an illegal search and seizure.[42] Many states voluntarily adhered to that ruling, and in 1961 the remaining states were required to do so by the decision of the Supreme Court in *Mapp v. Ohio.*[43] But under the relentless pressure of drug prosecutions and the frequent attempts of Congress to repeal or restrict the exclusionary rule, the Courts have whittled away at the protections afforded to individual privacy.

Notwithstanding the independence of the judicial branch, the Courts have in effect joined the war on drugs. Most notably, the U.S. Supreme Court gave its approval to just about every challenged drug enforcement technique. For example, the Court upheld the power of drug agents to use the airport drug courier profile to stop, detain and question citizens without probable cause;[44] to subject a traveller's luggage to a sniffing examination by drug-detector dogs without probable cause;[45] to make

---

[39]18 U.S.C. § 3142(e) (Supp. 1986).
[40]Kennedy, 'Foreword to Symposium on the Crime Control Act of 1984', 22 Am. Crim. L. Rev. vi, viii n. 4 (1985).
[41]Wald, 'Pretrial Detention and Ultimate Freedom: A Statistical Study', 39 N.Y.U. L. Rev. 631 (1964).
[42]*Weeks v. United States,* 232 U.S. 383 (1914).
[43]367 U.S. 643 (1961).
[44]*Florida v. Royer,* 460 U.S. 491, 493 (1983); see also *United States v. Montoya,* 473 U.S. 531 (1985); *Florida v. Rodriguez,* 469 U.S. 1, 5 (1984). Drug courier profiles are based on an informal compilation of traits commonly associated with drug smugglers; they have been criticized for allowing impermissible intrusions on fourth amendment rights based solely on an agent's 'hunch'. See Note, 'Drug Courier Profiles in Airport Stops', 14 S.U.L. Rev. 315, 316–317 & n. 23 (1984). For further criticisms, see Note, 'Search and Seizure: Defining the Outer Boundaries of the Drug Courier Profile', 17 *Creighton Law Review* 973 (1985).
[45]*United States v. Place,* 462 U.S. 696, 706 (1983).

warrantless searches of automobiles and closed containers therein;[46] to conduct surveillance of suspects by placing transmitters or beepers in containers in vehicles;[47] to search at will without cause ships in inland waterways;[48] and to obtain a search warrant based on an undisclosed informant's tip.[49] The Supreme Court also adopted a 'good-faith exception' to the exclusionary rule for evidence seized in searches made pursuant to defective warrants.[50] It authorized warrantless searches of open fields and barns adjacent to a residence.[51] It significantly enlarged the powers of police to stop, question, and detain drivers of vehicles on the highways on suspicion less than probable cause[52] or with no suspicion at all at fixed checkpoints or road blocks.[53] The Court also validated warrantless aerial surveillance, that is airplane overflights of private property,[54] the warrantless search of a motor home occupied as a residence,[55] and the warrantless search of the purse of a public school student.[56] In the realm of search and seizure, there is hardly a drug case that the government failed to win. Indeed, the Supreme Court in *Albernaz* apparently placed its imprimatur on the turn-the-screw approach of the U.S. Congress. Thus, the crackdown mentality prevails not only in the political realm but, to use Madison's phrase, in "the least dangerous branch" as well.

———————

[46]*United States v. Ross*, 456 U.S. 798, 821 (1982); see also *Colorado v. Bertine*, 107 S.Ct. 738 (1987).

[47]*United States v. Knotts*, 460 U.S. 276, 282 (1983).

[48]*United States v. Villamonte-Marquez*, 462 U.S. 579, 593 (1983).

[49]*Illinois v. Gates*, 462 U.S. 213 (1983). Gates replaced the principles of probable cause established in *Aquilar v. Texas*, 378 U.S. 108 (1964) and *Spinelli v. United States*, 393 U.S. 410 (1969) with a more loosely structured 'totality of the circumstances' test. *Gates*, 462 U.S. at 230.

[50]*United States v. Leon*, 468 U.S. 897, 905 (1984). To similar effect are *Illinois v. Krull*, 107 S.Ct. 1160 (1987), and *Maryland v. Garrison*, 107 S.Ct. 1013 (1987). For criticism of the good faith exception, see 1 W. LaFave, *Search and Seizure: A Treatise on the Fourth Amendment* § 1.3(c)–(d), at 51, 58–59 (1987) (arguing that the *Leon* Court overestimated the costs of adherence to the exclusionary rule based on "intuition, hunches, and occasional pieces of partial and often inconclusive data").

[51]*United States v. Dunn*, 107 S.C. 1134 (1987) (barn); *Oliver v. United States*, 466 U.S. 170 (1984) (open fields).

[52]*United States v. Sharpe*, 470 U.S. 675 (1985).

[53]*Texas v. Brown*, 460 U.S. 730 (1983).

[54]*California v. Ciraolo*, 106 S.Ct. 1809, 1813 (1986).

[55]*California v. Carney*, 471 U.S. 386, 390 (1985).

[56]*New Jersey v. T.L.O.*, 469 U.S. 325, 333 (1985).

One further example of the crackdown atmosphere prevailing in the U.S. comes from the Anti-Drug Abuse Act of 1986,[57] in which Congress not only created new crimes but added to the penalties which already existed. The effect of the Act is that drug crimes now rank among the most seriously punished offenses in the United States Criminal Code. For example, the Act provides mandatory minimum penalties of five and ten years in prison depending upon drug and weight involved; in the case of possession with intent to distribute five kilograms of cocaine, the penalty is a minimum of ten years up to a maximum of life imprisonment. Even as little as five grams of cocaine base require not less than five years in prison and a maximum of 40 years. In both cases, the range of penalties rises to a minimum of 20 years and a maximum of life if death or serious bodily injury results from the use of such substances. It should be emphasized that these penalties apply to *first-time* drug offenders; those with a prior state or federal drug conviction must receive a *mandatory life term* under these circumstances.

The fact that these penalties are so severe, more stringent in fact than sentences typically meted out to robbers or rapists,[58] illustrates one of the themes of this statement: people in the U.S. are so fearful and angry about their inability to contain drug trafficking that they are resorting to extremist, desperation measures. More than one public official has proposed simply shooting suspected drug-carrying planes out of the sky. The atmosphere is perhaps best conveyed by the judicial opinion of a respected federal judge in Miami who, in an order denying bail pending appeal, condemned drug dealers as "merchants of misery, destruction, and death" whose greed has wrought "hideous evil" and "unimaginable sorrow" upon the nation. Their crimes, he wrote, are "unforgivable".[59] And if drug crimes are literally "unforgivable", traditional constitutional

---

[57]Pub. L. No. 99–750, reprinted in 1986 U.S. Code Cong. & Admin. News (No. 10A) (codified as amended in scattered sections of U.S.C.).

[58]A not untypical example comes from a prominent 1988 news story. Larry Singleton had been convicted of raping a teenager and hacking off the arms of a teenager between wrist and elbow. He was convicted in California and given the maximum sentence of 14 years and served 8. In Florida, a person convicted of possession of 400 grams of cocaine or other similar drug trafficking offense would receive a non-parolable mandatory term of 15 years. With typical gain time and work credits, he might serve approximately 7 years in prison.

[59]*United States v. Miranda,* 442 F. Supp. 786, 795 (S.D. Fla. 1977).

and statutory protections for individual rights can be discounted or discarded. One congressman in fact complained about the extent to which legal protections interfered with the prosecution of drug cases: "[I]n the War on Narcotics we have met the enemy and he is the U.S. code. I have never seen such a maze of laws and hangups . . ."[60] In that spirit, and in the spirit of the angry judge just quoted, the punitive measures I have described, along with dozens of others, such as forfeiture of defense attorney's fees,[61] have become 'logical' measures in an endless cycle of crackdowns and failures.

Perhaps if these repressive laws applied only to drug defendants, who could be dismissed as an alien 'them', few would care and fewer still would protest. But this kind of reactionary force cannot be contained, cannot apply only to those accused of drug crime. In fact, the tentacles of drug enforcement have already spread out to reach into the lives of ordinary people, not just to those involved in the drug underworld. These intrusions into the lives of civilian society take many forms. One of the most obvious is the rapid proliferation of mandatory drug testing of employees and job applicants in the U.S. Civil Service,[62] state and local civil services, and in the private sector as well. Some 40 percent of *Fortune* 500 companies now subject their applicants or employees to urinalysis.[63] Government surveillance is on the increase in the form of wiretaps and the maintenance of 1.5 million or more names in NADDIS,

---

[60]Financial Investigation of Drug Trafficking: Hearings Before the House Select Comm. on Narcotics Abuse and Control, 97th Cong., 1st Sess. 58 (1981) (statement of Congressman Hutto).

[61]*United States v. Caplin & Drysdale,* 814 F.2d 905 (4th Cir. 1987).

[62]President's Message Announcing the Goals and Objectives of the National Campaign Against Drug Abuse, 22 Weekly Comp.Pres. Doc. 1040, 1041 (August 4th, 1986).

[63]General Dynamics, General Motors, Greyhound, E.F. Hutton, IBM, Mobil, *The New York Times,* The Teamsters, and United Auto Workers are but a few of the enterprises that have recently instituted some type of workplace drug testing. Ross, 'Drug Testing at Work Spreading—and Likely to Spread Further', *L.A. Daily Journal,* June 6th, 1985, p. 4.

See generally, 'Testing for Drugs in the American Workplace', 11 *Nova Law Review* 291 (1987); Wisotsky, 'The Ideology of Drug Testing', 11 *Nova Law Journal* 763 (1987).

One rationale for requiring that urinalysis be predicated upon individual suspicion is the not-unlikely possibility of a false positive result: "Two Navy doctors were almost drummed out of the service [in 1984] because they tested positive for morphine, the result of having eaten too many poppy seed bagels. Indeed, the Navy program has seen huge errors—over 4,000 men and women were recalled at full back pay [in 1985] because they were discharged on the basis of a [false positive]." (Ross, *supra.*)

a drug investigative data bank. On a more prosaic level, the War on Drugs hampers the mobility of travellers, who are subjected to road blocks, detained for questioning at airports, and whose luggage can be diverted for sniffing by drug-detector dogs.

One of the latest repressive anti-drug initiatives to emerge from Washington is called 'zero tolerance', begun by the Customs Service on March 21st. It means, in a nutshell, punishing drug users to promote 'user accountability' and to reduce 'the demand side of the equation'. One manifestation of this policy occurs in the effort to promote federal criminal prosecution of persons found in possession of small amounts of drugs for which they formerly would have escaped prosecution or been referred to local authorities for prosecution. On March 30th, 1988 Attorney General Meese sent a memorandum to all United States Attorneys encouraging the selective prosecution of "middle and upper class users" in order to "send the message that there is no such thing as 'recreational' drug use . . ."

More widely known is the seizure and forfeiture of cars, planes, or boats of persons found in possession of even trace amounts of illegal drugs; these forfeited assets in effect impose massive fines far greater than would ordinarily be imposed upon a criminal conviction for drug possession; but as civil forfeiture is in *rem*, no conviction or prosecution is required at all. Some examples: On April 30th, the Coast Guard boarded and seized the motor yacht *Ark Royal*, valued at $25 million, because 10 marijuana *seeds* and two stems were found aboard. Public criticism prompted a return of the boat upon payment of $1,600 in fines and fees by the owner. The 52-foot *Mindy* was impounded for a week because of cocaine dust in a rolled-up dollar bill. The $80 million oceanographic research vessel *Atlantis II* was seized in San Diego when the Coast Guard found 0.01 ounce of marijuana in a crewman's shaving kit. It was returned also. But a Michigan couple returning from a Canadian vacation lost the wife's 1987 Cougar when Customs agents found two marijuana cigarettes in the pocket of her husband. No charges were filed, but the car was kept by the government. In Key West, Florida, David Phelps, a shrimp fisherman, lost his 73-foot shrimper to the coast guard who found three grams of cannabis seeds and stems aboard. Under the law, the boat is forfeitable whether or not Phelps had any responsibility for the drugs. Three weeks later, the boat had not been returned. There are many other ways, too numerous to mention in this statement, that the War on Drugs has choked off civil liberties in the U.S.

In 1987, the United States celebrated the bicentennial of its Constitution. The framers of the Constitution were animated by the spirit of William Pitt's dictum that "unlimited power is apt to corrupt the minds of those who possess it."[64] They therefore created a constitutional structure in which governmental power was limited in the first instance and constrained in the second by the system of checks and balances. The Bill of Rights, the first 10 amendments to the Constitution, were added in 1791 to further secure personal freedom from governmental oppression. The War on Drugs has substantially undermined the American tradition of limited government and personal autonomy. Since the early 1980s, the prevailing attitude, both within Government and in the broader society, has been that the crackdown on drugs is so imperative that extraordinary measures are justified. The end has come to justify the means. The result is that Americans have significantly less freedom than they did only five or six years ago.

Developments in 1988: Polarization

Election year politics continues to ratchet the War on Drugs machinery tighter and tighter. In June the Administration declared its goal of a "drug-free America".[65] During the month of April, the Senate voted 93 to 0 to adopt the Anti-Drug Abuse Act of 1988, creating a $2.6 billion special reserve fund for anti-drug programs over and above the regular annual budget of three-plus billion dollars. (As noted above, the regular budget represents a manifold increase in the level of funding that prevailed when the war on drugs was declared.) The frustration of Congress with drug-producing nations of Latin America, crystallized by the stalemate with General Noriega in Panama, has produced a number of

---

[64]Speech, Case of Wilkes (January 19th, 1770).
[65]National Drug Policy Board, 'Toward a Drug Free America' (1988).

controversial proposals involving the threat of sanctions[66] and the use of military force to destroy coca crops or to capture fugitives from U.S. drug charges. Secretary Carlucci's opposition to arrest powers for the military services may tone down the final bill, but an expanded military surveillance role seems likely. At the state level, the National Guard has already been deployed on anti-drug search and destroy missions.

The President on April 19th "call[ed] upon the House and Senate to vote promptly on my bill providing for capital punishment when a death results from drug dealing, and when a . . . law enforcement officer is murdered." In the latest piece of fundamentalist-style anti-drug zealotry, the House on September 22nd voted 375–30 to adopt capital punishment, for a drug exception to the exclusionary rule, to deny college student loans to anyone convicted of possessing drugs, to impose without trial up to $10,000 in "civil fines" for a person caught in possession of drugs, and to impose a mandatory five-year prison sentence on anyone convicted of possession of crack cocaine. Other "zero tolerance" style bills abound. A House Republican Task force has introduced a bill calling for confiscation of 25 percent of the adjusted gross income and net assets of anyone caught possessing illegal substances. It would also cut off federal highway funds to states that do not suspend drivers' licenses of persons convicted of using drugs.[67] As we get closer to the November election, one can predict with confidence that more of these proposals will surface and that their extremist nature will increase.

But at the same time there is movement in the opposite direction. Respected journalists and other opinion leaders have begun to break ranks with the War on Drugs, in some cases suggesting that it be abandoned altogether. Here are some notable examples. David Boaz, Vice President for public policy at libertarian-oriented Cato Institute, wrote an op-ed piece for the *New York Times* (March 17th) "Let's Quit the Drug War". In it he denounced the war on drugs as "unwinnable"

---

[66]In February, the House Foreign Affairs Committee Task Force on International Narcotics Control demanded that the State Department impose sanctions against Colombia, Peru, Bolivia and other nations in order to force them to intensify their drug enforcement efforts.
[67]'The Drug Enforcement Report', June 23rd, 1988, p.2.

and destructive to other values such as civil liberties and advocated a "withdrawal" from the war. Edwin M. Yoder Jr. of the *Washington Post* Writers Group called the war on drugs "dumb" and compared it to the prohibition of alcohol for "encouraging and enriching mobsters" (March 4th, 1988). On March 10th, 1988, Richard Cohen of the *Los Angeles Times* Syndicate published a piece endorsing the idea of a plan for the government distribution of drugs in order to "recognize the drug problem is with us to stay—a social and medical problem, but not necessarily a law-enforcement one. We've been making war on drugs long enough. It's time we started making sense instead." By May and June, articles of this type became a staple item in newspapers all over the country as editors hopped aboard the "legalization" bandwagon.

This sample of articles shows the emergence of a significant body of opinion opposed to the war on drugs. What is perhaps even more significant is that the opposition transcends the liberal/conservative split. Traditionally, conservatives have advocated strict law enforcement and liberals have been identified with a permissive approach to the drug issue. Now highly respected conservative spokesmen have also begun to dissent from the War on Drugs.

Even before the recent spate of articles described above, prominent conservative columnist William F. Buckley Jr. had reversed his position and advocated the legalization of drugs as the only effective course of governmental action. Nobel Prize-winning economist Milton Friedman has made public statements advocating more market-oriented approaches to the regulation of drugs. *National Review*, the most prominent organ of conservative opinion, through its editor Richard Vigilante, published a piece (December 5th, 1986) exposing the Anti Drug Abuse Act of 1986 as a manifestation of public panic and criticizing the intrusiveness of drug testing and other enforcement measures. He also rejected the war on drugs as intolerant and politically unwise: "Embracing the drug hysteria requires a rejection of essential conservative principles." In the same issue of NR is an article by Richard C. Cowan, entitled 'How the Narcs Created Crack', arguing as follows: "Any realistic approach to the drug problem must begin with the legalization of small scale cultivation and sale of marijuana so that it is separated from the other, more dangerous drugs. . . . We need not fear that if we stop the lying and hypocrisy, the American people are going to destroy themselves with drugs."

This debate has captured the attention of the mainstream media.[68] Clearly, the challenge to the monopoly status of the War on Drugs is gaining ground. Nothing approaching this level of dissent has been seen or heard since the War on Drugs started.

The dissent has also begun to spill over to the political sector. For example, the *ABA Journal* (January 1st, 1988) reported that the New York County Lawyers Association Committee on Law Reform published a report advocating the decriminalization of heroin, cocaine, and marijuana. New York State Senator Joseph L. Galiber, from a district in the drug-ravaged Bronx, introduced on April 18th a bill in the New York State legislature to decriminalize the possession, distribution, sale, and use of all forms of controlled substances under the aegis of a State-Controlled Substance Authority. At a speech at the National Conference of Mayors and again on a May 10th, 1988, broadcast of ABC's 'Nightline', the Mayor of Baltimore called for congressional hearings to study the issue. Other mayors and a few congressmen supported him. And, surprisingly, Congressman Charles Rangel, Chairman of the House Select Committee on Narcotics Abuse and Control, scheduled a one-day hearing for September 29th, 1988, clearly inadequate for the task at hand, yet perhaps a harbinger of the future. Even if nothing constructive can emerge amidst election year maneuvering, at least the genie of change is out of the bottle.

There are also pressures beginning to come from abroad. For example, the attorney general of Colombia said in a telephone interview with the *Miami Herald* (February 23rd, 1988) that Colombia's battles against drug-trafficking rings have been a failure, calling them "useless". He suggested that legalizing the drug trade is something that the government "may have to consider" in the future. The *Economist* magazine ran a cover story (April 2–8) called 'Getting Gangsters Out of Drugs', advocating the legalized and taxed distribution of controlled substances. It followed up with similar commentaries on May 21st and

---

[68]*Time* magazine ran a cover story on the debate called 'Thinking the Unthinkable' (May 30th, 1988). *Newsweek* did a similar piece. The *New York Times* and the *Miami Herald* both ran front page stories on the same subject in May.

June 4th. *El Pais,* the most influential Spanish newspaper, also recommended "La legalizacion de la droga" in an editorial (May 22nd, 1988).

What accounts for this trend? Negative experience with the War on Drugs certainly plays a role. In the *Structure of Scientific Revolutions,* Thomas S. Kuhn argued that "the process by which a new candidate for paradigm replaces its predecessors" occurs "only after persistent failure to solve a noteworthy puzzle has given rise to crisis" (pp. 144–45). There is little doubt that the perception that the War on Drugs is a failure at controlling drug supply has spread significantly. Uncritical acceptance of the War on Drugs is no longer possible. And the perception that it has negative side effects, breeding crime, violence and corruption, has spread even to the comic pages of the daily newspapers.[69] In a more serious vein, Ted Koppel's "Nightline" broadcast a special three-hour "National Town Forum" on the subject of legalization. Perhaps we have already reached Kuhn's stage of "persistent failure and crisis", in which the war on drugs has been dislodged as the only conceivable paradigm for the control of drugs in the U.S. What now should be done?

Toward a New Beginning in Drug Control

One historically tested model of exploring policy reform is the appointment of a National Study Commission of experts, politicians and lay leaders to make findings of fact, canvass a full range of policy options, and recommend further research where needed. The precedent set by the National Commission on Marijuana and Drug Abuse in the early 1970s offers a model that might usefully be emulated in many respects. At the very least, a National Commission performs a vital educational function: its public hearings and attendant media coverage inform the public, bringing to their attention vital facts and a broader array of policy options. The level of public discourse is almost certain to be elevated. Only those who prefer ignorance to knowledge could possibly oppose the commission process.

---

[69]The syndicated strip 'Bloom County', for example, satirized the issue on at least two separate occasions. The April 18th, 1988, strip portrayed a scenario in which a lobbyist for smugglers makes contributions to anti-drug candidates for political office as a way to keep drug prices high. "Nothing makes us madder than some liberal talking drug legalization."

What should be the agenda of such a commission? Its over-riding goal should be to develop policies directed toward the objectives of 1. reducing drug abuse and 2. reducing the black-market pathologies resulting from the billions in drug money generated by drug law enforcement. In pursuit of these dual goals, the commission's study might benefit from adherence to the following five points:

I. DEFINE THE DRUG PROBLEM

What exactly is the problem regarding drugs in the U.S.? The absence of an agreed-upon answer to this question is one of the primary sources of incoherence in present law and policy. People now speak of "the drug problem" in referring to at least five very different phenomena: 1. the mere use of any illegal drug; 2. especially by teenagers; 3. the abuse of illegal drugs, or use which causes physical or psychological harm to the user; 4. drug-induced misbehavior that endangers or harms others, such as driving while impaired; and 5. drug-trafficking phenomena (crime, violence, and corruption) arising from the vast sums of money generated in the black market in drugs. This confusion in the very statement of the problem necessarily engenders confusion in solving it. The "drug problem" as Edward Brecher reminds us in his classic *Licit and Illicit Drugs* is itself a problem. Therefore, it does not and cannot lead to the formulation of useful solutions. It would be a real breakthrough if the Congress or the next President would generate a meaningful statement of the "drug problem". Otherwise, we are condemned to confirm the truth of Eric Sevareid's quip that the chief cause of problems is solutions.

II. STATE YOUR GOALS

A creative definition or redefinition of the drug problem would of itself carry us toward a (re)statement of goals. Rational policy-making is impossible without a clear articulation of the goals sought to be achieved. Part of that impossibility arises from the inconsistency between, for example, pursuit of existing goal number one by an attack on the drug supply and pursuit of goal number five, the suppression of drug money. Pursuit of the first creates a crime tariff which makes pursuit of the last more or less impossible. Instead, the result of drug enforcement is a black market estimated by the government to be over $100 billion per year, money that funds or gives rise to homicidal violence, street corruption by addicts, corruption of public officials and international narco-terrorism. It is therefore essential to distinguish between problems arising from drugs and problems arising from drug money. For example, how much criminality is attributable not to the psychopharmacology of drugs but to the excessive prices intentionally caused by the prohibition of drugs? Rational policy-makers have to distinguish between the two and acknowledge the trade-offs between the two lines of attack.

III. SET REALISTIC AND PRINCIPLED PRIORITIES BASED ON TRUTH

The suppression of drugs as an end in itself is frequently justified by arguments that drugs cause addiction, injury and even death in the short or long run. Granted that all drug use has the potential for harm, it is clear beyond any rational argument that most drug use does not cause such harm. DEA Director John Lawn to the contrary ("Drugs are illegal because they are bad"), drugs are not harmful *per se*. Exposure to drugs is not the same as exposure to radioactive waste.[70] Rather, the overwhelming majority of incidents of drug use are without lasting personal or societal consequence, just as the overwhelming majority of drinking causes no harm to the drinker or to society.

Accepting the truth of that premise means that not all drug use need

---

[70]Truth-based legislation will also have to acknowledge that 'recreational' drugs also have beneficial uses, most notably medicinal ones. Respectable authorities in the U.S. and abroad endorse heroin for pain relief for terminally ill patients. Francis Young, the chief administrative law judge of DEA, recommended this summer that marijuana be re-classified to permit doctors to prescribe it for relief of nausea from chemotherapy and for other purposes. His opinion concludes that marijuana is "far safer than many foods we commonly consume" and that its medical benefits are "clear beyond any question". Judge Young had previously recommended that MDMA ('ecstasy') be removed from Schedule I and be made legally available to psychiatrists for use in treating their patients.

Medical uses are not the only beneficial effects of drugs. An AP wire from Frankfurt reported that the U.S. Air Force allows its pilots to take Dexedrine "so that they are able to fly when they haven't gotten enough sleep or don't feel fit enough." Hundreds of thousands of 'drug abusers' similarly stimulate themselves with amphetamines and cocaine. Over a century ago, Sigmund Freud discovered in self-experiments that moderate doses (one tenth of a gram) of cocaine improved his muscular strength and reaction time. See Byck, *Cocaine Papers: Sigmund Freud* (New York: New American Library, 1974), pp. 98, 103.

be addressed by the criminal law, and that society might actually benefit from a policy of benign neglect respecting some forms of drug use. I have in mind the Dutch model, where nothing is legal but some things are simply ignored, cannabis in particular. NORML estimates that there are approximately one half-million arrests per year for marijuana, almost all for simple possession or petty sale offenses. Depending upon the age of consent chosen, most of these arrests could be eliminated from the criminal justice system, thereby achieving a massive freeing of resources for the policing of real crime.

Because we live in a world of limited resources, it is not possible to do everything. It is therefore both logical and necessary to make distinctions among things that are more or less important. I have in mind at least five basic dichotomies: 1. drug use by children (top priority) versus drug use by adults (low priority); 2. marijuana smoking (low priority) versus use of harder drugs (higher priority); 3. public use of drugs (high priority) versus private use of drugs at home (low priority); 4. drug consumption (no priority) versus drug impairment (high priority); 5. occasional use (low priority) versus chronic or dependent use (higher priority).

From these general criteria for drug policy, I would commend to the National Commission five specific goals for an effective, principled drug policy:

1. *Protect the Children.* I think this priority is self-evident and needs no discussion. I would simply add that this is the only domain in which "zero tolerance" makes any sense at all and might even be feasible if enforcement resources were concentrated on this as a top priority.

2. *Get Tough on the Legal Drugs.* It is common knowledge that alcohol (100,000 annual deaths) and tobacco (360,000 annual deaths) far exceed the illegal drugs as sources of death, disease, and dysfunction in the U.S. Everyone knows that alcohol and tobacco are big business—the advertising budget alone for alcohol runs about $2 billion a year—and, what is worse, the states and federal government are in complicity with the sellers of these deadly drugs by virtue of the billions in tax revenues that they reap.

I am not, however, suggesting prohibition of these drugs. That is wrong in principle and impossible in practice, as experience teaches. Nonetheless, there are more restrictive measures that can and should be undertaken. One is to get rid of cigarette vending machines so that cigarettes are not so readily available to minors. A second is to require or recommend to the states and localities more restrictive hours of sale. A third is to levy taxes on these products that are consistent with their social costs—billions of dollars in property damage, disease, and lost productivity.[71] Those costs should be financed largely by the sale of these products; at present prices, society is clearly subsidizing those products by providing police, fire, ambulance services for road accidents; medicare and medicaid reimbursement for therapy, surgery, prothesis or other medical care; and many other hidden costs effectively externalized by the industries from smoker and drinker to society as a whole. Precise numbers need to be derived from studies, but I wouldn't be surprised to find cigarettes at, say, $10 a pack and hard liquor at, say, $30–$50 a bottle to be priced more consistently with their true social costs. Such taxes would have the additional salutary effect of reducing the consumption of these dangerous products to the extent that demand is elastic.

3. *Public Safety and Order.* Here we need policies directed toward protection of the public from accident and injury on the highway, in the workplace and from unruly disruptions in public streets, public transport, parks and other gathering places. Programs specifically tailored to accomplish this more focused goal make a lot more sense than futile and counter productive "zero tolerance" approaches. Street-level law enforcement practices need to be reviewed to see to what extent they may actually encourage hustling drugs in the street to avoid arrests and forfeitures that might follow from fixed points of sale.

Promotion of driving and workplace safety require more knowledge. Nothing should be assumed. Drug use, as the Air Force's and Freud's examples show, does not automatically mean that a pilot or driver is impaired. Even with marijuana there is ambiguous evidence as to its effect on motor co-ordination.[72] Responsible research is required.

---

[71]The Research Triangle Institute estimated the annual costs of alcohol abuse to society at $116 billion in 1983. Conference Board, 'Corporate Strategies for Controlling Substance Abuse' 13 (Axel, ed., 1986). With 1,000 daily deaths from lung cancer and other diseases often preceded by years of medical treatment, there must be billions more in social costs attributable to tobacco.
[72]See Knepper, 'Puff the Dangerous Drug', *Car and Driver,* June 1980, p. 43.

4. *Protect Public Health.* The emphasis here is on the word "public". Policy should be directed toward 1. treatment of addicts on a voluntary basis and 2. true epidemiological concerns such as the use of drugs by pregnant women and the potential for transmission of AIDS by I.V. drug users. Addiction treatment is now shamefully underfunded, with months-long waiting lists in many cities.

Purely individualized risks are not in principle a public health matter and are in any case trivial in magnitude compared to those now accepted from alcohol and tobacco. Judge Young found no known lethal dose of marijuana. Even with cocaine, which has lethal potential, less than 2,000 deaths per year result even though billions of lines or puffs of cocaine are consumed every year. (Other long-term harms may result but are not systematically known at this time.) In any event, harmfulness is not the sole touchstone of regulation; the requirements of goal number five, listed below, demand considerable deference to individual choice in this domain.

5. *Respect the Value of Individual Liberty and Responsibility.* The current administration's goal of a drug-free America, except for children, is both ridiculous—as absurd as a liquor-free America—and wrong in principle. This is not a fundamentalist Ayatollah Land after all. A democratic society must respect the decisions made by its adult citizens, even those perceived to be foolish or risky. After all, is it different in principle to protect the right of gun ownership, which produces some ten to twelve thousand homicides per years and thousands more non-fatal injuries? Is it different in principle to protect the right of motorcyclists, skydivers or mountain climbers to risk their lives? Is it different to permit children to ride bicycles which "cause" tens of thousands of crippling injuries and deaths per year? To say that something is "dangerous" does not automatically supply a reason to outlaw it. Indeed, the general presumption in our society is that competent adults, with access to necessary information, are entitled to take risks of this kind as part of the right to life, liberty, and the pursuit of happiness. Why are drugs different?

It would be truly totalitarian if the government could decide these matters. After all, if the government is conceded to have the power to prohibit what is dangerous, does it not then have the power to compel what is safe? More specifically, if one drug can be prohibited on the ground that it is dangerous to the individual, would it then not be permissible for the government to decree that beneficial doses of some other drug must be taken at specified intervals?

The freedom of American citizens has already been seriously eroded by the War on Drugs.[73] More civil liberties hang in the balance of the 1988 Omnibus Anti-Drug Abuse Act pending in Congress and further legislation in years to come. Is the defense of Americans from drugs to be analogized to the defense of the Vietnamese from Communism, that it was necessary to destroy the city of Hue in order to save it? The National Commission should give serious weight to this value in its policy recommendations.

IV. FOCUS ON THE BIG PICTURE

Present drug policy suffers from a kind of micro-think that borders on irresponsibility and is sometimes downright silly. This typically manifests itself in proud administration announcements or reports to congressional committees of a new initiative or new accomplishment without regard to its impact on the bottom line. The examples are endless—a joint strike force with the government of the Bahamas; shutdown of a source of supply; the Pizza Connection case, the largest organized crime heroin trafficking case ever made by the federal government; a new bank secrecy agreement with the Caymans; a new coca eradication program in Bolivia or Peru, and so on. But none of these programs or "accomplishments" has ever made any noticeable or lasting impact on the drug supply. Even now, as the Godfather of Bolivian cocaine resides in a Bolivian prison, is there any observable reduction in the supply of cocaine?

The lack of insistence that enforcement programs should make a difference in the real world produces fatuous reports like this 1979 report by GAO to the Congress: "Gains made in Controlling Illegal Drugs, Yet The Drug Trade Flourishes."[74] In what sense is it meaningful

---

[73]*See* Wisotsky, 'Crackdown: The Emerging "Drug Exception" to the Bill of Rights', 38 *Hastings Law Journal* 889 (1987).
[74]GGD-80-4 (October 25th, 1979).

to say that gains are made if the bottom line grows worse and worse? This is reprehensible doubletalk or Newspeak that should not be tolerated by responsible public officials.

The whole drug enforcement enterprise needs to be put on a more businesslike basis, looking to the bottom line and not to isolated "achievements" of the war on drugs. In fact, the investor analogy is a good one to use: if the war on drugs were incorporated as a business enterprise, with its profits to be determined by its success in controlling drug abuse and drug trafficking, who would invest in it? Even if its operating budget were to be doubled to $6 billion per year, or doubled again to $12 billion per year, would it be a good personal investment? If not, why is it a good social investment?

This kind of hard-headed thinking is exactly what is lacking and has been lacking throughout the War on Drugs. No attention has been paid to considerations of cause and effect, or to trade-offs, or to cost-benefit analysis. New anti-drug initiatives are not subjected to critical questioning: what marginal gains, if any, can be projected from new programs or an additional commitment of resources? Conversely, how might things worsen? For example, many law enforcement officials believe that the coast guard's "successful" interdiction of marijuana coming from Jamaica and Colombia in the early 1980s had two negative side-effects: the substitution of domestic cultivation of more potent marijuana in California (and throughout the U.S.) and the diversion of smugglers into more compact and more readily concealable cocaine. Was that interdiction initiative therefore truly successful? Weren't those side-effects reasonably foreseeable? There are other examples. Drug gangs are probably far more ruthlessly violent today than in the 1970s because they have learned to adapt to aggressive law-enforcement methods. The friendly governments of Colombia, Peru, Bolivia are far weaker today, far more corrupt, and far more subject to narco-terrorist subversion because of similar adaptations there by the drug cartel and its associates. Has our national security been thus advanced by the War on Drugs?

For these reasons, it is important to abjure meaningless, isolated "victories" in the war on drugs and to focus on whether a program or policy offers some meaningful overall impact on the safety, security and well-being of the American people. In this respect, does it really matter that the DEA has doubled the number of drug arrests from 6,000 to 12,000 during the 1980s? Or that the Customs Service has dramatically increased its drug seizures to over 100,000 pounds of cocaine? Or that kingpins like Carlos Lehder Rivas have been convicted and imprisoned for life plus 135 years? Might it not be that the resources devoted to those anti-drug initiatives were not merely wasted but actually counter-productive?

Similarly, it is critical to pay scrupulous attention to cause and effect. Throughout the war on drugs, administration officials have been making absurd claims about the effects of anti-drug policies. Recently President Reagan asserted that the War on Drugs is working. His evidence? Marijuana smoking is down to 18 million per year and experimentation with cocaine by high school seniors in the University of Michigan survey declined by 20 percent. Everyone trained in logic knows that this is the fallacy of *post hoc ergo propter hoc*. But one need not be trained in logic to realize that there is no provable correlation between law enforcement initiatives and levels of drug consumption. Indeed, the same University of Michigan survey shows that marijuana consumption peaked in 1979, three years before the War on Drugs even began. Cocaine is purer, cheaper, and more available than ever before. If use is down, it is not because of successful law enforcement. Most categories of drug use are down and will most likely continue to go down as people become more educated and more concerned about health and fitness, fueled in some immeasurable degree by media reports of celebrity overdose deaths such as those of David Kennedy, John Belushi, Len Bias, and Don Rogers.[75]

Another important factor is the aging of the baby boom generation.

---

[75]About the only category of drug use that appears to be up is crack, and even that may be confined in large part to urban ghettos. See the *New York Times,* July 10th, 1988. The overall decline, of course, is a positive development so long as it is not offset by a corresponding rise in other drug use, such as alcohol or tobacco, or suicide or other forms of health-endangering behavior. In this regard, the National Commission should fund research directed toward the development of some meaningful index of health and well-being by somehow combining total morbidity/mortality data from all major causes. It would be a true Big Picture accomplishment if we could somehow confirm that specified demographic segments were not only using drugs less but were also happier and healthier.

That demographic bulge leaves fewer young people behind and thus contributes to the aging of the population as a whole. An older population is simply one that is less likely to use cocaine, marijuana, and heroin.

To attribute these changes to law enforcement levels is at the least unprofessional. The liberalization of marijuana laws in California, Oregon, Maine, and elsewhere in the early 1970s produced no observable rise in consumption (either new users or increased frequency) of marijuana compared to other states.[76] The connection between law and individual behavior at this level is remote. Government policies are no more responsible for the current decline in drug use than they were for the boom in the 1970s and early 1980s. Drug use will almost certainly decline in the 1990s, no matter what law enforcement does, for roughly the same reasons that cigarette smoking has declined dramatically without any change in the law.

V. SUBSTITUTE STUDY FOR SPECULATION

The War on Drugs has produced a siege mentality. Senators from large states speak of invasions and national security threats. Even professionals who should know better succumb to anti-drug hysteria. A former director of the National Institute of Drug Abuse claimed that without the War on Drugs to restrain the people, we would have 60–100,000,000 users of cocaine in this country.[77] Now this is extremely unlikely; because of the stimulant nature of the drug, it appeals mostly to younger people, the population is aging, there is already a downward trend in cocaine except for crack, and so forth. But rather than trading assertion and counter-assertion, the real question is epistemological: How does the Director know what he 'knows'? Clearly, there is no empirical basis for his claim. It must therefore be an expression of fear or perhaps political maneuver, but clearly something other than a statement of fact. Why would the Director of the public agency most responsible for informing the public on drugs take that tack? Whatever his reasons,

---

[76]Maloff, 'A Review of the Effects of the Decriminalization of Marijuana', *Contemporary Drug Problems*, p. 132 (Fall, 1981).
[77]Brinkley, 'The War on Narcotics: Can It Be Won?', *New York Times*, September 14th, 1984.

wild speculation is not the path to informed judgment and intelligent, workable policy. Why not truly confront the question of what less restricted availability of cocaine would mean in terms of increased drug use, taking account of both prevalence and incidence.[78]

There are a number of ways in which this might be done if we truly want to know the answers. One way is market research. A standard technique of market research is to conduct surveys and ask people about what they desire in a product in terms of price, quality, and other features. How much will they buy at various prices? The same techniques are adaptable, *mutatis mutandis,* to illegal drugs.

What about the effects of the drug? Is it addictive? Longitudinal studies of the kind pioneered by Ronald Siegel of UCLA should be encouraged.[79] NIDA Household Surveys register only gross numbers and do not track users. (They do not even cover group quarters, such as college dormitories and military barracks, where drug use may be higher than average.) At the present time we have almost no real-world knowledge of the experience of past and present cocaine users, except those unrepresentative few who come forward as former or recovering addicts. Even NIDA has conceded that we lack any estimate of the relative proportions of addictive use versus experimental or other non-consequential use in the total population of cocaine users.[80] Isn't that critical information in regulating the drug? (Drug users should be systematically interviewed, but they will be loath to step forward in the current climate of repression.) Useful experiments might also be performed using volunteers from the prison population (for instance, those

---

[78]To speak of a rise or fall in drug use is simplistic. It is important to distinguish between prevalence (the number of users) and incidence (the frequency of use). In measurable health consequences, it may be meaningless if the number of people who try cocaine goes up or down; conversely a change in the amounts and frequency of consumption may significantly alter morbidity and mortality.

[79]In a 1984 paper for NIDA (Research Monograph 50), Siegel concluded that the "hypothesis that long-term use of cocaine is inevitably associated with an escalating dependency marked by more frequent patterns of use is not supported by the findings." Instead he found that "social recreational drug users maintained relatively stable patterns of use" in the face of ready supplies and increased income as they aged.

[80]Jerome H. Jaffe, 'Foreword', *Cocaine Use in America: Epidemiologic and Clinical Perspectives* (NIDA, 1985). Other research agendas should include the possibility of addiction maintenance treatment and other therapeutic uses of cocaine.

serving life sentences without parole) and perhaps volunteers from the military services. How would men behave and how would their health fare with abundant access to cocaine? Would it be used widely or intensively or both? Finally, comparative studies from countries such as Holland can tell us a great deal about the effects of more freely available cannabis and heroin, although not so with respect to cocaine. We have a lot to learn from the Dutch.

Conclusion

I endorse a substantial measure of relaxation of drug laws in some respects simultaneously with a substantial measure of intensification in other respects: the enforcement of laws to protect children, along with more stringent laws regarding the sale of liquor and tobacco. As to the first point, some measure of relaxation of drug laws is both correct in principle and pragmatically necessary in the real world of limited resources. But this is not a 'surrender' in the War on Drugs. There is a paradox here: that the use of less force may actually result in producing more control over the drug situation in this country.

Consider the analogy of a panic stop in an automobile. In a typical scenario, a driver observes a sudden obstruction in his path and slams on the brakes in order to avoid a collision. If he uses too much force on the pedal, the sudden forward weight transfer will very likely induce front-wheel lockup. At that point, the car starts skidding out of control. If the driver turns the wheel left or right, the car will simply keep on skidding forward toward the very obstacle that he is trying to avoid. In this moment of panic, the 'logical' or instinctive thing to do is to stomp the brake pedal even harder. But that is absolutely wrong. The correct thing to do to stop the skid is to modulate the break pedal, releasing it just enough to permit the front wheels to begin rolling again so that steering control is restored. Thus, the correct and safe response is counter-intuitive, while the instinctive response sends the driver skidding toward disaster. I leave it to the Committee to decide whether this has any relevance in the re-making of drug policy.

7

OFFICIAL RESPONSES:
A MAYOR AND
A 'CZAR'

INTRODUCTION

In April 1988, at the U.S. Conference of Mayors, Baltimore Mayor Kurt L. Schmoke called on Americans at least to consider the option of legalization and called on Congress to hold hearings to debate the issue. A few months later hearings were indeed held, but perhaps more importantly, Mayor Schmoke may have provided the hottest spark to what has become a period of serious debate over legalization, with which this anthology is concerned. Since then, few other government officials have argued for legalization of any kind. A former Secretary of State, George Schultz, has done so. So too has a U.S. district judge, Robert W. Sweet of the Southern District, New York.

No public official, however, has written so forthrightly in support of the legalization debate as has Mayor Schmoke. We present here an article by the mayor, followed by an article by the then chief government official responsible for drug policy, William J. Bennett, director ('Czar') of the Office of Drug Control Policy. In the last-mentioned article, Dr. Bennett responds generally to critics of the government's policy, expressing some irritation at what he considers the "intellectual chorus" for legalization.

Decriminalizing Drugs: It Just Might Work—And Nothing Else Does

Kurt L. Schmoke

Baltimore Mayor Kurt L. Schmoke argues in favor of Congressional (and presumably other) debates on the issue of legalization. Although Mayor Schmoke rejects the libertarian argument for legalization (that people have a moral right to injure themselves) on the grounds that drugs "pose a danger to third parties", he thinks that the economic and medical arguments for legalization are "compelling enough for Congress at least to study the question."

As a result of his prosecuting and winning convictions against thousands of defendants for drug-related crimes, Mayor Schmoke has learned some "important lessons": that drug traffickers "care very little about the sanctions of the criminal-justice system, since they normally view going to jail as a business expense"; that drug dealers are more afraid of each other than of police (who are required to give them due process); and that the engine driving drug traffickers is a profit that is so large that they are willing to bear any risks, including not only risks of legal punishment but also the risks of murder, extortion, and kidnapping by their fellow dealers.

Like many other proponents of legalization, Mayor Schmoke thinks that we should treat using illegal drugs as we treat cigarette-smoking— as a potentially harmful habit that requires education but not punishment.

'Decriminalizing Drugs: It Just Might Work—And Nothing Else Does' by Kurt L. Schmoke (*Washington Post*, May 15th, 1988, pp. B1, B2). Used by permission.

Has the time come to add America's 'war on drugs' to the long list of history's follies? In the view of historian Barbara Tuchman, to qualify as folly, a policy must not only be unsuccessful, it must also be plainly against the interests of those in whose name it is being carried out. And folly has one more characteristic: Nobody wants to recognize it.

Whether the drug policies of the United States have reached the point of folly, I'm not prepared to say. But this much seems apparent: Political maturity, intellectual honesty and justifiable concern about drug-related violence make raising the question long overdue.

This is why I asked the U.S. Conference of Mayors last month to adopt a resolution calling upon Congress to hold hearings on whether to decriminalize narcotics.

The details—which drugs would be legalized, and how and by whom they could be purchased—would be left to Congress and state legislatures to decide after first concluding on the basis of research and testimony that some form of decriminalization is warranted.

Many who oppose decriminalization argue that it will serve as an open invitation to use drugs. If there is evidence to that effect, then it should be dispassionately presented to Congress and other policymakers, but it should not stand in the way of a public debate about decriminalization.

The time has come to admit that the emperor has no clothes. The war on drugs is being lost, notwithstanding President Reagan's recent claim that we are digging our way out. And continuing our present policy—even with more money—is unlikely to make any difference.

There are three basic arguments in favor of decriminalization: libertarianism, economics, and health. I don't subscribe to the libertarian view that people should have a right to injure themselves with drugs if they so choose. Drugs—even if decriminalized—also pose a danger to third parties. But the other two arguments are compelling enough for Congress at least to study the question.

The Economics Argument

Just as Prohibition banned something millions of people want, our current drug laws make it illegal to possess a commodity that is in very high demand. As a result, the price of that commodity has soared far beyond its true cost.

This has led to enormous profits from illegal drugs and turned drug trafficking into the criminal enterprise of choice for pushers and manufacturers alike.

I know this because for more than seven years I made a living putting people in jail. As an assistant U.S. attorney, and later state's attorney for Baltimore, I prosecuted and won convictions against thousands of defendants for drug-related crimes. Those crimes included murder of police officers and civilians; the victims included innocent bystanders and children caught up in criminal enterprises whose danger they could never appreciate.

During my years as a prosecutor, as I watched drug crime change the character of America's cities, I learned some important lessons.

First, drug traffickers—no matter how high-up or how venal—care very little about the sanctions of the criminal-justice system. Going to jail is just part of the cost of doing business. It's a nuisance, not a deterrent.

Second, drug dealers fear one another far more than they fear law-enforcement officials. They know that the police must give them due process, but competing drug dealers will kill them at a moment's notice.

Finally, profit is the engine driving drug trafficking. Neither criminal sanctions nor even the competitive business practices (murder, extortion, kidnapping) of their fellow dealers have much, if any, effect on people who trade in drugs.

But take the profit out of their enterprise—and you'll get their attention. Perhaps it's time to fight the crime epidemic associated with drug trafficking by communicating with the drug underground in the only language they understand: Money.

Decriminalization would take the profit out of drugs and greatly reduce, if not eliminate, the drug-related violence that is currently plaguing our streets. Decriminalization will not solve this country's drug abuse problem, but it could solve our most intractable crime problem.

It is very easy for people living in communities where drugs are not a problem (and those are becoming fewer all the time), to argue that drug-related violence cannot justify decriminalization. But if you have to live with that violence day in and day out—as millions of people in large urban areas do—and live in terror of being gunned down, robbed, or assaulted, or having the same occur to one of your loved ones, you soon start wanting results.

Taking the profit out of drugs would have a detrimental impact on those who are now producing and selling drugs. Drug lords would no longer risk prison for a commodity that was not making them a profit.

The Health Argument

Some will argue that the public-health risks from drugs will only worsen if they are decriminalized. Again, this is a question Congress would need to resolve, but there is every reason to believe that decriminalization would improve public health.

First, violent crime associated with illegal sale of drugs would fall dramatically. For those who doubt that, imagine how violent crime would increase if we once again made the use and sale of alcohol illegal.

Secondly, decriminalization would allow billions of dollars now used for interdiction and enforcement to be redirected toward prevention and treatment.

Smoking kills over 300,000 people every year, but we have made the policy decision to treat tobacco as a health problem, not a crime problem, and we are making real progress. The number of people smoking continues to fall because of a concerted public education campaign about the health effects of smoking.

There is no reason that we could not do the same with drugs. And then we could find the money we need to educate our young people on the harmful effects of drugs and treat those who are currently addicted, instead of engaging in a wildly expensive cat-and-mouse game that the mouse is winning 90 percent of the time.

To make matters worse, the Reagan administration has continuously tried to cut drug programs aimed at the prevention and treatment of drug abuse. It was Congress, through its passage of the anti-drug abuse act of 1986, that enabled the United States to make an even modestly credible effort to treat and prevent drug abuse. But it is doubtful that even the effort of Congress will make much difference. Several hundred million dollars to fight the health effects of an enterprise earning billions is not sufficient. Only by applying a substantial portion of the more than three billion dollars invested in the total federal drug program can we begin to treat those currently addicted—many of whom now have AIDS—and properly educate our children about the harmful effects of drugs.

Many political and opinion leaders will resist the notion that our current drug policy is folly, and perhaps they're right. But all the signs are there: We're spending billions of dollars in an effort that is enriching the very people we're trying to stop. And in the meantime, millions of people continue to use drugs and millions more have lost all confidence that they can live securely in their neighborhoods.

It takes great maturity and willpower for a society to step back from a policy that on the surface seems noble and justified, but in reality has only compounded the problem it is attempting to solve. On the subject of drugs, such maturity and willpower may now be in order. At the very least, we need a sober national debate on the subject.

Mopping Up After the Legalizers: What the 'Intellectual' Chorus Fails to Tell You

William J. Bennett

Dr. William J. Bennett, former director of the Office of Drug Control Policy, claims that the arguments of drug legalizers are weak and, if accepted, dangerous: "They are, at bottom, a series of superficial and even disingenuous ideas that more sober minds recognize as a recipe for a public-policy disaster."

According to Dr. Bennett, a number of assumptions popularly used by legalization proponents are mistaken. For example, while legalizers argue that legalization will take the profit out of the illegal drug trade, this assumption, according to Dr. Bennett, is questionable, since "instances of drug dealers actually earning huge sums of money are relatively rare." He goes on to argue that most people in the crack business are low-level "runners" who turn only small profits, and that in fact steady workers at McDonald's can make more money than many drug dealers.

For Bennett, what drug legalizers often ignore, or simply do not realize, is that laws against drugs deter many people from selling or using drugs because many people realize that "dealing drugs invariably leads to murder or prison". And according to Dr. Bennett, "that's exactly why we have drug laws—to make drug use a wholly unattractive choice." While he believes in education

'Mopping Up After the Legalizers: What the "Intellectual" Chorus Fails to Tell You' by William Bennett (*Washington Times*, December 15th, 1989). Used by permission.

and treatment, he argues that no amount of treatment or education will be effective against drugs unless they are supplemented by law enforcement.

Though it has no bearing on the merits of the argument, it is a striking fact for the history of the debate that whereas Dr. Bennett had referred in September to "a small number of journalists and academics" favoring legalization (p. 53 above), three months later he repeatedly alludes to the large proportion of intellectuals and opinion-leaders advocating legalization.

What I read in the opinion columns of my newspaper or in my monthly magazine or what I hear from the resident intellectual on my favorite television talk show is something like a developing intellectual consensus on the drug question. That consensus holds one or both of these propositions to be self-evident: 1. that the drug problem in America is absurdly simple, and easily solved; and 2. that the drug problem in America is a lost cause.

As it happens, each of these apparently contradictory propositions is false. As it also happens, both are disputed by the *real* experts on drugs in the United States—and there are many such experts, though not the kind the media like to focus on. And both are disbelieved by the American people, whose experience tells them, emphatically, otherwise.

Right and Left for Legalization

The consensus has a political dimension, which helps account for its seemingly divergent aspect. In some quarters of the far right there is a tendency to assert that the drug problem is essentially a problem of the inner city, and therefore that what it calls for, essentially, is quarantine. "If those people want to kill themselves off with drugs, let them kill themselves off with drugs," would be a crude but not too inaccurate way of summarizing this position. But this position has relatively few adherents.

On the left, it is something else, something much more prevalent. There we see whole cadres of social scientists, abetted by whole armies of social workers, who seem to take it as catechism that the problem facing us isn't drugs at all; it's poverty, or racism, or some other equally large and intractable social phenomenon. If we want to eliminate the drug problem, these people say, we must first eliminate the 'root causes' of drugs, a hopelessly daunting task at which, however, they also happen to make their living.

Twenty-five years ago, no one would have suggested that we must first address the root causes of racism before fighting segregation. We fought it, quite correctly, by passing laws against unacceptable conduct. The causes of racism posed an interesting question, but the moral imperative was to end it as soon as possible and by all reasonable means: education, prevention, the media, and not least of all, the law. So, too, with drugs.

What unites these two views of the drug problem from opposite sides of the political spectrum is that they issue, inevitably, in a policy of neglect. Let me pause here to note one specific issue on which the left/right consensus has lately come to rest; a position around which it has been attempting to build national sentiment. That position is legalization.

It is indeed bizarre to see the likes of Anthony Lewis and William F. Buckley lining up on the same side of an issue; but such is the perversity that the so-called legalization debate engenders. To call it a 'debate', though, suggests that the arguments in favor of drug legalization are rigorous, substantial, and serious. They are not. They are, at bottom, a series of superficial and even disingenuous ideas that more sober minds recognize as a recipe for a public-policy disaster. Let me explain.

Most conversations about legalization begin with the notion of 'taking the profit out of the drug business'.

But has anyone bothered to examine carefully how the drug business works? As a recent *New York Times* article vividly described, instances of drug dealers actually earning huge sums of money are relatively rare. There are some who do, of course, but most people in the crack business are the low-level 'runners' who do not make much money at all.

In many cases, steady work at McDonald's over time would in fact be a step *up* the income scale for these kids. What does straighten them out, it seems, is not a higher minimum wage, or less-stringent laws, but the dawning realization that dealing drugs invariably leads to murder or prison. And that's exactly why we have drug laws—to make drug use a wholly unattractive choice.

Legalization, on the other hand, removes that incentive to stay away from a life of drugs. Let's be honest; there are some people who are going to smoke crack whether it is legal or illegal. But by keeping it illegal, we maintain the criminal sanctions that persuade most people that the good life cannot be reached by dealing drugs.

The big lie behind every call for legalization is that making drugs legally available would 'solve' the drug problem.

But has anyone actually thought about what that kind of legalized regime would look like? Would crack be legal? How about PCP? Or smokable heroin? Or ice? Would they all be stocked at the local convenience store, perhaps just a few blocks from an elementary school?

And how much would they cost? If we taxed drugs and made them expensive, we would still have the black market and the crime problems we have today. If we sold them cheap to eliminate the black market— cocaine at, say, $10 a gram—then we would succeed in making a daily dose of cocaine well within the allowance budget of most sixth-graders.

When pressed, the advocates of legalization like to sound courageous by proposing that we begin by legalizing marijuana. But they have absolutely nothing to say on the tough questions of controlling other, more powerful drugs, and how they would be regulated.

As far as marijuana is concerned, let me say this: I didn't have to become drug czar to be opposed to legalized marijuana. As Secretary of Education I realized that, given the state of American education, the last thing we needed was a policy that made widely available a substance that impairs memory, concentration, and attention span. Why in God's name foster the use of a drug that makes you stupid?

Drug Use Would Soar

Now what would happen if drugs were suddenly made legal? Legalization advocates deny that the amount of drug use would be affected. I would argue that if drugs are easier to obtain, drug use will soar. In fact, we have just undergone a kind of cruel national experiment in which drugs became cheap and widely available. That experiment is called the crack epidemic.

When powder cocaine was expensive and hard to get, it was found almost exclusively in the circles of the rich, the famous, or the privileged. Only when cocaine was dumped into the country, and a $3 vial of crack could be bought on street corners, did we see cocaine use skyrocket— this time largely among the poor and disadvantaged.

The lesson is clear: If you're in favor of drugs being sold in stores like aspirin, you're in favor of boom times for drug users and drug addicts. With legalization, drug use will go up, way up.

When drug use rises, who benefits and who pays? Legalization advocates think the cost of enforcing drug laws is too great. But the real question—the question they never ask—is what it costs *not* to enforce those laws.

The price that American society would have to pay for legalized drugs, I submit, would be intolerably high. We would have more drug-related accidents at work, on highways, and in the airways. We would have even bigger losses in worker productivity. Our hospitals would be filled with drug emergencies. We would have more school kids on dope, and that means more drop-outs. More pregnant women would buy legal cocaine, and then deliver tiny, premature infants. I've seen them in hospitals across the country. It's a horrid form of child abuse, and under a legalization scheme, we will have a lot more of it. For those women and those babies, crack has the same effect whether it's legal or not.

Now, if you add to that the costs of treatment, social welfare and insurance, you've got the price of legalization. So I ask you again, who benefits and who pays?

What about crime? To listen to legalization advocates, one might think that street crime would disappear with the repeal of our drug laws. They haven't done their homework.

Our best research indicates that most drug criminals were into crime well before they got into drugs. Making drugs legal would just be a way of subsidizing their habit. They would continue to rob and steal to pay for food, for clothes, for entertainment. And they would carry on with their drug trafficking by undercutting the legalized price of drugs and catering to teenagers, who, I assume, would be nominally restricted from buying drugs at the corner store.

Law Enforcement Works

All this should be old news to people who understand one clear lesson of Prohibition. When we had laws against alcohol, there was less consumption of alcohol, less alcohol-related disease, fewer drunken brawls and a lot less public drunkenness. And contrary to myth, there is no evidence that Prohibition caused big increases in crime. No one is suggesting that we go back to Prohibition. But at least we should admit that legalized alcohol, which is responsible for some 100,000 deaths a year, is hardly a model for drug policy. As Charles Krauthammer has pointed out, the question is not which is worse, alcohol or drugs. The question is: Can we accept both legalized alcohol *and* legalized drugs? The answer is no.

So it seems to me that on the merits of their arguments, the legalizers have no case at all. But there is another, crucial point I want to make on this subject, unrelated to costs or benefits.

Drug use—especially heavy drug use—destroys human character. It destroys dignity and autonomy, it burns away the sense of responsibility, it subverts productivity, it makes a mockery of virtue. As our Founders would surely recognize, a citizenry that is perpetually in a drug-induced haze doesn't bode well for the future of self-government.

Libertarians don't like to hear this, but it is a truth that everyone knows who has seen drug addiction up close. And don't listen to people who say drug users are only hurting themselves: They hurt parents, they destroy families, they ruin friendships. And drugs are a threat to the life of the mind; anyone who values that life should have nothing but contempt for drugs. Learned institutions should regard drugs as the plague.

The Surrender of the Intellectuals

That's why I find the surrender of many of America's intellectuals to arguments for drug legalization so odd and so scandalous.

Their hostility to the national war on drugs is, I think, partly rooted in a general hostility to law enforcement and criminal justice. That's why they take refuge in pseudo-solutions like legalization, which stress only the treatment side of the problem.

Whenever discussion turns to the need for more police and stronger penalties, they cry that our constitutional liberties are in jeopardy. Well, yes, they are in jeopardy, but not from drug *policy:* On this score, the guardians of our Constitution can sleep easily. Constitutional liberties are in jeopardy, instead, from drugs themselves, which every day scorch the earth of our common freedom.

When we are not being told by critics that law enforcement threatens our liberties, we are being told that it won't work.

Let me tell you that law enforcement does work and why it must work. Several weeks ago I was in Wichita, Kansas, talking to a teenage boy who was now in his fourth treatment program. Every time he had finished a previous round of treatment, he found himself back on the streets, surrounded by the same cheap dope and tough hustlers who had gotten him started in the first place. He was tempted, he was pressured, and he gave in.

Virtually any expert on drug treatment will tell you that, for most people, no therapy in the world can fight temptation on that scale. As long as drugs are found on any street corner, no amount of treatment, no amount of education can finally stand against them. Yes, we need drug treatment and drug education. But drug treatment and drug education need law enforcement. And that's why our strategy calls for a bigger criminal justice system: as a form of drug *prevention.*

America's intellectuals—and here I think particularly of liberal intellectuals—have spent much of the last nine years decrying the social programs of two Republican administrations in the name of the defenseless poor. But today, on the one outstanding issue that disproportionately hurts the poor—that is wiping out many of the poor—where are the liberal intellectuals to be found?

They are on the editorial and op-ed pages, and in magazines like this month's *Harper's,* telling us with a sneer that our drug policy won't work.

The current situation won't do. The failure to get serious about the drug issue is, I think, a failure of civic courage—the kind of courage shown by many who have been among the main victims of the drug scourge. But it betokens as well a betrayal of the self-declared mission of intellectuals as the bearer of society's conscience. There may be reasons for this reluctance, this hostility, this failure. But I would remind you that not all crusades led by the U.S. government, enjoying broad popular support, are brutish, corrupt and sinister. What is brutish, corrupt and sinister is the murder and mayhem being committed in our cities' streets. One would think that a little more concern and serious thought would come from those who claim to care deeply about America's problems.

8

THE SCOPE AND SEVERITY OF ADDICTION: TWO SCIENTISTS' DIVERGENT VIEWS

INTRODUCTION

How addictive are illegal drugs? How many addicts would there be with legalization? Historically and medically, what is the impact of the use and misuse of narcotics? Doctors Michael S. Gazzaniga and Gabriel G. Nahas reach opposite conclusions to those questions.

The Opium of the People: Crack in Perspective

Michael S. Gazzaniga

Dr. Michael Gazzaniga, a professor of psychiatry who specializes in neuroscience, argues in favor of at least trying legalization. On the basis of his understanding of neuroscience and the social sciences, as well as the relevant statistics, Dr. Gazzaniga argues that a small (relatively fixed) percentage of the population will misuse drugs to the point of addiction, regardless of whether certain drugs are made more or less available. He claims that, while greater availability of drugs might mean more use (at least initially), the more widespread use of drugs will most likely not—in and of itself—substantially increase the number of people who become addicted:

> The central point is that human beings in all cultures tend to seek out means of altering their mental state, and that although some will shop around and lose the powers of self-discipline, most will settle down to a base rate of use, and a much smaller rate of abuse, and those rates are pretty much what we have in the United States right now.

Dr. Gazzaniga argues for trying legalization not only because of the social costs of proscription but also because he believes that drug laws will inevitably be ineffective in reducing the incidence of addiction.

Notice that the interviewer envisions legalization in the form of government monopoly stores selling drugs to the public, whereas Dr. Gazzaniga does not endorse this proposal.

'The Opium of the People: The Federal Drugstore' by Michael S. Gazzaniga (*National Review*, February 5th, 1990, pp. 34–41). Used by permission.

Q: Professor Gazzaniga, as you know, there are those who have recommended the decriminalization of drugs. Before we take up a concrete proposal coming in from that quarter, we want to ask you a question or two, the answers to which will shed light on any such proposal. The first question is this:

It is said that the drug crack is substantively different from its parent drug, cocaine, in that it is, to use the term of Professor van den Haag, "crimogenic". In other words a certain (unspecified) percentage of those who take crack are prompted to—well, to go out and commit mayhem of some kind. Is that correct?

GAZZANIGA: No, not in the way you put it. What you are asking is, Is there something about how crack acts on the brain that makes people who take it likelier to commit crime?

Let's begin by making it clear what crack is. It is simply cocaine that has been mixed with baking soda, water, and then boiled. What this procedure does is to permit cocaine to be smoked. Now any drug ingested in that way—absorbed by the lungs—goes more efficiently to the brain, and the result is a quicker, more intense experience. That is what crack gives the consumer. But its impact on the brain is the same as with plain cocaine and, as a matter of fact, amphetamines. No one has ever maintained that these drugs are 'crimogenic'.

The only study I know about that inquires into the question of crack breeding crime reports that most homicides involving crack were the result not of the use of crack, but of dealer disputes. Crack did not induce users to commit crimes. Do some crack users commit crimes? Of course. After all, involvement in proscribed drug traffic is dangerous. Moreover, people who commit crimes tend to use drugs at a high rate, though which drug they prefer varies from one year to the next.

Q: You are telling us that an increase in the use of crack would not mean an increase in crime?

GAZZANIGA: I am saying that what increase there would be in crime would not be simply the result of the pharmacology of that drug. Look, let's say there are 200,000 users/abusers of crack in New York City—a number that reflects one of the current estimates. If so, and if the drug produced violent tendencies in all crack users, the health-care system would have come to a screeching halt. It hasn't. In fact, in 1988 the hospitals in New York City (the crack capital of the world) averaged only seven crack-related admissions, city-wide, a day. The perception of crack-based misbehavior is exaggerated because it is the cases that show up in the emergency rooms that receive public notice, and the whole picture begins to look very bleak. All of this is to say: when considering any aspect of the drug problem, keep in mind the matter of selection of the evidence.

It is prudent to recall that, in the past, dangerous and criminal behavior has been said to have been generated by other drugs, for instance marijuana (you remember 'Reefer Madness'). And bear it in mind that since cocaine is available everywhere, so is crack available everywhere, since the means of converting the one into the other are easy, and easily learned. It is important to note that only a small percentage of cocaine users actually convert their stuff to crack. Roughly one in six.

Q: Then would it follow that even if there were an increase in the use of crack, legalization of it would actually result in a decrease in crime?
GAZZANIGA: That is correct.

Q: Isn't crack a drug whose addictive power exceeds that of many other drugs? If that is the case, one assumes that people who opt to take crack do so because it yields the faster and more exhilarating satisfactions to which you make reference.
GAZZANIGA: That is certainly the current understanding, but there are no solid data on the question. Current observations are confounded by certain economic variables. Crack is cheap . . .

Q: Why? If cocaine is expensive, how can crack be cheap?
GAZZANIGA: Cocaine costs $1,000 per ounce if bought in quantity. One ounce can produce one thousand vials of crack, each of which sells for $5. The drug abuser is able to experience more drug episodes. Crack

being cheap, the next high can come a lot more quickly and since there is a down to every up, or high, the cycle can become intense.

So yes, crack is addictive. So is cocaine. So are amphetamines. The special punch of crack, as the result of going quickly via the lungs to the brain, may prompt some abusers to want more. By the way, it is the public knowledge that crack acts in this way that, as several studies document, causes most regular cocaine users to be cautious about crack. The casual-to-moderate user very clearly wants to stay in that category. So, all you can say is that there is a *perception,* widely shared, that crack is more addictive. Whether it is, isn't really known. One thing we do know is that crack does not begin to approach tobacco as a nationwide health hazard. For every crack-related death, there are three hundred tobacco-related deaths.

Q: You are confusing us. You say that because of the especially quick effects that come from taking crack, there is a disposition on the part of the user to want more. Isn't that a way of saying that it is more addictive? If someone, after smoking, say, ten cigarettes, begins to want cigarettes every day, isn't tobacco 'addictive', as you say it is? Or are you saying that crack finds most users indifferent to the highs it brings on, and for *that* reason it can't be said to be more addictive than cocaine?

GAZZANIGA: The current, official definition of an addict is someone who compulsively seeks psychoactive drugs. The definition, you will note, focuses on human behavior, not on pharmacologic action on the brain. In respect of crack, there are factors that might lead to a higher rate of addiction. Some of these factors are certainly social in nature and some may be pharmacologic. The purported higher rate of addiction among crack users could be due to social values, for instance the low cost of crack. We simply don't know as yet.

Keep in mind our experience with LSD. When it was fashionable to take it, droves did so. But LSD has unpleasant side-effects, and eventually the use of it greatly diminished. In drugs, as in much else, there is a strong tendency to follow the herd. Sorting out the real threat from the hyperbole takes time.

Another example of hyperbole is the recent claim that there were 375,000 'crack babies' born last year; how could that possibly be, when the government (the National Institute on Drug Abuse) informs us that there were only 500,000 crack *users* last year? Exaggeration and misinformation run rampant on this subject.

Q: Well, if crack were legally available alongside cocaine and, say, marijuana, what would be the reason for a consumer to take crack?

GAZZANIGA: You need to keep your drug classifications straight. If your goal were, pure and simple, to get high, you might try crack or cocaine, or some amphetamine. You wouldn't go for marijuana, which is a mild hallucinogen and tranquilizer. So, if you wanted to be up and you didn't have much time, you might go to crack. But then if it were absolutely established that there was a higher addiction rate with crack, legalization could, paradoxically, diminish its use. This is so because if cocaine were reduced to the same price as crack, the abuser, acknowledging the higher rate of addiction, might forgo the more intensive high of crack, opting for the slower high of cocaine. Crack was introduced years ago as offering an alluring new psychoactive experience. But its special hold on the ghetto is the result of its price. Remember that—on another front—we know that 120-proof alcohol doesn't sell as readily as the 86-proof, not by a long shot, even though the higher the proof, the faster the psychological effect that alcohol users are seeking.

Q: The basic question, we take it, has got to be this: It is everywhere assumed that if drugs were legal, their consumption would increase. That guess is based on empirical observations of a past phenomenon. Mr. Bennett, for instance, has said that when Prohibition ended, the consumption of alcohol increased by 400 percent. What are your comments on that?

GAZZANIGA: Books and even careers have been built around studies of the Eighteenth Amendment. Arguments about its meaning continue to rage in the scientific journals. Arguments always continue when available data are inconclusive.

Most experts insist that the rate of alcohol use before Prohibition was the same as after. Some qualify that assertion by pointing out that the pre-Prohibition rate of consumption was not realized again until years after Prohibition was over. From this we are invited to conclude that, in that sense, Prohibition was really successful—it interrupted many potential drinkers on their way to the saloon. And then some point out that although alcohol was freely available during Prohibition, it was harder to get in some parts of America. Even so, overall consumption was rising (some say to pre-Prohibition levels) toward the middle and end of Prohibition.

Frankly, here is what's important: *There is a base rate of drug abuse, and it is achieved one way or another.* This is so even though there are researchers who point to different rates of abuse in different cultures. The trouble with that generality is that it is usually made without taking into account correlative factors, such as national traditions, the extent of education programs available, and so on. In which connection, I think the Federal Government should establish a study group to collect drug information from different cultures in an effort to get useful leads.

Q: Is there evidence that the current consumption of drugs is restrained by their illegality? We have read that 90 million Americans have experimented, at one time or another, with illegal drugs. Would more than 90 million have experimented with them if drugs had been legal?

GAZZANIGA: I think illegality has little if anything to do with drug consumption—and, incidentally, I am certain that far more than 90 million Americans have at some point or other experimented with an illegal drug.

This gets to the issue of actual availability. Drugs are everywhere, simply everywhere. In terms of availability, drugs might just as well be legal as illegal. Now it has been argued that legalization will create a different social climate, a more permissive, more indulgent climate. It is certainly conceivable, primarily for that reason, that there would be greater initial use—the result of curiosity. But the central point is that human beings in all cultures tend to seek out means of altering their mental state, and that although some will shop around and lose the powers of self-discipline, most will settle down to a base rate of use, and a much smaller rate of abuse, and those rates are pretty much what we have in the United States right now.

Q: Then the factor of illegality, in your opinion, does not weigh heavily? But, we come to the critical question, if 90 million, or more, Americans have experimented with the use of drugs, why is drug abuse at such a (relatively) low level?

GAZZANIGA: If you exclude tobacco, in the whole nation less than 10 percent of the adult population abuses drugs. That is, 9 to 12 million adult Americans abuse drugs. That figure includes alcohol, by the way, and the figure remains fairly constant.

Consider alcohol. In our culture alone, 70 to 80 percent of us use alcohol, and the abuse rate is now estimated at 5 to 6 percent. We see at work here a major feature of the human response to drug availability, namely, the inclination to moderation. Most people are adjusted and are intent on living productive lives. While most of us, pursuing that goal, enjoy the sensations of euphoria, or anxiety reduction, or (at times) social dis-inhibition or even anaesthesia, we don't let the desire for these sensations dominate our behavior. Alcohol fills these needs for many people and its use is managed intelligently.

It is worth noting that the largest proportion of this drug is sold to the social drinker, not the drunk, just as most cocaine is sold to the casual user, not the addict. Now, early exposure to alcohol is common and inevitable, and youthful drinking can be extreme. Yet studies have shown that it is difficult to determine which drunk at the college party will evolve into a serious alcoholic. What is known is that the vast majority of early drinkers stop excessive drinking all by themselves. In fact, drug use of all types drops off radically with age.

Q: Wait a minute. Are you telling us that there is only a 10 percent chance that any user will become addicted to a drug, having experimented with it?

GAZZANIGA: The 10 percent figure includes all drugs except tobacco. The actual risk for abuse of some drugs is much lower. Consider last year's National Household Survey (NHS), which was carried out by the National Institutes on Drug Abuse. It is estimated that some 21 million people tried cocaine in 1988. But according to the NHS only three million defined themselves as having used the drug at least once during the month preceding their interview. Most of the three million were casual users. Now think about it. *All* the cocaine users make up 2 percent of the adult population, and the addicts make up less than one-quarter of one percent of the total population. These are the government's own figures. Does that sound like an epidemic to you?

Q: But surely an epidemic has to do with the rate at which an undesirable occurrence is increasing. How many more cocaine users were there than the year before? Or the year before that?

GAZZANIGA: The real question is whether or not more and more Americans are becoming addicted to something. Is the rate of addiction to psychoactive substances going up? The answer to that is a flat 'No.' Are there fads during which one drug becomes more popular than another as the drug of abuse? Sure. But, when one drug goes up in consumption, others go down. Heroin use is down, and so is marijuana use. That is why the opiate and marijuana pushers are trying to improve their purity—so they can grab back some of their market share, which apparently they have done for heroin in New York City.

But, having said that, you should know that the actual use of cocaine and all other illicit drugs is on the decline, according to the NHS. The just-published National High School Survey carried out by the University of Michigan reports that the same is true among high-school students. Crack is used at such a low rate throughout the country that its use can hardly be measured in most areas.

Q: Well, if a low addiction rate is the rule, how do we come to terms with the assertion, which has been made in reputable circles, that over 40 percent of Americans fighting in Vietnam were using heroin and 80 percent marijuana?

GAZZANIGA: Stressful situations provoke a greater use of drugs. Vietnam was one of them. But what happens when the soldiers come home?

That point was examined in a large study by Dr. Lee Robbins at Washington University. During the Vietnam War, President Nixon ordered a study on the returning vets who seemed to have a drug problem. (Nixon didn't know what he was looking for, but he was getting a lot of flak on the point that the war was producing a generation of drug addicts.) Dr. Robbins chose to study those soldiers returning to the United States in 1971. Of the 13,760 Army enlisted men who returned and were included in her sample, 1,400 had a positive urine test for drugs (narcotics, amphetamines, or barbiturates). She was able to re-test 495 men from this sample a few months later. The results were crystal clear: Only 8 percent of the men who had been drug positive in their first urine test remained so. In short, over 90 percent of them, now that they were back home, walked away from drug use. And all of them knew how to get hold of drugs, if they had wanted them. Incidentally, Dr. Robbins did a follow-up study a couple of years later on the same soldiers. She reported there had not been an increase in drug use.

Q: Aha! You are saying that under special circumstances, the use of drugs increases. Well, granted there was stress in Vietnam. Isn't there stress also in American ghettos?

GAZZANIGA: Floyd Bloom of the Scripps Medical Institute—one of the foremost brain scientists in the country—has posited that most psychoactive drugs work on the brain's reward systems. There is good neurobiologic research to support this idea. It is an idea that can easily be understood and applied to everyday life.

What it tells you is that some people want artificial ways of getting their kicks out of life, but also that some people need those artificial crutches. If you live in poverty and frustration, and see few rewards available to you, you are likelier than your better-satisfied counterpart to seek the escape of drugs, although the higher rate of consumption does not result in a higher rate of addiction. Virtually every study finds this to be the case with one possibly interesting twist. A recent Department of Defense study showed that drug use in the military was lower for blacks than for whites, the reverse of civilian life. (It is generally agreed that the military is the only institution in our country that is successfully integrated.) In short, environmental factors play an important role in the incidence of drug use.

Q: So you are saying that there are social circumstances that will raise the rate of consumption, but that raising the rate of consumption doesn't in fact raise the rate of addiction. In other words, if 50 percent of the troops in Vietnam had been using crack, this would not have affected the rate at which, on returning to the United States, they became addicted. They would have kicked the habit on reaching home?

GAZZANIGA: That's the idea. Drug consumption can go up in a particular population, fueled by stress, but the rate of addiction doesn't go up no matter what the degree of stress. Most people can walk away from high drug use if their lives become more normal. Of course, the stress of the ghetto isn't the only situation that fuels high drug consumption. Plenty of affluent people who for some reason or another do not find their lives rewarding also escape into drugs.

Q: If it is true, then, that only a small percentage of those who take crack will end up addicted, and that that is no different from the small percentage who, taking one beer every Saturday night, will become alcoholics, what is the correct way in which to describe the relative intensity of the addictive element in a particular drug?

GAZZANIGA: That is an interesting question and one that can't satisfactorily be answered until much more research is done. There are conundrums. Again, it is estimated that 21 million people tried cocaine in 1988. Yet, of those, only 3 million currently use it, and only a small percentage are addicted. As for crack, it is estimated that 2.5 million have used it, while only a half-million say they still do, and *that* figure includes the addicted and the casual user. Some reports claim that as many as one half of crack users are addicted. As I have said, crack is cheap, and for that reason may be especially attractive to the poor. That is a non-pharmacological, non-biological factor, the weight of which we have not come to any conclusions about. We don't even have reliable data to tell us that crack creates a greater rate of addiction then, say, cocaine. My own guess is that it doesn't. Remember that the drug acts on the same brain systems that cocaine and amphetamines do.

What is needed, in order to answer your question, is a science of comparative pharmacology where the various psychoactive drugs could be compared against some kind of common physiological/psychological measure. Doing that would be difficult, which is one of the reasons why those data don't exist. How do you capture fluctuating moods and motivations? There are times when the smallest dose of a drug can have a sublime effect on someone, while at another time it takes ten times the dose to have any noticeable effect. These are tough problems to quantify and study, even in the laboratory.

Q: To what extent is the addictive factor affected by education? Here is what I mean by this: Taking a drug, say heroin or cocaine or crack—or, for that matter, alcohol—is a form of Russian roulette, using a ten-cartridge revolver. Now, presumably, an educated person, concerned for his livelihood, wouldn't take a revolver with nine empty cartridges and one full cartridge, aim it at his head, and pull the trigger. But granted, decisions of that kind are based on ratiocinative skills. And we have to assume these skills don't exist even among college students. If they did, there would be no drinking in college, let alone drug taking. Comments?
GAZZANIGA: Most people perceive themselves as in control of their destiny. They do not think the initial exposure will ruin their lives, because of their perceived self-control, and they are right. Take the most difficult case, tobacco—the most highly addictive substance around. In a now classic study, Stanley Schachter of Columbia University formally surveyed his highly-educated colleagues at Columbia. At the same time, he polled the working residents of Amagansett, a community on Long Island where he summered. He first determined who were ongoing smokers, and who had been smokers. He took into account how long they had smoked, what they had smoked, and all other variables he could think of.

It wasn't long before the picture began to crystallize. Inform a normally intelligent group of people about the tangible hazards of using a particular substance and the vast majority of them simply stop. It wasn't easy for some, but in general they stopped, and they didn't need treatment programs, support programs, and all the rest. Dr. Schachter concluded, after this study, that it is only the thorny cases that show up at the treatment centers, people who have developed a true addiction. For those people, psychological prophylactics, including education, are of little or no value. Yet it is these people that are held up as examples of what happens when one uses drugs. This is misleading. It creates an unworkable framework for thinking about the problem. Most people can voluntarily stop using any psychoactive substance, and those people who do continue to use it can moderate their intake to reduce the possibility of health hazards. This is true, as I say, for most substances, but I repeat, less true for tobacco because of its distinctively addictive nature. The people who unwisely continue to use tobacco tend to smoke themselves into major illness even though they are amply warned that this is likely to happen.

Q: So no matter how widely you spread the message, it is in fact going to be ignored, both by PhDs and by illiterates?

GAZZANIGA: If they are real abusers, yes. That is the reason for the high recidivism rate among graduates of drug treatment centers. Here we are talking about the true addicts. Education appears not to help the recalcitrant abusers, who are the ones that keep showing up at health centers.

Yet, manifestly, education contributes to keeping the abuse rate as low as it is. I think the message gets to the ghetto, but where there are other problems—the need for an artificial reward—drugs are going to be taken by many people because the excruciating pain of a current condition overrides long-term reason. In short, the ghetto citizen or the psychologically isolated person might well decide that the probability of living a better life is low, so grab some rewards while you can.

Q: At what level of intelligence is a potential drug user influenced to take a less dangerous, rather than a more dangerous, drug? I mean, if it were known to all PhDs that crack was more dangerous than marijuana, that the small percentage who became addicted to crack would suffer greater biological damage from it, up to and including death, in contrast to comparatively lenient sentences from addiction to marijuana, what percentage of PhDs would be influenced to stay away from the hard stuff, compared to illiterate 17-year-old ghetto dwellers?

GAZZANIGA: Again, this is difficult to answer because the educational message interacts with innumerable social problems. For example, drug abuse is three times greater among the unemployed. Someone who is unemployed on Monday might be re-employed on Friday, and this may stop, or reduce, his use of drugs. Gainful employment has a bigger effect in a case like this than education does. But in general, education plays a big role, and this is established. Remember, we are a health-oriented society, and we do care about our bodies and minds, by and large. Marijuana is a mild drug, compared to crack, for a variety of biological and psychological reasons. There are studies showing that casual-to-moderate cocaine users will not go the crack route because of fear of a greater chance of addiction or of an immediate physiological crisis. A recent issue of the *New England Journal of Medicine* reports that cocaine use contributes to heart disease in a rather muted way. However, crack may have a far greater impact and be responsible for a much more serious increase in drug-related heart failures. Does that kind of thing influence a kid in the ghetto? I think the message does get there. It certainly gets to Park Avenue first, however.

Q: In that case, education, even in the popular media, is likely to influence primarily the educated classes. That has to mean that the uneducated class will suffer more addiction than the educated class.
GAZZANIGA: Well, again, people in the lowest socio-economic status will continue to consume more drugs, but that doesn't change the addiction rate. Still, legalization shouldn't change the current figures, since drugs are literally available everywhere in the ghetto. They are also available on every college campus. They are available in prisons! I suppose if one wants to conjure up fresh problems brought on by legalization, they will center on the folks living on Park Avenue, where drugs are less easily secured, not the ghetto. Legalization of drugs would reduce crime in the ghetto, and much that is positive would follow.

Q: If the number of addicts would be increased by decriminalization, is the trade-off worth it? Is it wise to decriminalize, even if by doing so: we a. abort the $150 billion per year drug-crime business; b. release $10 billion in federal money now going to the pursuit of drug merchants; c. end the corruption of government subsidized by drug dealers; and d. come upon a huge sum of money available to give treatment to addicts? Is this, in your judgment, a moral recommendation to make, given our knowledge of the psychological problems we are talking about?

GAZZANIGA: Are you asking me to commit myself at this point to the question of whether that trade-off is wise?

Q: Well, no, not quite yet. Let me describe a situation, the concrete situation I spoke of a while ago, and ask you to comment on it in the light of the questions put to you above.

Suppose that drugs were made available. All of them, legally, in a Federal Drugstore. But above each of the common drugs—crack, cocaine, heroin, hash, marijuana, amphetamines, LSD, etc.—there was a graphic description of what addiction to that drug would do to you. Suppose a situation in which, for instance, over the punch bowl at the far left of the counter that contained crack were written: 'This drug will create an appetite to take another dose. That appetite is very strong. If you become an addict, you will want to take as many as 20 of these every day, and the results of doing so will be serious for your health. With overuse, you may suffer a heart attack and die.'

By contrast, let's say that the placard directly above the punch bowl that houses marijuana were to say: 'Not addictive, but chronic use may lead to cancer, chromosome damage, birth deformities in future children, memory loss, paranoia, and depression.' Is there any reason to suppose that this kind of merchandising will have the effect of propelling the majority of consumers either to taking no drugs at all, or to taking the less dangerous drugs? For example, marijuana over, say, cocaine?

GAZZANIGA: For those not intent on self-abuse, yes. After all, as I said, we are a health-oriented society. Hard liquor sales are down, and, for that matter, so are wine sales. You can now buy low-cholesterol popcorn and so on. We want our kicks, but within a knowledgeable health-safety framework. On the other hand, for those intent on self-abuse, drug consumption will continue. Self-abuse occurs at all levels of our society, not only in the ghetto. Remember, most people in America are not living in ghettos, and a certain percentage of them are addicted to something. I think we as a society ought to focus attention on addiction groups and see if some factors can be isolated that might help out. Currently, drug treatment programs, which should more accurately be called drug management programs, need a lot of help. Treatment is not a reality for most of these centers. As I have already indicated, the recidivism rate is high at drug centers and this in part reflects the fact the drug centers get only the tough cases, the hard-core abusers that can not stop abuse themselves. Much more research is key.

Q: All right then, presumably the price of the drugs available for sale at the Federal Drugstore will be low enough to discourage black-market activity. Would such Federal Drugstores eliminate black-market activity altogether?

GAZZANIGA: No, of course not. The criminal mind is ever inventive. Special services will be supplied, like home-delivery services, and the inevitable (and positively illegal) pushing to children. There will be new drugs dreamed up, and they will have their own market until they are isolated, and then will be sold legally. But, the vast majority of the crime network ought to crumble. The importance of that cannot be overestimated.

Q: So, the Federal Drugstores would obviously charge the cost of providing the drugs and the overhead of retailing them. Let's suppose that they could then double the acquisition cost without activating black-market competition; if double proved too much, they would simply lower the price. Whatever; profits would go to the treatment centers and toward more advertising of the dangers of drug abuse, and indeed of drug consumption. Do you have any difficulty with that?

GAZZANIGA: No, but I would caution against setting up a plan that found the government playing the role of pusher. If the drug-treatment centers were dependent on income from the Drugstore, the bureaucrats running the store might be tempted to increase profits. Once Congress comes around to thoughtfully considering legalization, the actual mechanisms will have to be carefully thought out.

Q: What would be your prediction, as a scientist, of what the advent of the Federal Drugstore, combined with a program of intensified education, would accomplish in the next ten years?

GAZZANIGA: Drug-consumption rates will bounce around, related as they are to environmental factors, fads, and a host of other factors. Drug-abuse rates will not change much, if at all. Yet many of the negative social consequences of keeping drugs illegal will be neutralized. The health costs of drug abuse will always be with us. We should try to focus on those problems with more serious neurobiologic and neurobehavioral research and help where we can to reduce the percentage that fall victim. I am an experimental scientist, and like most people can see that the present system doesn't work. We need to try another approach. If for whatever reason, legalization doesn't improve the situation, it would take five minutes to reverse it.

The Decline of Drugged Nations

Gabriel G. Nahas

Pharmacologist Gabriel G. Nahas, who opposes legalization, argues that the distinction between "licit" and "illicit" drugs is not arbitrary but based on documentable medical and historical facts. He submits that while nicotine and alcohol can harm people, "illicit addictive" drugs are "associated with a temporary impairment of brain mechanisms that results in distorted perceptions." He submits further that illicit drugs (for example, cocaine and heroin) can addict people with even very low exposure.

In short, Dr. Nahas argues that people who use such drugs as marijuana, hashish, cocaine, and opiates are more likely to damage their health than those who use alcohol, and that those drugs, if made more widely available through legalization, would do greater harm than they are doing now.

Americans seem agreed today that the rise in consumption of tobacco and alcohol, two legal addictive drugs, is associated with such staggering individual and social costs that restrictive measures to limit their consumption, especially by the young, should be considered. At the same time some prestigious opinion-makers suggest that illegal addictive drugs, such as marijuana, heroin, and cocaine, be made available commercially as well.

In this verbal tug-of-war it seems that opinions have replaced established facts derived from pharmacological, epidemiological and historical studies.

'The Decline of Drugged Nations' by Gabriel G. Nahas (*Wall Street Journal*, July 11th, 1988). Used by permission.

First, the distinction between licit and illicit addictive drugs is not arbitrary, as we might be led to believe. While both types of drugs have properties in common, they also have basic differences. In terms of similarities, they both induce certain biochemical changes in the brain that are usually pleasant and lead to a repeat experience; eventually, their use leads to daily drug-seeking and drug-consuming behavior. Once instilled, this behavioral pattern is difficult to alter. In the case of illicit addictive drugs, however, the pleasant experience is associated with a temporary impairment of brain mechanisms that results in distorted perceptions.

While the legal, addictive drugs tobacco (nicotine), alcohol (in small amounts), and coffee (caffeine) do not impair mental acuity, cocaine, heroin and marijuana do, even in minute quantities. Furthermore, the addictive potential of illicit addictive drugs is greater than for licit drugs. It takes very low exposure to cocaine or heroin to become dependent on these drugs, as reported in epidemiological studies of drug-consuming populations.

Moslems and Hashish

Among those who drink alcoholic beverages world-wide, 8 percent consume daily amounts that are damaging to their health and to society. Epidemiological studies of the populations of marijuana and hashish, cocaine and opiate consumers show that about 50 percent, 90 percent, and 95 percent, respectively, of the consumers will use these drugs daily, in doses damaging to their health and to society, when they are readily available. Finally, history shows that when illicit addictive drugs are socially accepted and easily available, they are widely consumed, and their use is associated with a high incidence of individual and social damage.

The use of cannabis in the Islamic-dominated world surfaced in the 11th century, when the Moslem Empire extended from the Atlantic to the Indian oceans. Historians of the twelfth to the sixteenth centuries have documented the damage done by the widespread use of hashish in Moslem medieval society. (An account of their writings has been compiled by Franz Rosenthal of Yale University in his book, *Hashish vs. Moslem Medieval Society.*

In the fifteenth century all restrictions against hashish were set aside. As a result, according to the contemporary historian Al Magrizi, a general debasement of the people was apparent. A large number of people from all walks of life were in a constant state of intoxication. All the scholars and religious leaders of the time condemned the weed—but the habit of hashish-taking had become ingrained in society and could not be eliminated.

In ancient Peru, the chewing of the coca leaf, which began 1,500 years ago, was restricted by the Inca leaders to religious ceremonies. After the Spanish conquest in 1554, this habit spread among the farmers and laborers, who were paid in coca leaves, which they chewed nearly continuously. As a result they were in a state of continuous low-grade intoxication. This drug use continues today. The farmers and miners of the Andes thus are able to work under the most adverse conditions with limited food intake. As a result, their social condition has not changed in centuries; their general health and life expectancy are poor.

In 1858, the legal trade of opium and the Opium Wars were imposed on China by British mercantilism. By 1900, 90 million Chinese were addicted to opium. It took a national revival at the turn of the century that stressed traditional Chinese values to stem the tide. The support of the U.S. and the international community stopped the international opium trade. But it took 50 years of coercive measures for the country to become opium-free. Today, opium and other dependence-producing drugs are banned from China, as well as from Taiwan and Singapore.

In Egypt in the 1920s, the unrestricted commercial availability of cocaine and heroin resulted in an epidemic use of these drugs. This use was curtailed in the 1930s following national and international interdiction, and punitive measures meted out to all addicts.

In the 1950s, Japan experienced a major epidemic of intravenous amphetamine use involving half a million addicts. A national campaign aimed at restricting demand and supply with sanctions applied against users and traffickers brought the number of addicts down to a few thousand within four years. A heroin epidemic was curtailed in the same manner in the 1960s, reducing the number of heroin addicts from several thousand to a few hundred.

In contrast, the British in 1925 adopted a medical model allowing physicians to prescribe heroin to heroin addicts. This "British system" worked satisfactorily as long as addicts were few in number and all registered: 500 a year between 1930 and 1960. It became unmanageable after 1960, when heroin had to be dispensed to more than 1,000 users of the drug. Each addict had to be provided with daily doses of heroin, as well as the equipment required for the injection of the drug four to six times a day.

Because of this logistical problem and because of the potential for diversion of the drug to nonregistered addicts, heroin began to be progressively replaced by methadone maintenance. (Methadone, a long-lasting opiate, needs to be absorbed only once a day, by mouth.) But the number of registered British addicts had grown by 1980 to 2,800, double the total seeking treatment seven years earlier. In 1985 there were an estimated 80,000 heroin addicts in Britain, most of whom were not in drug-treatment programs. Despite this failure of the British system, it is still advocated by some in the U.S.

These scientific and historical facts demonstrate that supply and demand reduction are needed in the U.S. to control the present epidemic of illicit drug use.

U.N. Assistance Needed

Supply reduction will require national and international interdiction measures. The gradual eradication of coca-bush plantations must be initiated in the producing countries, together with a program for planting basic food crops. Such a scheme calls for a new multibillion-dollar, ecologically sound United Nations assistance program (with the co-operation and contribution of the U.S.S.R.) staggered over many years.

At the same time, the consuming country must lower its demand by more strictly enforcing existing laws that ban use and possession of cocaine. Dealers should be subjected to the same sentences imposed on murderers; users should be forced to enter rehabilitation programs, as is currently done in Japan.

Such measures rely upon a strongly expressed sentiment of societal disapproval of cocaine and other illicit drug use by all segments of society. Prohibitive measures cannot be effective in a climate of cultural acceptance of "recreational" drug use which has led some opinion makers to advocate the legalization of all drugs. Only when the vital grass-roots forces of America, feeling their existence threatened, become determined to fight drugs will they be able to wage a war and win it.

The battle primarily will be one of the mind—for the constraints that have to be accepted by a progressive and free society. Americans need to know the truth about our common enemy and must be encouraged, as they were during the great wars, by the same unambiguous media that helped the nation to victory.

9

SCAPEGOATS, CYCLES, AND SOCIETY: THE VIEWS OF TWO PSYCHIATRISTS

INTRODUCTION

Here we look at two arguments, one by psychiatrist Thomas Szasz (for legalization) and one by professor of psychiatry David F. Musto (against legalization). Dr. Szasz argues that society has targeted drugs as its latest scapegoat. Dr. Musto argues that drug use is cyclical and therefore controllable (with criminal sanctions).

A Plea for the Cessation of The Longest War in the Twentieth Century—The War on Drugs

Thomas S. Szasz

Psychiatrist Thomas S. Szasz argues in favor of legalization, maintaining that people have a right to use drugs as they like, just as people have a right to choose what books they want to read. Dr. Szasz argues that our response to drugs is based not on a rational assessment of objective dangers but on the human need to find scapegoats:

> In the past we have witnessed religious or holy wars waged against people who professed the wrong faith; more recently, we have witnessed racial or eugenic wars, waged against people who possessed the wrong genetic make-up; now we are witnessing a medical or therapeutic war, waged against people who use the wrong drugs.

Dr. Szasz argues that human beings in general tend to proscribe all sorts of conduct that they invest with religious or political significance but that do not necessarily pose any objective threat to people. He mentions religious dietary laws covering pork (Judaism and Islam) and beef (Hinduism) and norms against birth control, masturbation, and religious heresy.
> *While Dr. Szasz grants that people can hurt themselves by misusing*

'A Plea for the Cessation of the Longest War of the Twentieth Century—The War on Drugs' by Thomas S. Szasz (*The Humanistic Psychologist*, vol. 16, no. 2, Autumn 1988, pp. 314–322). Used by permission.

drugs, he argues that the popular image of illegal drugs as corrupting or victimizing whoever uses them is false:

> The danger posed by so-called dangerous drugs is quite unlike that posed by hurricanes or plagues, but is rather like the danger posed (to some people) by, say, eating pork or masturbating . . . which strike[s] us down as "active victims", that is, only if we succumb to their temptation.

Szasz rejects the argument that the use of (illegal) drugs must be controlled for the benefit of society. He believes that prohibitions against drugs are no more justifiable than censorship of books or art, and that government prohibitions against drugs in effect treat adults as children. He holds that our government—as a consistent matter of principle—does not control or prohibit only those drugs that are addictive or dangerous, since it regulates the availability of insulin and penicillin. Moreover, the government, he claims, does not consistently prohibit other dangerous substances or activities, since poisons and guns, which are much more dangerous than narcotics (especially to others), are not prohibited.

Dr. Szasz believes that "we need private voluntary associations—or also, some might contend, the government—to warn us of the dangers of heroin, salt, or a high-fat diet." But, he contends, "it is one thing for our would-be protectors to inform us of what they regard as dangerous substances, and it is quite another thing for them to punish us if we disagree with them or defy their wishes."

> Was the government to prescribe to us our medicine and diet, our bodies would be in such keeping as our souls are now. Thus in France the emetic was once forbidden as a medicine, the potato as an article of food.—Thomas Jefferson, 1781/1944, p. 275

A Metaphorical War

Ostensibly, the war on drugs is a struggle against "dangerous" drugs. But the substances we call "drugs" are simply the products of nature (for example, coca leaves) or of human inventiveness (for example, Valium).

They are material objects: leaves and liquids, powders and pills. How then could human beings wage war against drugs? One would have to be blind not to recognize that the war on drugs must be a metaphorical war; actually, like any war, the war on drugs is aggression unleashed by some people against some other people. Tragically, the destructiveness of this war is obscured by modern man's stubborn refusal to come to grips with what a drug is, and by the modern politician's eagerness to exploit this. Seemingly, the word 'drug' is a part of the vocabulary of science; actually, it is now even more importantly a part of the vocabulary of politics. This explains why there is no such thing—why there can be no such thing—as a 'neutral' drug. A drug is either good or bad, effective or ineffective, therapeutic or noxious, licit or illicit. This is why we deploy drugs simultaneously as technical tools in our fight against medical diseases and as scapegoats in our struggle for personal security and political stability.

If history teaches us anything at all, it teaches us that human beings have a powerful need to form groups and that the sacrificial victimization of scapegoats is often an indispensable ingredient for maintaining social cohesion among the members of such groups. Perceived as the very embodiment of evil, the scapegoat's true nature is thus impervious to rational analysis. Since the scapegoat is evil, the good citizen's task is not to understand him (or her, or it), but to hate him and to rid the community of him. Attempts to analyze and grasp such a ritual purgation of society of its scapegoats is perceived as disloyalty to, or even an attack on, the 'compact majority' and its best interests.

In my opinion, the (American) 'war on drugs' represents merely a new variation in humanity's age-old passion to 'purge' itself of its 'impurities' by staging vast dramas of scapegoat persecutions (Szasz 1970, pp. 242–275). In the past, we have witnessed religious or holy wars waged against people who professed the wrong faith; more recently, we have witnessed racial or eugenic wars, waged against people who possessed the wrong genetic make-up; now we are witnessing a medical or therapeutic war, waged against people who use the wrong drugs.

Let us not forget that the modern state is a political apparatus with a monopoly on waging war: it selects its enemies, declares war on them, and thrives on the enterprise. In saying this I am merely repeating

Randolph Bourne's now classic observation that "war is the health of the State. It automatically sets in motion throughout society those irresistible forces for uniformity, for passionate co-operation with the Government in coercing into obedience the minority groups and individuals which lack the larger herd sense" (Bourne, 1977, p. 360).

Let us not forget, too, that only fifty years have passed since Hitler incited the German people against the Jews by 'explaining' the various ways in which the Jews were 'dangerous' to the Germans individually and to Germany as a nation. Millions of Germans—among them leaders in science, in medicine, in law, in the media—came to believe in the reality of the 'dangerous Jew': they loved the imagery of that racial myth, felt exhilarated by the increased self-esteem and solidarity it gave them, and were thrilled by the prospect of 'cleansing' the nation of its 'racial impurities'. Today, hardly anyone in Germany believes the myth of the 'dangerous Jew'—a change in point of view that surely had nothing to do with more research on, or fresh scientific discoveries about, the problem of 'dangerous Jews'.

Mutatis mutandis, every American president since John F. Kennedy, and countless other American politicians, have incited the American people—indeed people everywhere—against 'dangerous drugs' by 'explaining' the various ways in which such drugs threaten Americans individually and the United States as a nation. Millions of Americans—among them leaders in science, in medicine, in law, in the media—believe in the reality of 'dangerous drugs': they love the imagery of this pharmacological myth and are inspired by the prospect of cleansing the nation of illicit drugs. In short, we are now in the midst of a 'therapeutic' war waged against 'drugs' and the people who sell and buy them (Szasz, 1985).

From Self-Abuse to Drug Abuse

It is a grave error to view currently fashionable drug controls as their proponents portray them, namely, as similar to measures aimed against the spread of, say, typhoid fever by contaminated water or food. Instead of resembling controls based on objective (technical, scientific) considerations, contemporary drug controls resemble the prohibition of countless substances whose control rests on religious or political (ritual, social) considerations. In this connection, we must not forget that there is hardly any object or behavior that has not been prohibited somewhere at some time, and whose prohibition was not viewed by those who believed in it and enforced it as rational or valid. The following is but a brief and quite incomplete list of such prohibitions, with a few comments about them.

The Jewish dietary laws, set forth in the Old Testament, prohibit the ingestion of numerous edible things. Although conformity to these rules is now often rationalized on hygienic grounds, they have nothing whatever to do with health; instead, they have to do with holiness, that is, with being dutiful toward God, in an effort to gain His favor. By glorifying what one may or may not eat as a matter of the gravest concern to an all-caring deity, true believers elevate ordinary events—say, eating a shrimp cocktail—to acts that are, spiritually speaking, matters of life and death. Similar proscriptions of food characterize other religions. For example, Muslims are forbidden to eat pork, Hindus to eat beef. Most religious codes also proscribe, as well as prescribe, certain drinks. Jewish and Christian religious ceremonies require the use of alcohol, which, in turn, is forbidden in the Koran.

Like eating and drinking, sexual activity is a basic human urge whose satisfaction has also been closely controlled by custom, religion, and law. Among the forms of sexual activity that have been, or are still, forbidden, the following spring quickly to mind: masturbation; homosexuality; heterosexual intercourse outside of marriage; heterosexual intercourse with the use of condoms, diaphragms, or other 'artificial' birth-control devices; nongenital heterosexual intercourse; incest; and prostitution. For about two hundred years—well into the twentieth century—self-abuse (as masturbation was then called) was thought to be the greatest threat to the medical and moral well-being of mankind. Preoccupation with self-abuse, both popular and professional, has since been displaced by a similar preoccupation with drug abuse.

Verbal and pictorial representations of certain ideas or images are perhaps the prime products of human inventiveness prohibited by human inventiveness. This behavior, too, has its roots in religious ritual, exemplified by the Jewish prohibition against graven images, that is, making pictures of God and hence of man, created by His image. This is why, prior to the modern era, there were no Jewish painters or sculptors. With the development of literacy among the laity, the Catholic church quickly criminalized translating the Bible into the 'vulgar' tongues. Thus, in the fifteenth century, possessing a Bible in the English language was an offense much like possessing heroin is today, except that the penalty for it was death by burning at the stake. Since then, there followed an almost limitless variety of prohibitions against the spoken or printed word and the painted picture, such as prohibitions of blasphemy, heresy, subversion, sedition, obscenity, pornography, and so forth; these prohibitions have been implemented by such institutionalized interventions as the Roman Catholic Index of Prohibited Books, the Comstock laws (in the United States), the Nazi book burnings, and the censorship policies of the various totalitarian countries.

Money, as precious metal or paper, is another product of human inventiveness widely prohibited throughout history. Although the United States is regarded as the very pillar of the Western capitalist world, owning gold was, until recently, prohibited in this country. Private ownership of this metal (in forms other than personal ornaments) is, of course, prohibited in all communist countries; and so, too, is the free movement, across national boundaries, of paper money. Prohibitions against lending money at interest are deeply ingrained in the Christian and Muslim religions. Charging any interest was sometimes viewed as an evil that must be proscribed; at other times, only charging 'excessive' interest, called 'usury', was prohibited. Interest rates charged or paid by American banks today would, of course, have been considered usurious in the Middle Ages.

Although gambling was prevalent and permitted in antiquity, in the Christian worldview it, too, came to be seen as a sin and was generally prohibited. Conducted as a private enterprise, gambling is still treated as a criminal offense in most parts of the United States; however, if it is conducted by the state—offering much poorer odds for the gambler than do private gaming establishments—it is regarded as a positively virtuous undertaking, aggressively promoted by the government.

In short, there is virtually no material object or human behavior that has not been found to be 'dangerous' or 'harmful'—to God, king, the public interest, national security, bodily health, or mental health—and thus prohibited by religious, legal, medical, or psychiatric authorities. In every case of such prohibition, we are confronted with certain ceremonial-ritual rules rationalized and justified on pragmatic-scientific grounds. Typically, we are told that such prohibitions protect the health or well-being of particularly vulnerable individuals or groups. Actually, the rules protect the well-being—that is, the integrity—of the community as a whole (which is what is meant by saying that certain behavioral rules have a ceremonial function).

Perils and Profits of the Anti-Drug Crusade

In what way are drugs a danger to persons individually or to people collectively, as nations? What do the officially persecuted drugs—especially opium (heroin, etc.), cocaine, and marijuana—do that is so different from what other drugs do? And if these drugs pose such a grave danger today, why were they not a danger to mankind for thousands of years? Anyone who reflects on these matters must realize that our culturally accepted drugs—in particular, alcohol, tobacco, and mind-altering drugs legitimated as psychotherapeutic—pose a much graver threat, and cause much more demonstrable harm, to people than do the prohibited or so-called dangerous drugs.

There are, of course, complex religious, historical, and economic reasons, which I cannot consider here, that play a part in determining which drugs people use and which they avoid. But regardless of such cultural-historical determinants, and regardless of the pharmacological properties of the 'dangerous drugs' in question, one simple fact remains—namely, that no one has to ingest, inhale, or inject any of these substances unless he or she wants to do so. This simple fact compels one to see the 'drug problem' in a light totally different from that in which it is now officially portrayed. The official line is that 'dangerous drugs' pose an external threat to people—that is, a threat like a natural disaster, such as an erupting volcano or a hurricane. The inference drawn from this image is that it is the duty of a modern, scientifically-enlightened state to protect its citizens from such dangers, and it is the duty of the citizens to submit to the protections so imposed on them for the benefit of the community as a whole.

But 'dangerous drugs' pose no such threat. The danger posed by so-called dangerous drugs is quite unlike that posed by hurricanes or plagues, but is rather like the danger posed (to some people) by, say, eating pork or masturbating. The point is that certain threats—so-called natural disasters, in particular—strike us down as 'passive victims', whereas certain other threats—for example, forbidden foods or sexual acts—strike us down as 'active victims', that is, only if we succumb to their temptation. Thus, an orthodox Jew may be tempted to eat a ham sandwich and a devout Catholic may be tempted to use artificial contraception, but that does not make most of us view pork products or birth-control devices as 'dangers' from which the state should protect us. On the contrary, we believe that free access to such foods and devices is our right.

In actuality—that is, at the present time, and especially in the United States—the so-called 'drug problem' has several distinct dimensions. First, there is the problem posed by the pharmacological properties of the drugs in question. This problem is technical: all new scientific or practical inventions not only offer us certain solutions for old problems, but also create new problems for us. Drugs are no exception. Secondly, there is the problem posed to the individual by the temptation to use certain drugs, especially those believed to possess the power to 'give' pleasure. This problem is moral and psychological: some drugs offer us certain new temptations that we must learn to resist or enjoy in moderation. Thirdly, there is the problem posed by the prohibition of certain drugs. This problem is partly political and economic, and partly moral and psychological. Drug prohibition constitutes a type of scape-goating, as discussed earlier. It also creates vast new legal, medical, and social problems—problems predictably associated with authoritarian-prohibitionist meddling into what most people regard as their private lives.

In addition to all this, policies of drug prohibition generate a wide range of otherwise unavailable economic and existential options and opportunities. For members of the upper and middle classes, the war on drugs provides opportunities for gaining self-esteem, public recognition for benevolence, life meaning, jobs, and money; for example, it enables the wives of American presidents to play a combination of Santa Claus and Doctor Schweitzer *vis-à-vis* their involuntary beneficiaries, who, without the compassion and largesse of these ladies, are ostensibly unable to abstain from illegal drugs. Similarly, it enables physicians, especially psychiatrists, to claim special skills in treating the mythical disease of drug abuse, a claim politicians and others are only too eager to authenticate. These examples are, of course, only the tip of the proverbial iceberg: there is no need to list the numerous jobs in the 'drug rehabilitation' racket, and their ripple effects on the economy, with which we are only too familiar.

For members of lowest and lower classes, the war on drugs is perhaps even more useful; for example, for unemployed and unemployable youngsters, the war provides an opportunity for making a living as drug dealers and, after they have recovered from 'drug abuse', as drug abuse counselors; for unskilled but employable persons, it provides countless opportunities for staffing and running the infrastructure of the drug abuse empire. Last but not least, for persons at all levels of society, the war on drugs offers a ready-made opportunity for dramatizing their lives and aggrandizing their individuality by defying certain modern medical taboos.

The role of defiance in so-called drug abuse is, indeed, quite obvious. It is clearly displayed in the various contemporary subcultures' righteous rejection of conventional or legal drugs and its passionate embrace of the use of unconventional or illegal drugs. The perennial confrontation between authority and autonomy, the permanent tension between behavior based on submission to coercion and the free choice of one's own course in life—these basic themes of human morality and psychology are now enacted on a stage on which the principal props are drugs and laws against drugs.

The Censorship of Substances

Americans regard freedom of speech and religion as fundamental rights. Until 1914, they also regarded the freedom of choosing their diets and drugs as fundamental rights. Obviously, this is no longer true today. What is behind this fateful moral and political transformation, which has resulted in the rejection, by the overwhelming majority of Americans, of their right to self-control over their diets and drugs? How could it have come about in view of the obvious parallels between the freedom to put things into one's mind and its restriction by the state by means of censorship of the press, and the freedom to put things into one's body and its restriction by the state by means of drug controls?

The answer to these questions lies basically in the fact that our society is therapeutic in much the same sense in which medieval Spanish society was theocratic. Just as the men and women living in a theocratic society did not believe in the separation of church and state but, on the contrary, fervently embraced their union, so we, living in a therapeutic society, do not believe in the separation of medicine and the state but fervently embrace their union. The censorship of drugs follows from the latter ideology as inexorably as the censorship of books followed from the former. That explains why liberals and conservatives—and people in that imaginary center as well—all favor drug controls. In fact, in the United States, persons of all political and religious convictions, save libertarians, now favor drug controls.

Viewed as a political issue, drugs, books, and religious practices all present the same problem to a people and its rulers. The state, as the representative of a particular class or dominant ethic, may choose to embrace some drugs, some books, and some religious practices and reject the others as dangerous, depraved, demented, or devilish. Throughout history, such an arrangement has characterized most societies. Or the state, as the representative of a constitution ceremonializing the supremacy of individual choice over collective comfort, may ensure a free trade in drugs, books, and religious practices. Such an arrangement has traditionally characterized the United States, but does so no longer.

Ironically, throughout the so-called free western world today, the censorship of words and pictures is generally regarded as a moral and political anachronism, rejected by virtually all intellectuals and politicians; whereas precisely the opposite is the case for the censorship of drugs. The argument, such as it is, that people need the protection of the state from dangerous drugs but not from dangerous ideas is unpersuasive. No one has to ingest any drug he does not want, just as no one has to read a book or look at a picture he does not want. Insofar as the state assumes control over such matters, it can only be in order to subjugate its citizens—by protecting them from temptation, as befits children, and by preventing them from assuming self-determination over their lives, as befits an enslaved population. How have we come to this sorry pass?

Conventional wisdom now approves—indeed, assumes as obvious—that it is the legitimate business of the state to control certain substances we take into our bodies, especially so-called psychoactive drugs. According to this view, as the state must, for the benefit of society, control dangerous persons, so it must also control dangerous drugs. The obvious fallacy in this analogy is obscured by the riveting together of the notions of dangerous drugs and dangerous acts: as a result, people now 'know' that dangerous drugs cause people to behave dangerously and that it is just as much the duty of the state to protect its citizens from dope as it is to protect them from murder and theft. The trouble is that all these supposed facts are false.

Clearly, the argument that heroin or cocaine is prohibited because it is addictive or dangerous cannot be supported by facts. For one thing, there are many drugs, from insulin to penicillin, that are not addictive but are nevertheless also prohibited: they can be obtained only through a physician's prescription. For another, there are many things, from poisons to guns, that are much more dangerous than narcotics (especially to others) but are not prohibited. It is possible, in the United States, to walk into a store and walk out with a shotgun, but it is not possible to walk into a store and walk out with a bottle of barbiturates or with an empty hypodermic syringe. We are now deprived of these options because we have come to value medical paternalism more highly than the right to obtain and use drugs without recourse to medical intermediaries.

I submit that our so-called drug-abuse problem is an integral part of our present social ethic that accepts 'protections' and repressions justified by appeals to health similar to those which medieval societies accepted when they were justified by appeals to faith. Drug abuse (as we now know it) is one of the inevitable consequences of the medical monopoly over drugs—a monopoly whose value is daily acclaimed by science and law, state and church, the professions and the laity. As formerly the church regulated man's relations to God, so medicine now regulates his relations to his body. Deviation from the rules set forth by the church was then considered heresy and was punished by appropriate theological sanctions; deviation from the rules set forth by medicine is now considered drug abuse (or 'mental illness') and is punished by appropriate medical sanctions, called treatment.

To be sure, drugs are potentially potent influences, for good or ill, on our bodies as well as on our minds. Hence, we need private voluntary associations—or also, some might contend, the government—to warn us of the dangers of heroin, salt, or a high-fat diet. But it is one thing for our would-be protectors to inform us of what they regard as dangerous substances, and it is quite another thing for them to punish us if we disagree with them or defy their wishes.

According to the formula made famous by the Caesars, the masses of mankind need only two things: *panem et circenses,* bread and circuses. This is still true. Today, farms and factories supply us with an abundance of 'bread', while drugs and drug controls give us our 'circuses'. In other words, the contemporary preoccupation with the use and abuse of drugs, together with the persecution of (illicit) drugs, addicts, and pushers, is best understood as a secular ritual that amuses, fascinates, terrorizes, and satisfies people today, much as gladiatorial contests and Christian wonder-workings fascinated and satisfied the Romans.

Sadly, the war on drugs has offered, and continues to offer, modern man much of what he seems to crave: fake compassion and genuine coercion; pseudo-science and real paternalism; make-believe disease and metaphorical treatment; opportunistic politics and unctuous hypocrisy. It is hard for me to see how anyone who knows anything about history, about pharmacology, and about the fundamental human struggle for self-discipline and the seemingly equally intense human need to reject it and replace it with submission to a coercively paternalistic authority— how any such person could escape the conclusion that the war on drugs is simply another chapter in the natural history of human stupidity (Mackay 1962).

An End to this Stupid and Unwinnable War

I believe that just as we regard freedom of speech and religion as fundamental rights, so should we also regard freedom of self-medication as a fundamental right; and that, instead of mendaciously opposing or mindlessly promoting illicit drugs, we should, paraphrasing Voltaire, make this maxim our rule: 'I disapprove of what you take, but I will defend to the death your right to take it!'

In closing, the war on drugs is the longest, most protracted formally declared war of this turbulent century: it has already lasted longer than the first and second World Wars, and the wars in Korea and Vietnam combined—and its end is nowhere in sight. Indeed, because this war is a war on human desire, it cannot be won in any meaningful sense of that term. Finally, since its principal beneficiaries are the politicians who wage it, we must, against all odds, try to enlist some honest and humane politicians in our quest to lay before the people the case that peace, after all, is better than war—even if the 'enemy' is stupidly called 'drugs'.

REFERENCES

Bourne, R. 1977. *The Radical Will: Selected Writings, 1911–1918*. New York: Urizen.

Jefferson, T. 1944. 'Notes on the State of Virginia'. In A. Koch & W. Peden (eds.), *The Life and Selected Writings of Thomas Jefferson*. New York: Modern Library (Originally published, 1781).

Mackay, C. 1962. *Extraordinary Popular Delusions and the Madness of Crowds*. New York: Noonday Press.

Szasz, T.S. 1970. *The Manufacture of Madness: A Comparative Study of the Inquisition and the Mental Health Movement*. New York: Harper and Row.

Szasz, T.S. 1985. *Ceremonial Chemistry: The Ritual Persecution of Drugs, Addicts, and Pushers* (Rev. Ed.). Holmes Beach, FL: Learning Publications.

Testimony of David F. Musto to the Select Committee on Narcotics Abuse and Control

David F. Musto

Dr. David F. Musto, professor of psychiatry and the history of medicine at the Yale School of Medicine, argues against legalization, because, according to him, drugs such as cocaine and heroin can harm people mentally, physically, and psychologically.

He concedes, however, that opponents of illegal drugs, including government officials, have at times so exaggerated the dangers of drugs that they have lost much credibility, and that, historically, opposition to drug use has been linked with racial hostility (as when many southern whites during the turn of this century stereotyped blacks as cocaine addicts). With the foregoing points granted, he submits nonetheless that, even in the absence of turf wars and other consequences of criminalization, the use of many drugs creates problems, often destroying the body and disintegrating the personality.

Much of Musto's thought is based on his analysis of the history of drug use, especially in the United States. Basing his views on that history, he submits that when Americans could legally buy and sell cocaine and opiates (as they could during the nineteenth century), people came increasingly to misuse those drugs. During the latter part of that century (1880s and 1890s) the use of

'Testimony of David F. Musto, M.D., professor of psychiatry (Child Study Center) and of the History of Medicine, Yale School of Medicine; Senior Policy Consultant, APT Foundation, prepared for delivery to the House Select Committee on Narcotics Abuse and Control, 29th September, 1988, (pp. 115–125).

cocaine and opium was widespread. Gradually people's attitudes changed so that they no longer regarded the use of opiates and cocaine as desirable and came increasingly to see them as physically destructive. He contends that this shift from "chemical liberation" to "chemical conservatism" is cyclical: "[A] drug is initially seen as being a tonic, a stimulant to the body, and helpful in attaining insight or relaxation. The claims for drugs are positive and their use, if someone knows nothing more than the claims, seems reasonable." Maintains Dr. Musto: "The road from this initial positive attitude to refusing to try drugs, is a long one."

Dr. Musto asserts that if we can change American attitudes toward drug use, just as others have changed those attitudes in the past, we can make drug use less fashionable. To make it less fashionable, we can, according to him, legitimately use the law to deter people from using illegal drugs and to express social disapproval.

Mr. Chairman, thank you for your invitation to testify today about the history of the drug problem in the United States. This is a broad subject extending more than a century into our past, but I will try to extract those features most relevant to the current debate over the legalization of drugs such as cocaine. I discuss these matters in much greater detail in my book *The American Disease*.

The first point to be made is that narcotics were legal in the United States last century. There were several reasons for this. Strict construction of the Constitution left police powers—like curbing careless physicians or prohibiting dispensing of certain drugs—to the states. Furthermore, although U.S. consumption of opium and its active ingredient morphine grew continuously during the nineteenth century, levels and consequences did not alarm the public until the use of the hypodermic syringe exploded after the 1860s. We reached a level of opium and opiate consumption in the mid-1890s which is arguably the highest per capita level in our history. Some steps at the state level, in some states, were taken by 1900 to limit access to morphine, but the effectiveness was modest if not invisible. Drugs were available from mail-order houses and a wide choice of hypodermic kits could be purchased from the Sears, Roebuck Catalog and elsewhere.

A fear of the effects of morphine and opium appears to have begun a reduction in per capita consumption after the 1890s. We entered what has been called the Progressive Era, a time in many ways like our own today. Americans became increasingly concerned about the environment and what we took into our bodies. The conservation movement, battles for clean air and streams, pure food and drugs, and a curbing of industrial disregard for the waste products of factories energized Americans. Many of the basic laws in these fields were enacted around the turn of the century. Included in this concern was the effect of narcotics on the individual, family, and community.

But it was not just morphine or, after 1898, heroin that worried Americans. A new drug, a powerful stimulant, had arrived in the 1880s: cocaine. At first cocaine was considered harmless. Experts in the drug and medical areas assured Americans that cocaine not only safely energized the weary and cheered the melancholy, but that there was no such thing as cocaine addiction. Sometimes the praise was slightly tempered by the advice that cocaine should be taken 'in moderation', at other times this bow toward common sense was lacking.

Cocaine rapidly spread through American society. At first it was rather expensive, but in about ten years or so the price of cocaine had dropped enough that it was available to almost everyone. It became a standard remedy for sinusitis and hay fever. It had been in Coca-Cola from the beginning until about 1900 when cocaine's reputation began plummeting. Its damage, especially among young people, was most visible in the cities. In Chicago, Jane Addams was appalled by the effect of cocaine on children she and her co-workers were trying to help. One example she gave: "He had been in our kindergarten as a handsome merry child, in our clubs as a vivacious boy, and then gradually there was an eclipse of all that was animated and joyous and promising, and when I last saw him in his coffin [at the age of 17], it was impossible to connect that haggard shriveled body with what I had known before." Jane Addams succeeded in getting a stronger state law in Illinois in 1907, 81 years ago.

Chicago's poor neighborhoods did not differ much from the worst inner-city areas of today. One observer called Chicago "first in violence, deepest in dirt; loud, lawless, unlovely, ill-smelling, new . . ." Cocaine was everywhere, from soda pop to sniffing powders. But Ms. Addams, who would later become the first American woman to receive the Nobel Peace Prize, did not abandon these difficult neighborhoods to cocaine. She was spurred to action by the effect of cocaine on the minds and bodies of young people. And eventually, after years of struggle, she and the neighborhoods won. As a result of the anti-cocaine attitude expressed in several state laws, such as the Al Smith anti-cocaine law of New York in 1913, and then at the national level the Harrison anti-narcotic Act of 1914, the attack on cocaine eventually succeeded, although more slowly than an impatient America wished. Cocaine's availability in the 1930s was far less than in 1910 and by the 1940s and 1950s, cocaine had become a memory for the vast majority of Americans.

In the time from 1885 to about 1905, 20 years, cocaine had moved from a harmless tonic to a drug which was seen as dangerous to take even once. This was a fundamental shift in popular attitudes that underlay the decline in demand. Such a changed perception of a drug from being a help to a hindrance occurred in the United States in other cycles of drug use.

In fact, the United States has a long history of slowly alternating attitudes toward drugs. If we include alcohol, these cycles of tolerance and intolerance toward drugs extend back to the earliest days of our nation. What can I say briefly about these cycles? That a drug is initially seen as being a tonic, a stimulant to the body, and helpful in attaining insight or relaxation. The claims for drugs are positive and their use, if someone knows nothing more than the claims, seems reasonable. The road from this initial positive attitude to refusing to try drugs, is a long one. We find any reason to reject the dangerousness of drugs and overlook or explain away the bad effects. Because the use of drugs is in general an individual decision, a lot of minds must change in order to reduce demand.

This move toward seeing drugs as harmful to achieving productive goals in life affects all the institutions of society. Schools, the police, courts, churches, and other institutions co-operate and reinforce one another in the rejection of drugs. In the first stage of drug use these institutions may not have taken the problem very seriously or not even have seen drug use as a problem. Gradually, the pressure of these institutions makes drug use less easy, less desirable, and less approved.

Peer pressure can be as much against drugs as for them. Slowly, drug use declines.

The last time this happened, about 1920 to 1950, we strove to erase the memory of the earlier drug epidemic from our minds and our textbooks. With a very natural response to a scourge Americans hoped would never recur, we settled on three strategies; extreme punishment, silence, or exaggeration. The effect of these measures may have been sadly and paradoxically to create new generations coming of age in the 1960s knowing nothing of the reality of drugs. The official information contained such exaggerated descriptions of their dangers that the government lost all credibility among young people discovering they had been grossly misled.

I believe we have moved in the current epidemic, as in the last, toward rejection of drugs as helpful and harmless. We can see signs of this in many areas from the decline in approval of marijuana since 1978 to a more recent drop in cocaine among high-school seniors. Public opinion polls on the legalization of marijuana have paralleled these changes. With this shift from seeing a drug like cocaine being relatively harmless in the mid-1970s to our current perception, legalizing the drug is a proposal simply out of step with public attitudes. The first cocaine epidemic shows that widespread use should not lead us to helplessness and hopelessness: use can be reduced. Further, the actual physiological and mental effects of cocaine as well as the actual effects of heroin are destructive to neighborhoods, community organization and to families as well as to the individual addicted. It is not just the price of drugs or turf wars that create problems—although those are an easily visible side of the drug question. It is the slowly, quietly destructive effect of the drugs on social cohesion that is the greatest and most lasting destruction of all.

The question arises: does the great profit from illegal drugs make demand reduction impossible? Is the damage done by fighting for turf between gangs worth the legal restraints on drugs? This is a decision Congress and the nation must make. My belief is that the popular attitude which is growing so powerfully against drug use in this country is in the long run more determinative than profits or even foreign supply. Coca bushes grew in Bolivia and Peru before, during, and after the first cocaine epidemic. As for profits, there were profits in the past, both legitimate when cocaine was legal and by pushers when illegal. Eventually, the fear engendered by cocaine along with the legal and institutional restraints did bring the epidemic under control. I believe legal sanctions are as necessary and appropriate to support this shift of attitude toward drugs as in the struggle against racial discrimination.

The problems we have had regarding cocaine and illicit profits certainly arise from cocaine's illegality in a period of tolerance toward the drug. Many saw no real evil in providing that which they considered harmless—in moderation. If we had maintained the earlier antagonism toward cocaine through the 1960s, based on a vivid knowledge about its actual effects, one wonders whether we would have had such a serious problem a second time.

This brings me, in this brief opening statement, to the near and more distant futures. The immediate task is to support families and communities besieged by drug dealing and crime, and co-ordinate social institutions opposing drug use. If we once again reduce drug use to a much lower level in the United States, we must not again revert to extreme punishments, silence or exaggeration.

Finally, we must recognize that the decline phase contains the potential for serious public policy errors. The reduction in drug use earlier this century did not proceed smoothly but rather was tarnished with prejudice and overkill. For example, although both Blacks and Whites used cocaine around the turn of the century, the drug became, in the popular mind, closely linked with Black hostility to Whites in the South. Since that period coincided with the peak of lynching and the removal of voting rights from Blacks, cocaine served as a chemical excuse for repression. The fear of drugs can be so extreme, perhaps intensified by the frustrating slowness of decline, that drug use becomes a reason for almost any negative social activity. Drug use can also be ascribed to a whole group, like Southern Blacks before World War One, with little appreciation of how unfair or how inaccurate such labelling might be. We cannot forget that even if drugs were eliminated from the inner-cities, the landscape of poor education and lack of opportunity would remain.

With this in mind, we should be concerned that as middle-class drug use declines and antagonism to drugs grows, which apparently is happening, the inner cities of our nation are not written off as a collection of drug users unworthy of support and investment by more abstinent Americans. The middle-class are the earliest to turn against drugs when drugs interfere with home life or employment. The reasons for this gradual antagonism toward drugs, though, rests in large part on the goals of work, home, and education. To the extent this is absent among the inner city residents while drug-dealing remains an available employment opportunity, we cannot be optimistic that drug use will decline there at the same rate as in middle America. We must understand that in many ways, the best attack on drug abuse is to provide a community in which drug use is irrelevant, a handicap in the path toward satisfying personal goals.

A second concern is that our anti-drug attitude will lead to excessive and ill-informed drug testing in our search for drug users. When the vast majority of Americans are anti-drug, our judgment may be skewed so that we engage in overkill, causing problems rather than resolving them.

A third concern is that basic research into drugs will lose steady funding in a trend toward law enforcement and a conviction that the only important goal is separating people from drugs. There is an enormous amount we do not understand about drug and bodily reactions. We should provide reasonable research support that is steady over the years and not subject to the swings of funding which have characterized past years.

Finally, another reaction to a blanket opposition to drugs is the phenomenon of patients refusing pain-killing medication because they have come to see drugs like morphine as too dangerous to accept even in a medical setting. This has been an unpleasant surprise to the staff at such prestigious institutions as the Memorial Sloan-Kettering Cancer Center.

In this brief statement I have been able to touch on only some of the great issues confronting our nation and its drug problem. Although I can empathize with those who out of frustration wish to legalize drugs, I believe the history of America's battles with drugs gives us hope that we can overcome the present difficulties. The fundamental change of attitude toward drugs which undergirds a reduction in demand is currently underway. We must be careful to not let our antagonism get out of hand. We can overcome drugs and achieve a more cohesive, productive nation.

10

THE JOURNALISTS: A 'CONSERVATIVE' AND A 'LIBERAL' VIEW

INTRODUCTION

Hundreds of commentaries about the debate over legalization have been written by journalists in almost every newspaper and magazine in the country. *National Review* and *The New Republic,* however, represent the quintessential 'conservative' and 'liberal' publications, respectively. We here present a sample of opinions from editors of the two magazines: first, *National Review* editor-in-chief William F. Buckley Jr., and then one of *The New Republic*'s senior editors, Morton M. Kondracke. Note that, in at least this case, the 'liberal' opposes legalization and the 'conservative' favors legalization.

Drug Talk Across the Way

William F. Buckley Jr.

William F. Buckley Jr., editor-in-chief of National Review, *favors trying legalization and emphasizes that being in favor of legalization is compatible with opposing the misuse of drugs. He agrees with Michael Massing that the current approach overtaxes every branch of our legal system ("law enforcement, bench, and bar") and does not alleviate the drug problem.*

The Kentucky Center for the Arts brought together four men of varied experience to discuss the question whether drugs ought to be legalized, and Dr. Robert DuPont, a psychiatrist, gave the impression that he had disposed of any question by his initial asseveration. To wit, "Name me one politician in the United States who has run successfully for political office who believes in legalizing drugs."

There are two preliminary difficulties with that statement. The first is that Mayor Kurt Schmoke of Baltimore believes in drug legalization, as does Marion Barry, the mayor of Washington, D.C.—or so it was contended by the moderator, National Public Radio's Bob Edwards—and they are successful politicians. But the second difficulty faced by Dr. DuPont is that a politician may well believe in legalizing drugs, which does not mean that he will disclose his private belief other than to his wife or his priest. One participant asked how many politicians running for office in 1800 came out for abolition? A third participant (a professor) favored legalization, a fourth opposed it for non-addicts, favored it for the addict population.

'Drug Talk Across the Way' by William F. Buckley Jr. (*National Review*, May 5th, 1989, p. 63). Used by permission.

What proved most curious is that there was a substantial lobby that night, among the literati of Louisville, for every position. For rigid, diehard, call-in-the-Marines suppression; for complete legalization, together with heightened educational efforts to cure and to dissuade; for submitting everyone to random testing; for not submitting anyone to random testing; for executing certain classes of drug vendors; and for not doing so. If Louisville is representative of the nation, on the drug issue the people are divided.

Are we absolutely certain that the candidate who came out for drug legalization—on the grounds that to do so would permit government agents rather than criminals to dole out the poison to those who will not do without it—would automatically lose in any political race? Certainly he would lose, and would deserve to do so, if he were identified as a drug-lover. For a generation, anyone running in the South identified as a 'nigger-lover' would automatically lose an election. Gradually it became clear that a so-called nigger-lover was someone who believed that blacks were human beings entitled to civil liberties. Not inconceivably, in years ahead it will dawn on reluctant intelligences that those who wish to legalize drugs may be just as heartily opposed to their consumption, but are more highly mobilized than the prohibitionists concerning the mounting problem of drug crime.

The gentleman who ventured the opinion that legalization is hardly worth talking about given the unanimity of political opinion opposed to it is not merely a practicing psychiatrist, but also a former public servant who was himself what they now call William Bennett, the 'Drug Czar'. His title was director of the National Institute on Drug Abuse. What does he propose doing?

How are we doing in our war on drugs? Michael Massing writes in the current issue of *The New York Review of Books:* "[Prosecutor] Giuliani's office spent five years gathering evidence in the [Pizza Connection] case. . . . His associates videotaped meetings, gathered airline passenger seat lists, recovered ticket stubs, pored over hotel registers, kept surveillance logs, and retrieved immigration records. Teams of six agents listened to 47 telephones around the clock, taping a total of 55,000 conversations; the nine hundred most important were transcribed and collated in nine bound volumes. So vast was the evidence that it took a full year to be presented in court.

"In the end, the government was rewarded for its pains. All but two of the defendants were convicted, and most were sentenced to long terms. Still, as [author Shana] Alexander observes, the case 'did not make the slightest dent in the nation's desperate drug problem. More heroin, and more cocaine, is on the streets today than before [the trial began]. The trial severely overtaxed every branch of our legal system—law enforcement, bench, and bar—and taxed the unfortunate jurors most of all.'"

The meeting in Louisville took place one night after William Bennett, the new Drug Czar, went on *Meet the Press* to announce his much-heralded recommendations. But that morning, *Meet the Press* was pre-empted in Louisville; NBC instead showed a high-school debate.

What is gathering in America is a deep frustration. The people do not listen any more to a George Bush promising at his inauguration to do away with the "scourge" of drugs. They do not tune in to hear the new Drug Czar. And, listening to four points of view on the subject, they can only agree that no politician can be elected who recommends the one thing that hasn't been tried.

Don't Legalize Drugs: The Costs are Still Too High

Morton M. Kondracke

Morton M. Kondracke of The New Republic *argues against legalization, proposing that we must continue to wage a war against drugs but must wage it more seriously and intelligently than we have so far because of the medical and social costs due directly to drugs and not simply to their prohibition. He holds that prohibition decreased the consumption of alcohol, and that its repeal increased consumption. Accordingly, he argues that, if drugs are legalized, we shall see a dramatic increase in drug use, drug addiction, and such attendant evils as domestic crime, child abuse and neglect, and drug-related accidents.*

While he believes that the advocates of legalization may be right about some of the social benefits of legalization, he believes that they are almost certainly wrong about the extent and severity of the likely negative consequences of legalization.

Mr. Kondracke concludes by approving of drug testing for people with sensitive jobs or workers involved in accidents, lifting driver's licenses, and requiring treatment. "These are," he maintains, "not nosy moralistic intrusions on people's individual rights, but attempts by society to protect itself from danger."

The next time you hear that a drunk driver has slammed into a school bus full of children or that a stoned railroad engineer has killed 16 people in a train wreck, think about this: if the advocates of legalized drugs have

'Don't Legalize Drugs: The Costs are Still Too High' by Morton M. Kondracke (*The New Republic*, June 27th, 1988, pp. 16–19). Used by permission.

their way, there will be more of this, a lot more. There will also be more unpublicized fatal and maiming crashes, more job accidents, more child neglect, more of almost everything associated with substance abuse: babies born addicted or retarded, teenagers zonked out of their chance for an education, careers destroyed, families wrecked, and people dead of overdoses.

The proponents of drug legalization are right to say that some things will get better. Organized crime will be driven out of the drug business, and there will be a sharp drop in the amount of money (currently about $10 billion per year) that society spends to enforce the drug laws. There will be some reduction in the cost in theft and injury (now about $20 billion) by addicts to get the money to buy prohibited drugs. Internationally, Latin American governments presumably will stop being menaced by drug cartels and will peaceably export cocaine as they now do coffee.

However, this is virtually the limit of the social benefits to be derived from legalization, and they are far outweighed by the costs, which are always underplayed by legalization advocates such as the *Economist*, Princeton scholar Ethan A. Nadelmann (see 'Shooting Up', TNR, June 13th), economist Milton Friedman and other libertarians, columnists William F. Buckley and Richard Cohen, and Mayors Kurt Schmoke of Baltimore and Marion Barry of Washington, D.C. In lives, money, and human woe, the costs are so high, in fact, that society has no alternative but to conduct a real war on the drug trade, although perhaps a smarter one than is currently being waged.

Advocates of legalization love to draw parallels between the drug war and Prohibition. Their point, of course, is that this crusade is as doomed to failure as the last one was, and that we ought to surrender now to the inevitable and stop wasting resources. But there are some important differences between drugs and alcohol. Alcohol has been part of Western culture for thousands of years; drugs have been the rage in America only since about 1962. Of the 115 million Americans who consume alcohol, 85 percent rarely become intoxicated; with drugs, intoxication is the whole idea. Alcohol is consistent chemically, even though it's dispensed in different strengths and forms as beer, wine, and 'hard' liquor; with drugs there's no limit to the variations. Do we legalize crack along with snortable cocaine, PCPs as well as marijuana, and LSD and 'Ecstasy' as well as heroin? If we don't—and almost certainly we won't—we have a black market, and some continued crime.

But Prohibition is a useful historical parallel for measuring the costs of legalization. Almost certainly doctors are not going to want to write prescriptions for recreational use of harmful substances, so if drugs ever are legalized they will be dispensed as alcohol now is—in government-regulated stores with restrictions on the age of buyers, warnings against abuse (and, probably, with added restrictions on amounts, though this also will create a black market).

In the decade before Prohibition went into effect in 1920, alcohol consumption in the United States averaged 2.6 gallons per person per year. It fell to 0.73 gallons during the Prohibition decade, then doubled to 1.5 gallons in the decade after repeal, and is now back to 2.6 gallons. So illegality suppressed usage to a third or a fourth of its former level. At the same time, incidence of cirrhosis of the liver fell by half.

So it seems fair to estimate that use of drugs will at least double, and possibly triple, if the price is cut, supplies are readily available, and society's sanction is lifted. It's widely accepted that there are now 16 million regular users of marijuana, six million of cocaine, a half million of heroin, and another half million of other drugs, totaling 23 million. Dr. Robert DuPont, former director of the National Institute on Drug Abuse and an anti-legalization crusader, says that the instant pleasure afforded by drugs—superior to that available with alcohol—will increase the number of regular users of marijuana and cocaine to about 50 or 60 million and heroin users to ten million.

Between ten percent and 15 percent of all drinkers turn into alcoholics (ten million to 17 million), and these drinkers cost the economy an estimated $117 billion in 1983 ($15 billion for treatment, $89 billion in lost productivity, and $13 billion in accident-related costs). About 200,000 people died last year as a result of alcohol abuse, about 25,000 in auto accidents. How many drug users will turn into addicts, and what will this cost? According to President Reagan's drug abuse policy adviser, Dr. David I. McDonald, studies indicate that marijuana is about as habit-forming as alcohol, but for cocaine, 70 percent of users become addicted, as many as with nicotine.

So it seems reasonable to conclude that at least four to six million people will become potheads if marijuana is legal, and that coke addicts will number somewhere between 8.5 million (if regular usage doubles and 70 percent become addicted) and 42 million (if DuPont's high estimate of use is correct). An optimist would have to conclude that the number of people abusing legalized drugs will come close to those hooked on alcohol. A pessimist would figure the human damage as much greater.

Another way of figuring costs is this: the same study (by the Research Triangle Institute of North Carolina) that put the price of alcoholism at $117 billion in 1983 figured the cost of drug abuse then at $60 billion—$15 billion for law enforcement and crime, and $45 billion in lost productivity, damaged health, and other costs. The updated estimate for 1988 drug abuse is $100 billion. If legalizing drugs would save $30 billion now being spent on law enforcement and crime, a doubling of use and abuse means that other costs will rise to $140 billion or $210 billion. This is no bargain for society.

If 200,000 people die every year from alcohol abuse and 320,000 from tobacco smoking, how many will die from legal drugs? Government estimates are that 4,000 to 5,000 people a year are killed in drug-related auto crashes, but this is surely low because accident victims are not as routinely blood-tested for drugs as for alcohol. Legalization advocates frequently cite figures of 3,600 or 4,100 as the number of drug deaths each year reported by hospitals, but this number too is certainly an understatement, based on reports from only 75 big hospitals in 27 metropolitan areas.

If legalization pushed the total number of drug addicts to only half the number of alcoholics, 100,000 people a year would die. That's the figure cited by McDonald. DuPont guesses that, given the potency of drugs, the debilitating effects of cocaine, the carcinogenic effects of marijuana, and the AIDS potential of injecting legalized heroin, the number of deaths actually could go as high as 500,000 a year. That's a wide range, but it's clear that legalization of drugs will not benefit human life.

All studies show that those most likely to try drugs, get hooked, and die—as opposed to those who suffer from cirrhosis and lung cancer—are young people, who are susceptible to the lure of quick thrills and are terribly adaptable to messages provided by adult society. Under pressure of the current prohibition, the number of kids who use illegal drugs at least once a month has fallen from 39 percent in the late 1970s to 25 percent in 1987, according to the annual survey of high school seniors conducted by the University of Michigan. The same survey shows that attitudes toward drug use have turned sharply negative. But use of legal drugs is still strong. Thirty-eight percent of high school seniors reported getting drunk within the past two weeks, and 27 percent said they smoke cigarettes every day. Drug prohibition is working with kids; legalization would do them harm.

And, even though legalization would lower direct costs for drug law enforcement, it's unlikely that organized crime would disappear. It might well shift to other fields—prostitution, pornography, gambling or burglaries, extortion, and murders-for-hire—much as it did in the period between the end of Prohibition and the beginning of the drug era. As DuPont puts it, "Organized crime is in the business of giving people the things that society decides in its own interest to prohibit. The only way to get rid of organized crime is to make everything legal." Even legalization advocates such as Ethan Nadelmann admit that some street crimes will continue to occur as a result of drug abuse—especially cocaine paranoia, PCP insanity, and the need of unemployable addicts to get money for drugs. Domestic crime, child abuse and neglect surely would increase.

Some legalization advocates suggest merely decriminalizing marijuana and retaining sanctions against other drugs. This would certainly be less costly than total legalization, but it would still be no favor to young people, would increase traffic accidents and productivity losses—and would do nothing to curtail the major drug cartels, which make most of their money trafficking in cocaine.

Legalizers also argue that the government could tax legal drug sales and use the money to pay for anti-drug education programs and treatment centers. But total taxes collected right now from alcohol sales at the local, state, and federal levels come to only $13.1 billion per year—which is a pittance compared with the damage done to society as a result of alcohol abuse. The same would have to be true for drugs—and any tax that resulted in an official drug price that was higher than the street price would open the way once again for black markets and organized crime.

So, in the name of health, economics, and morality, there seems no alternative but to keep drugs illegal and to fight the criminals who traffic in them. Regardless of what legalization advocates say, this is now the overwhelming opinion of the public, the Reagan administration, the prospective candidates for president, and the Congress—not one of whose members has introduced legislation to decriminalize any drug. Congress is on the verge of forcing the administration to raise anti-drug spending next year from $3 billion to $5.5 billion.

There is, though, room to debate how best to wage this war. A consensus is developing that it has to be done both on the supply side (at overseas points of origin, through interdiction at U.S. borders and criminal prosecution of traffickers) and on the demand side (by discouraging use of drugs through education and treatment and/or by arrest and urine testing at workplaces). However, there is a disagreement about which side to emphasize and how to spend resources. Members of Congress, especially Democrats, want to blame foreigners and the Reagan administration for the fact that increasing amounts of cocaine, heroin, and marijuana are entering the country. They want to spend more money on foreign aid, use the U.S. military to seal the borders, and fund 'nice' treatment and education programs, especially those that give ongoing support to professional social welfare agencies.

Conservatives, on the other hand, want to employ the military to help foreign countries stamp out drug laboratories, use widespread drug testing to identify—and, often, punish—drug users, and spend more on police and prisons. As Education Secretary William Bennett puts it, "How can we surrender when we've never actually fought the war?" Bennett wants to fight it across all fronts, and those who have seen drafts of a forthcoming report of the White House Conference for a Drug Free America say this will be the approach recommended by the administration, although with muted emphasis on use of the U.S. military, which is reluctant to get involved in what may be another thankless war.

However, DuPont and others, including Jeffrey Eisenach of the Heritage Foundation, make a strong case that primary emphasis ought to be put on the demand side—discouraging use in the United States rather than, almost literally, trying to become the world's policeman. Their argument, bolstered by a study conducted by Peter Reuter of the RAND

Corporation, is that major profits in the drug trade are not made abroad (where the price of cocaine triples from farm to airstrip), but within the United States (where the markup from entry point to street corner is 12 times), and that foreign growing fields and processing laboratories are easily replaceable at low cost.

They say that prohibition policy should emphasize routine random urine testing in schools and places of employment, arrests for possession of drugs, and 'coercive' treatment programs that compel continued enrollment as a condition of probation and employment. DuPont thinks that corporations have a right to demand that their employees be drug-free because users cause accidents and reduce productivity. He contends that urine testing is no more invasive than the use of metal detectors at airports.

"Liberals have a terrible time with this," says DuPont. "They want to solve every problem by giving people things. They want to love people out of their problems, while conservatives want to punish it out of them. What we want to do is take the profits out of drugs by drying up demand. You do that by raising the social cost of using them to the point where people say, 'I don't want to do this.' This isn't conservative. It's a way to save lives."

It is, and it's directly parallel to the way society is dealing with drunk driving and cigarette smoking—not merely through advertising campaigns and surgeon general's warnings, but through increased penalties, social strictures—and prohibitions. Random testing for every employee in America may be going too far, but testing those holding sensitive jobs or workers involved in accidents surely isn't, nor is arresting users, lifting driver's licenses, and requiring treatment. These are not nosy, moralistic intrusions on people's individual rights, but attempts by society to protect itself from danger.

In the end, they are also humane and moral. There is a chance, with the public and policy-makers aroused to action, that ten years from now drug abuse might be reduced to its pre-1960s levels. Were drugs to be legalized now, we would be establishing a new vice—one that, over time, would end or ruin millions of lives. Worse yet, we would be establishing a pattern of doing the easy thing, surrendering, whenever confronted with a difficult challenge.

11

HALF-MEASURES?
SOME PROPOSALS
BETWEEN THE
EXTREMES

INTRODUCTION

In any public debate, there is a tendency for the issues to become simplified into a straight choice between two alternatives: in this case, legalize all drugs or proceed with the traditional 'war on drugs'. While such a polarization of positions can be helpful to the clarity of the debate, it can also cause various intermediate alternatives to be overlooked. There is not merely a simple choice between legalization and present policies. Legalization could conceivably take many different forms, and present policies could be dramatically changed without legalization. The following three articles look at some of the intermediate positions often neglected in the heat of the legalization battle.

Should Drugs be Legalized?
The Perils at the Extremes

Daryl Frazell

While it may be an oversimplification to describe arguments for legalization as one 'extreme' and anti-legalization arguments as the opposite 'extreme', there is, we believe, some value in examining a position that expresses concern over both legalization and our present policy. Daryl Frazell, an editor with the St. Petersburg Times, *offers some suggestions.*

While frustrated by the current drug situation, Mr. Frazell fears that our government might adopt one of two 'extreme' approaches: either 1. using the military in an "all-out effort to block the supply of drugs from abroad", or 2. legalizing drugs. Before we seriously think about adopting either approach, he wants us to try a third approach, in his eyes much less risky: to effect a change in our attitude toward illegal drugs so that their use is considered not chic but rather a matter of shame and dishonor. He believes that just as we changed attitudes toward cigarettes and drunken driving, so we can and must change attitudes toward illegal drugs.

I recognize that current efforts to control the nation's drug problem are like trying to dam the Mississippi River by throwing rocks at it. I understand that people are tired of waiting for somebody to do something, anything that might work. But the extreme measures being advocated today make me shudder at the dangers of going too far.

The frustrated public is beginning to pull in two directions in its eagerness to find some sort of balm for its anguish. One faction would

---

use the armed forces in an all-out effort to block the supply of drugs from abroad. Congress and the administration are moving in this direction.

Under a bill passed by the Senate, soldiers would make civilian arrests. Only specially trained troops would be used. Presumably they would be taught to respect civil rights. Presumably only smugglers would be treated as invading enemies. But soldiers and sailors and airmen are not normally trained to give the enemy any kind of break. The mission of the military is to coerce and, when necessary, kill.

I am haunted by the thought of the 'wrong-house raids' committed by various police agencies in the past. Even highly trained drug enforcement officers make mistakes. They kick down the wrong door, rough up the wrong people. Do we really want to give the military that kind of power against American citizens?

How far we have come since the days when the nation was, as a matter of policy, unprepared for war. Americans kept their standing army small and weak to avoid institutionalizing militarism, which they believed would endanger their liberties and increase the likelihood of going to war. All that changed after World War II, of course, and U.S. armed forces now stand ready not only on their own soil but also at outposts around the world.

They are there to protect the national interest against foreign enemies. The prospect of their intervention in a law enforcement problem that is basically domestic should worry everybody who cares about civil liberties.

"Let no one believe that we're going to pass a piece of legislation and solve the drug problem, but we can improve it," Senator Sam Nunn, (Democrat, Georgia), was quoted as saying in regard to the Senate bill.

Improve it at what cost? How much freedom must we give up to protect ourselves from ourselves?

At the other extreme from those who advocate sending in the Marines is a growing faction that speaks of legalizing drugs, an idea that was considered irresponsible until recently. The argument, as advanced by Baltimore Mayor Kurt Schmoke on Page 1-D, is that legalization would bring the drug-trafficking crime machine to a halt by cutting off its fuel, money.

Schmoke favors treating drug abuse as a health problem, not a crime problem, in the same way we deal with other addictions such as alcoholism. This would actually improve public health, he says, by reducing crime and releasing enforcement funds to be used for treatment and education programs.

To make this work we would have to make drugs easily available and cheap. This would put the drug dealers out of business, but what would it do to the population? Would cocaine be dispensed to anyone who asked, including children?

Today, cocaine users disregard the danger of this highly addictive and potentially lethal narcotic because they want to get high. Would this reaction spread with legalization, as more and more people tried it and liked it? Would we have a coke problem that would make alcoholism seem tame? Nobody knows, and there is no way to find out without experimenting with legalization.

The prospect scares some people. "I would be terrified to live in a cocaine legalized society," Yale University researcher Frank H. Gawin said recently, as quoted in the *New York Times*.

Clearly we have reached a point where something new should be tried, but both extremes pose risks that we should accept only after cool and careful consideration, and not in an attitude of hysterical desperation.

There is one risk-free remedy that would surely help the situation, if only we could bring it about. It is simple to state if difficult to accomplish: Change the image of drugs.

Today, despite all the political posturing and the 'just say no' campaign, drugs are in style. They are used openly in the streets, and not just by hopeless addicts. It is hardly unusual to encounter the odor of marijuana smoke in public places.

Some people are attracted by the image of drugs as naughty and adventurous. The attitude is that a little bit can't hurt, as long as you know when to stop, and anyway, drugs are no worse than liquor or cigarettes.

Changing that image would require demeaning drugs, labeling them as medicine for the sick, crutches for the weak-willed. Their use would become a matter of shame and dishonor.

I have seen something similar happen with tobacco. Not so long ago newsrooms were smoke-filled. People seemed to think they could not work without cigarettes smoldering at their fingertips. Any substantial reversal of this particular profession's taste for tobacco seemed highly improbable.

Yet it happened. Today the air is clear. Smokers are forced to stand in the corners, next to ventilators. A once-fashionable practice has become socially unacceptable.

We seem to be moving in the same direction with drinking and driving. Could we do it to drugs? I think we could if we tried.

Let Koop Do It: A Prescription for the Drug War

Taylor Branch

Many arguments for legalization call for regulating currently illegal drugs in much the same way as alcohol or cigarettes are now regulated. In the following New Republic *article, freelance writer Taylor Branch first argues that many people are naive or hypocritical in condemning illegal drugs while they condone legal ones (including alcohol, tobacco, and prescription medicines, many of which "in combination with alcohol kill more people by overdose than heroin"). She then suggests applying former surgeon general Charles Everett Koop's techniques for regulating tobacco and alcohol to currently illegal drugs.*

According to Ms. Branch, to adapt Dr. Koop's techniques to illegal drugs, we would do, among other things, the following:

> [L]icense private distributors carefully and tax the drugs as heavily as possible, ideally to the point just short of creating a criminal black market. . . . [T]ry to ban commercial advertising for harmful drugs, even though their sale is legal. . . . [C]oncentrate police powers on two tasks: prohibiting sales to children, and enforcing strict sanctions against those who cause injury to others while under the influence.

Branch further suggests that if we are serious about developing a rational drug policy, we shall want government officials to be more honest and objective in discussing drugs and to be careful to avoid exaggerating the properties of drugs and the risks they pose to users. Indeed, she attributes the declining

---

'Let Koop Do It: A Prescription for the Drug War' by Taylor Branch (*The New Republic*, October 24th, 1988, pp. 22–26). Used by permission.

popularity of smoking in the U.S. to the credence most people give to the government's cigarette warnings. "By contrast," she argues, "official propaganda against cocaine and marijuana still meets with skepticism and ridicule."

Ms. Branch concludes by arguing that the people who categorically oppose any form of legalization are objectionably paternalistic, assuming without warrant that "most people cannot follow their own best interests without force of external authority."

Only two years after the last bombs-away overhaul, and 15 years after President Nixon announced that we had turned the corner in the war on drugs, Congress and the White House are concocting a new drug law that would unleash the military and the death penalty. Among other measures that would fall heavily on addicts and teetotalers alike, the law would deny federal contracts to any firm lacking an approved policy against drugs in the workplace. Also, having flattened whole South American governments under the weight of American-fed drug mobs richer than Capone ever dreamed, we would flatten them again by defoliating their countryside. The newest dragnet would get the government off our backs and into our bathrooms, requiring random urinalysis for nearly everyone, even though the tests have been fooled by substances ranging from Advil to poppy-seed bagels. (The Pentagon once admitted that nearly half its 9,000 urine-based disciplinary cases may have involved false results.)

Officials refuse to predict that any of this would actually reduce the use of drugs. They are unsure whether they want to drive the price of drugs up or down, whether to give users 20 years or treatment. A maze of drug bureaucracies are locked in turf battles and even real ones, arresting one another's undercover agents. Ed Meese's task force on the drug problem found government complicity in only three countries—Cuba, Nicaragua, and Bulgaria—and made no mention at all of corruption within American law enforcement.

We are unnerved, ready to try anything. Baltimore Mayor Kurt Schmoke proved that last spring when he suggested that we might do better to legalize illicit drugs. As the first major officeholder who dared to suggest such an idea, he scrambled the accepted image of the problem. An Ivy League black man and a former prosecutor who had spent years putting dealers behind bars, Schmoke announced that he was tired of going to the funerals of police officers killed by drug dealers. As mayor of the city with the nation's highest teenage murder rate, he tried to distinguish between the evils of drug consumption *per se* and the unintended evils caused by society's prohibitions. He said the law itself has turned the inner city into a war zone. Anti-drug enforcement has created a netherworld of stupendous, artificial profit that now sucks children into a deadly version of NBA fool's gold. Legalizing drugs would eliminate this undertow just as swiftly as the repeal of Prohibition wiped out the speakeasy gangsters. "I don't know of any kid who is making money running booze," said Schmoke.

Still, few are persuaded. According to a recent Gallup Poll, about 80 percent of Americans oppose legalizing even marijuana. So far, the debate between crackdown and legalization has merely advertised a nearly universal desire to do something drastic.

Schmoke's appeal to the logic of Prohibition reminds us how thoroughly we have banished that astonishing drama from historical memory. Prohibition is a lost epoch of tenacious sincerity and forgotten effect. In revolt against the toxic, demoralizing properties of alcohol, Americans sacrificed almost half of all federal revenues (alcohol taxes produced some $240 million in 1916, compared with income taxes of only $68 million), and we cut the booze habit so deeply that per capita alcohol consumption did not regain pre-Prohibition levels until 1970. Yet, we changed our minds, and undid our fundamental instrument of government for the first and only time. For all that, you have to squint to find Prohibition in standard histories as anything more than an 'experiment', leavened by unfortunate but colorful gangland entertainment. We are sensitive about our Puritanism, and especially about our mad lurchings between liberty and repression. Future historians most likely will see the current drug debate as an all-too-human comedy in pain, like the contortions of Prohibition. On no other subject except race are we so evasive about our past, and none other remains so contemporary.

One aspect of our drug history that ought to be reviewed, especially by the legalizers, is the checkered performance of the health industry.

Organized medicine opposed—then secured loophole privileges within
—both the Volstead Act (Prohibition) and the first federal ban on
narcotics in 1914. These laws arrived together in the Woodrow Wilson
era as liberal reforms, over-riding conservative fears of intrusive government. At a time when medicine still cured few diseases, doctors,
pharmacists, and other competing factions of the health profession were
struggling to raise their historically low status. Most 'drug stores' were
just that, and many offered nothing but preparations with narcotics, such
as "Hooper's Anodyne, the Infant's Friend," and "Mrs. Winslow's
Soothing Syrup." Doctors resented the druggists for 'recommending'
remedies such as their laudanum elixirs and their cocaine-based hemor-
rhoid balms, while the druggists in turn resented the physicians who ran
high-volume dispensaries from their back door. Eventually they reached
a compromise to protect each other and the drug companies, shutting out
the street vendors, mail-order houses, and other lowbrow competitors.

The health industry brought all the major illicit drugs into popular
usage. A predecessor of Merck began manufacturing morphine compounds in 1832. Parke-Davis (now Walker Lambert) introduced its
famous Coca Cordial along with its cocaine ointments and sprays.
Parke-Davis also invented PCP in 1957, as an animal anesthetic. Even
LSD, imported from a German pharmaceutical house, was hailed by
health professionals in the early 1960s as a wonder drug that promised
scientifically maintained positive attitudes for all Americans. Most of the
narcotics prosecutions early in this century targeted the notorious 'dope
doctors' and their confederates in the medicinal trade.

By the late Prohibition years, bacteriology and other miracles of
legitimate medicine had earned doctors greater public stature than the
federal enforcers themselves enjoyed. In 1930 the Bureau of Narcotics
ordered its agents to leave doctors and pharmacists alone and arrest only
the uneducated smugglers. Seven years later, when the government's
"Reefer Madness" campaign secured the first ban on marijuana, the
AMA made only a half-hearted effort to protect cannabis corn plasters
and other marijuana-based prescriptions.

Doctors gradually abandoned their right to dispense most of the
banned drugs, each of which carried the political stigma of a hated,
lower-class minority (from 'opium-addled Chinese' immigrants to 'co-

caine-crazed Negro rapists'). But medicine never spurned the desire of upstanding patients to manipulate their moods through chemistry. Quite apart from tobacco, alcohol, and illicit narcotics, health experts have made Americans a heavily drugged people even in proportion to wealth. In 1986 retail pharmacists alone filled 1.56 *billion* prescriptions for restricted drugs. The two leading categories—cardiovascular regulators and antibiotics—are reassuringly medical, but next come 132 million "psychotherapeutics", a medical euphemism for uppers and downers; prescriptions for 112 million "anti-depressants", led by an expensive pick-me-up called Elavil, have risen fivefold in the past generation.

Prescription drugs in combination with alcohol kill more people by overdose than heroin. Codeine-based medicines produce nearly as many overdose deaths as cocaine. A single depressant, diazepam, kills far more people by pharmaceutically pure overdoses than street-stomped, bootleg PCP.

All through this hay fever season, advertisements have promoted a new, drowsiness-free antihistamine, suitable for the general public, in broadcasts ending "See your doctor". Sneezers are thus invited to pay an office-visit fee of $40 or so for the prescribed right to visit a pharmacist acting as intermediary for the patent-holder and ad-maker, Merrill-Dow, to whom they can pay about $60 for 25 Seldane pills. This pricing structure bears a disturbing resemblance to the heavily populated markup chain for illegal substances. Indeed, the overall record of the health industry in the field of mentally active chemicals ought to be a sober warning to today's advocates of legalized drugs, nearly all of whom tout a 'medical approach' to drug users. Health officials, like wardens, prefer to hold the keys. They might be willing to prescribe a 'proper dose' of cocaine or marijuana, but they reserve the right to define the terms, to change their minds, and to collect a fee for treatment.

Charles Rangel, chairman of the House Select Committee on Narcotics Abuse and Control, opposes legalization. He knows that junkies, potheads, and even yuppie experimenters would rebel against a 'See your doctor' alternative. If enough of them stuck with their black market dealers, the illicit market would continue, with the health industry tagging along for legal profit. Rangel has been able to confound legalizers simply by asking practical questions: Where would drugs be distributed—at hospitals, pharmacies, convenience stores? What would be the allowable doses? Who would be allowed to buy medicinal drugs—admitted addicts only, recreational users, new users, kids? In response, advocates of the medical approach have fumbled for a dignified blend of whoopee and whoa.

Rangel expresses shrill urgency in all directions. He calls for tougher anti-drug laws and huge leaps in the enforcement budget, saying the country is flooded with poison because we have not yet begun to fight. Yet he also says that the excesses of the drug war already have "trampled the Constitution." Rangel evokes George Patton on war and William Kunstler on civil liberties. While heaping scorn on a bankrupt anti-drug policy from both directions, he nevertheless defends its tested logic against the dangerously muddled ideas of the drug legalizers. Even then, his bombastic derision is well chosen for possible retreat or adjustment. Rangel never denounces legalization in principle. He merely demands from it a detailed, logical practicality that escapes the lab-coated reformers and the dungeon-stuffing draconians alike.

The problem with legalization, however, is not its practical mechanics. Surgeon General Everett Koop has shown that in his relatively obscure war on tobacco and alcohol. Koop's rules of engagement are democratic and simple. You license private distributors carefully and tax the drugs as heavily as possible, ideally to the point just short of creating a criminal black market. You try to ban commercial advertising for harmful drugs, even though their sale is legal. You concentrate police powers on two tasks: prohibiting sales to children, and enforcing strict sanctions against those who cause injury to others while under the influence.

Although Koop has taken no position in the recent debates over illegal drugs, the logic of his approach applies to them as well. Does Koop want to require drinkers to get a Prohibition-style doctor's prescription for gin, vodka, and beer? Ridiculous—even though in 1984 alcohol took the lives of 11,111 Americans for every death even vaguely associated with marijuana. Does Koop recommend outlawing the manufacture and sale of cigarettes? No, he resists the temptations—even though alcohol and tobacco together kill more than 300 Americans for every one who dies from all illegal drugs put together, including heroin and cocaine. Would Koop or even the most slack-brained drug legalizer recommend that heroin be sold in restaurant vending machines? Of course not. Such machines currently make a mockery of state laws against the sale of cigarettes to minors. Koop would outlaw them.

Koop's latest government studies argue scientifically that nicotine is as addictive as morphine and heroin. Even so, he has not called in the doctors or the Untouchables. For a generation, the campaign against tobacco consumption has illustrated the democratic power of communication. The smoking rate fell from 30.4 percent to 26.5 percent in 1986 alone, and continues to fall—largely because people have come to accept the government's health warnings. By contrast, official propaganda against cocaine and marijuana still meets skepticism and ridicule.

The legal status of alcohol and tobacco allows Koop to tell people exactly what they are consuming, and what the risks are. With street drugs, purity and contents are guesswork for the government and Len Bias alike. Also, there is no room for Koop's credible, objective discernment regarding currently illegal drugs because their criminal status almost obliges authority figures to exaggerations of demonology. Officials obscure their own truths in brittle, hysterical cant, as in the extraordinary obsession with professional athletes. Impressionable youths wonder how athletes can perform amazing feats of mental and physical prowess under the influence of drugs that are presented as deadly poisons. The elaborate drug enforcement programs advertise sensitivity and doubt rather than virtue. Public relations and criminal repression lie down poorly together.

Koop believes that cigarettes can be licked by common sense and willpower. His grim studies showing that nicotine is as addictive as heroin have a logical flip side: kicking heroin is no tougher than kicking cigarettes. This perspective humanizes the evil, which lies somewhere within nearly everyone but can be refused or fought, as ex-smokers and struggling smokers may attest. There are some 30 million fewer smokers now than a decade ago—an extraordinary decline attributable to quitters, tobacco deaths, and to younger people who have refused to start. More than likely, the minuscule support for drug legalization owes much to their accomplishment. Among the abstainers, many baby boomers turning 40 may dimly believe that they have outlived their most dangerous propensities.

Early in Prohibition, a Texas senator declared that "there is as much chance of repealing the 18th Amendment as there is for a hummingbird to fly to the planet Mars with the Washington Monument tied to its tail." Only when Pierre du Pont, John D. Rockefeller Jr., and other pillars of conservative wealth converted to the cause of repeal did organized agitation begin in 1927. It took two more years before well-financed repealers began cranking out propaganda studies claiming that we could more than wipe out the federal deficit by taxing alcohol instead of chasing Capone. The industrial magnates reached an unlikely alliance with the immigrant-soaked Democratic Party. Even then, only the catastrophe of Depression brought the wets to victory. It is barely conceivable that a similar constituency of dollar-minded conservatives, reformers, and goodtimers might prevail someday regarding other drugs. If they did, Koop would get a chance to become not only public servant of the decade but also of the century.

Looking Back on Legalization

Legalization on the Koop model would produce numerous immediate benefits. Some are obvious, and the speculative, non-fearful side of our brains can perceive others through the fog of present understanding. Looking back on an imaginary Year One of legalization, we see first that a staggering $140 billion made its way back from the drug chieftains through the pushers to the buyers and into the above-ground economy. Some $25 billion went straightway to the federal Treasury, solving a Gramm-Rudman problem that had paralyzed Congress for months. This was only an accountant's relief, however, compared with the swift and magnificent destruction of the drug empire. Acres upon acres of pleasure boats and private airplanes were reclaimed at fire-sale prices by members of the legitimate topsider class. Whole warehouses of .38s, sawed-off shotguns, and—from the big guys—Uzis and AK-47s rusted in benign disuse, along with the most sophisticated electronic tools of the smuggler's trade. A generation's painstaking investment in human machinery —bribed judges, overseas connections, look-the-other-way cops, and fixed lawyers—collapsed into a useless, unsightly heap of corruptions bought but undelivered. Nearly 40 percent of all organized crime activity vanished. The livelihoods of some 700,000 assorted street and parlor pushers disappeared, including an estimated 180,000 jobs for cocaine dealers.

The value of illicit drugs plummeted toward zero. A batch of the ghetto brainscorcher 'loveboat', which had fetched more than $500,000 when packaged as drug-soaked parsley joints, suddenly was worth little more than the $500 in chemicals required to make a gallon of the active ingredient, PCP. As the prices of other drugs shrank by factors of ten to 100, drug users left with their rightful owners the money and goods they otherwise would have stolen to pay 90 to 98 percent of the underworld's former demands. Drug gangs and sinister cartels no longer killed policemen, bystanders, and each other in wars over outlaw riches. Homicide rates in many cities dropped 60 percent overnight. In New York law enforcement officers tore up more than 80 percent of their search warrants, freeing themselves from their most hazardous assignments and the courts from a mountain of paperwork. Policemen threw down their new anti-pusher Green Beret flak jackets and 9 mm semi-automatics. They looked like policemen again, instead of Beirut stormtroopers. Similarly, kids looked like kids. Twelve-year-olds turned in their beepers, pistols, and bulletproof vests, which they had come to wear under their $150 GorTex jackets.

The end of the illegal drug market arrived as salvation for bulging prisons, whose inmate population had doubled to 600,000 in the 1980s even as the drug traffic rose by half. More than 70,000 prisoners had been incarcerated for buying or selling drugs. In addition, going by police estimates that half the ordinary property crimes had been committed to service the astronomical costs of drug use, at least another 100,000 no longer had reasons to get locked up. A prison population that had been growing at a steady rate of 900 new prisoners per day—adding $18 million in annual service costs each morning, and demanding costly new construction—turned instead into a small exodus of those convicted of lesser trafficking crimes without violence. By parole, amnesty, and attrition, nearly a quarter of the prisoners were free within a year.

Law enforcement units felt proportionate relief. The U.S. attorneys, whose collective budget had grown sixfold under President Reagan, had 10,000 fewer cases to prosecute. Among many who found other work were the graphic artists who received $17,000 to chart the intricacies of the 'Pizza Connection' heroin ring for a jury. One thousand special agents of the FBI's new narcotics units were furloughed or re-assigned. Moreover, the majority of internal corruption cases disappeared at all levels. Since the heroin from the famous French Connection bust disappeared from the police evidence room in the 1970s, corruption had grown from a novelty into a crippling, everyday scourge. (No sooner had President Reagan revoked J. Edgar Hoover's lifelong order to keep FBI agents out of the 'dirty' drug war than the first drug-crooked FBI agent drew ten years for taking $850,000 in bribes. An elite Strike Force prosecutor had gone down for $210,000 and a sailboat. Corruption investigations of some 300 Justice Department officials reached public notice between 1983 and 1985. In Miami, after a shift of narcotics detectives was caught killing the dealers and stealing the drugs, a massive internal investigation 'purged' one-tenth of the entire police force.)

But the most immediate relief came to the civilians who had been wounded in the cross-fires of the drug wars. Aside from their feeling of safety and well-being, the victims had lost nearly $8 billion in cash and personal property. Spared these losses, these citizens also saw their insurance costs plummet.

Large as the $8 billion drug-robbery figure might sound, it represents only a small fraction of the $140 billion spent annually for illegal drugs. The huge balance points to two lessons about the trade: first, the consumers are more 'ordinary' than commonly conceived, spending mostly their own money to buy hideously expensive luxury goods; and second, many of the thefts for drug money probably go unreported. Studies show that an inner-city heroin addict commonly commits up to 2,000 muggings and burglaries a year. Getting 20 cents on the dollar to fence hot property, thieves had to strip nearly $25 billion worth of bare-bones possessions from the nation's poorest neighborhoods— usually uninsured—for each $5 billion of the drug balance that we might fairly ascribe to unreported crimes.

Although we would hope to have Koop, or someone like him, crusading to drive down consumption of the new drugs along with the old ones, there would be enormous new 'sin' tax revenues as well. At the modest rate of ten dollars per ounce, taxing marijuana alone would produce $20 billion at present levels of estimated consumption. Combined with savings in crime and enforcement, legalization would provide more than $100 billion of tax relief.

But what are the offsetting costs of legal, cheap drugs? Although predictions vary wildly, some experts see a 20-fold jump in heroin addicts to ten million, plus 60 or 70 million cocaine addicts. These gigantic numbers point to social doom. A Koop model of legalized drug war has received scant attention for one principal reason: fear. Chairman Rangel's last annual report put the matter most nakedly by declaring that people simply cannot resist the pleasure of drugs. "This human failing has proven to be universal," said the House select committee. "When drugs are available, they will be used; the more they are available, the more they will be used."

This credo takes us to the heart of the matter. If it is true, then the 'Just Say No' hoopla is a farce, because people lack the capacity to make a choice. The state must say no for them. The 'human failing' theory also strips some of the condescension from the anti-drug crusade. Puritans have always liked to call in the sheriff against those they see as threatening, moral inferiors, whether they be atheists, gamblers, addicts, or abortionists. Such power reinforces a sense of moral superiority in the controllers, and it is convenient to assume that temptation would ruin someone else—society's weaklings. However, the Rangel committee admits a dose of insecurity beneath the noblesse. It suggests that the Puritans themselves would succumb if they could pick up a packet of medical-quality cocaine or marijuana at the local vice market.

The fear catches all of us at some level. I worry about my children, even as I bridle at the notion that the government can protect them better than I can teach them to protect themselves. Why take the risk? It seems better to accept the hemorrhage of current laws and hope the menace will decline. Part of the apprehension is grounded in social norms; illicit drugs raise the fear of gutter depravity. There is no Rx respectability about addiction, no Dewar's Profile of a junkie.

To fight the entire drug war by Everett Koop's rules would require disciplined courage within individual citizens and enormous trust between them. But so does the practice of democracy itself. Whether or not we ever choose Schmoke's path, the debate over drug legalization ought to be valuable because it raises fundamental questions of political identity. Our whole theory of government is built on the conviction that citizens have the strength and the right to govern themselves. The drug laws, like royalist theory, rest on the contrary propostion that most people cannot follow their own best interests without force of external authority. They suggest an atomized nation of people who remain suckling babes anywhere outside their narrow expertise, in fields ranging from health to national security. Even if this admission goes down easily in the emotionally charged minefield of drugs, it may alert us to a more general collapse of democratic faith.

Tough Choices: The Practical Politics of Drug Policy Reform

Arnold S. Trebach

Arnold Trebach, law professor at American University, regards the arguments for "full legalization" of drugs as "more elegant" and "more rationally consistent" than calls for drug reforms that fall short of full legalization. Nonetheless, since he believes that full legalization is highly unlikely "within the foreseeable future" because of political obstacles, he thinks that it is important to present practical measures for immediate action: "Thus I suggest that we now think not of total repeal of drug prohibition as occurred with alcohol prohibition in 1933. Rather, we should think of a gradual series of small steps that will, in effect, disengage forces and begin building peaceful relations in an arena torn by conflict and violence."

He suggests that drug reformers organize opposition to "extremist officials and policies", including those of the White House drug policy office, the Alcohol, Drug Abuse, and Mental Health Administration, the Drug Enforcement Agency, and others. He calls for "tolerance, compassion, and help for [drug] users and abusers" and opposition to the policy of "zero tolerance". He calls on people also "to support increases in treatment facilities for legal and illegal drug abuse." He advocates "drug maintenance and needle-exchange programs" to prevent addicts from injecting themselves with the AIDS virus. Further, he supports allowing doctors to prescribe heroin and marijuana for people suffering from cancer, glaucoma, multiple sclerosis, and other diseases. He supports also experiments with "limited 'legalization'." ("In essence, all

'Tough Choices: The Practical Politics of Drug Policy Reform' by Arnold S. Trebach (*American Behavioral Scientist*, vol. 32, no. 3, January/February 1989, pp. 249–258). Used by permission of Sage Publications, Inc.©

drugs remain illegal; but peaceful users and small sellers are left alone; blatant sellers and those who are violent or connected with organized crime are arrested.") Finally, he recommends *"enlightened action that places greater legal and cultural controls on alcohol, tobacco, and caffeine."*

Dr. Trebach believes that following those recommendations will reduce overcrowded courts and jails, decrease street violence and police corruption, and improve the efficiency of the police and the criminal justice system.

During the past 15 years, I have written numerous articles, two books, congressional testimony, and other statements that proposed comprehensive reforms in our drug laws and policies. Each proceeded on the assumption that there was something terribly destructive about the American approach to drug control and each proposed sweeping reforms.

At times, this has been a very lonely position, especially in the midst of the drug hysteria of recent years when I would receive pleading calls from television producers saying they could find no other person to go on camera to take the opposition position. However, many good people preceded me in this effort and it is comforting to see others joining the cause.

We must constantly keep the public aware that there are other methods of approaching drug control than through the use of the criminal law—and that complete prohibition usually fails as a national policy of drug control. Indeed, I have found that it is often easier to make the case for fundamental reform, even for complete legalization, than for limited proposals. The full legalization argument is more elegant, more rationally consistent, and has fewer logical inconsistencies. By pushing it on the political hustings and in media appearances we should win almost every debate and give nothing away to the drug warriors. At the same time, there is only a tiny chance of winning in the real political battle to change significantly any of the laws in, say, the next four years or in this century.

Perhaps we should rather concentrate on winning a point or two that makes concrete progress, however small it may appear in the grand debate. Yet I worry that we weaken our fundamental position by working now for only limited goals rather than for outright repeal of drug prohibition, as alcohol reformers did in the thirties. Thus those of us in the loyal opposition to the war on drugs are faced with some tough choices when we enter, as we are now doing, the thicket of practical reform politics.

While the comprehensive strategies are not the main subject of my comments, I did want, at the outset, to summarize some of my conclusions at this broad level over the years.

The Heroin Solution

The first are the major findings and recommendations of my book, *The Heroin Solution* (1982). That book was based upon eight years of study of the history of heroin and of the intertwined stories of the development of British and American narcotic laws and policies. The study also included many months of field work in English drug clinics and on the streets of London and American cities, talking to addicts and police. I concluded that the British approach, while full of problems, worked better than the American because health considerations tended to dominate the national approach to the drug problem. The police and the criminal justice system had a role because crime was involved in the addiction problem there as here, but at a much lower level. Many addicts, I personally saw, were maintained on narcotics and managed to live decent lives. I also applauded their use of heroin in the treatment of people in pain, especially terminal cancer sufferers.

The Canadian government utilized that book and its findings as part of the scientific support for its historic action in 1986 that brought heroin back into medicine for pain treatment—as did the Australian Human Rights Commission in recommending similar reforms. The American government continues to ignore the findings.

The Great Drug War

The second set of recommendations is a summary of the major proposals from my latest book, *The Great Drug War* (1987). That book was based upon four years of study of the current American war on

311

drugs. In the course of that study, I traveled to some of the major fronts in our drug-control campaign and saw at first hand how it affects the police, addicts, other sick people, and ordinary citizens.

The book reported on how our police are often victims of the drug war in terms of threats of violence, the temptations of easy money, and personal stress from undercover work. It reported also how people in pain and addicts, sometimes the same people, were treated as enemies in our chemical civil war and sacrificed on its martial altar. As it happened, one was a Baltimore grandfather who was denied pain medicine by state medical authorities because he was an admitted heroin addict and who died in agony.

I invested a major effort in a review of all available data on drugs and other threats to the health of American society. That review turned up some familiar and some new, ironic twists of reality in terms of public perceptions. The federal data for 1985, for example, documented 2,177 deaths from the most popular illicit drugs: heroin, cocaine (including crack), PCP, and marijuana. Diseases related to alcohol and tobacco kill approximately 500,000 Americans every year.

Federal data for 1985 showed that in the entire country, 52 children between the ages of 6 and 17 died from all forms of drug overdoses. At a time when we were being told that our children were dying in droves from crack overdoses, the book documented how federal data could identify not a single crack death (they were merged in the cocaine numbers). The total of all known deaths from all forms of cocaine and crack abuse among children (ages 10 to 17) was seven in 1985.

I also reported in the book that, after reviewing all federal data, I had yet to encounter a single overdose death due mainly to marijuana abuse. The greatest threats to children, I said, are from accidents and from the dangers of life in a modern society, often from ignored threats. Toy balloons, for example. From the files of the U.S. Consumer Product Safety Commission I was able to document a minimum of 34 deaths of children from ingestion of toy balloons between 1981 and 1985. Or swimming pools. During 1985, CPSC data recorded 337 deaths of young people (through the age of 24) in swimming pools and another 249 in swimming accidents elsewhere. Or mothers and fathers. A special computer run of FBI crime reports came up with the grisly fact that 408 American children (from infants through the age of 14) were murdered by their parents in 1983, a fairly typical year. So also the modern fast food, massive fat diet that is being recognized as a major threat to the health of the nation and its children.

None of this data was meant to discount the health threat of illegal drugs. That health threat is real. But it has been exaggerated, especially in comparison with legal drugs and other threats. Too often the health threats of illegal drugs are confused with the extra threats caused by the use of the criminal law and pursuit of the war on drugs. Those extra threats expand the basic health threat of the illegal drugs from the level of a serious problem to that of an international disaster.

The experience of working on the book outraged and scared me. I became convinced that my country, its people, democratic institutions, and human rights were in danger because our leaders had lost their sense of balance over this problem. It was similar to my fears during the McCarthy bout of hysterical anticommunism and during the rabid segregationist battles of the 1950s and 1960s. Accordingly, I pleaded for calm and humane methods for dealing with the drug problem. I did not recommend legalization of all drugs as the answer but instead called for a bundle of peaceful compromises, in the best American tradition, that might receive practical support from Middle America.

Included in that bundle of peaceful compromises, among others, were the following proposals. Place greater controls on the sale and consumption of currently legal drugs, especially alcohol and tobacco. Place fewer controls on the currently illegal drugs. Put health warning labels on every container of alcohol, including beer and wine. Restrict all alcohol and tobacco advertising to agate-type listings in newspapers. Prohibit all smoking on airplanes and in many other public locations. Make marijuana use and cultivation legal for personal use by adults. Medicalize heroin and cocaine for addicts by prescription but do not make them legal for nonaddicts. Create new legal protections against the search for drugs in the homes, the lands, the bodies, and the bodily wastes of free citizens.

Initial Resolutions of the Drug Policy Foundation

My work on that book had one other impact on me. It convinced me that instead of another book, I wanted to 'write' a new reform organization. Accordingly, starting in late 1986, with the help of a few friends, I began work on the Drug Policy Foundation. It came into formal existence in April 1987. The foundation is a reformist think tank meant to provide a rallying point for what might be termed the loyal opposition to the war on drugs in America and other countries. We are now creating an enduring professional research and educational institution that will function beyond the time when this issue fades once again from the headlines.

At our first major meeting—the International Conference on Drug Policy Reform, held in London, England, in July 1987—we produced our first set of resolutions aimed at creating a dialogue on rethinking some of the most basic ideas about drug abuse control. Many people contributed to the process of drafting and redrafting that went into the current version of 'The Reform of Basic Drug Control and Treatment Policies.' That is the third set of reform proposals that I commend to your attention. They were debated and voted on by the participants in the International Conference on Drug Policy Reform held in October 20–23, 1988.

Those resolutions do not call for legalization of all drugs but rather recommend that the war on drugs be terminated everywhere and that peaceful experiments be encouraged in varying nations and localities that include different forms of legalization, medicalization, and decriminalization. Until major legal reforms occur, however, these draft Drug Policy Foundation resolutions recommend that existing laws be enforced in a selective and rational fashion. For example, every effort should be made to support and expand the efforts of law enforcement agencies in all countries to combat those predatory, violent criminal syndicates that traffic in drugs and other illegal commodities. However, less law enforcement attention should be paid to small dealers and simple users, who should be virtually ignored by the police unless they commit other crimes, such as robbery or burglary, or create public nuisances by interfering with normal street traffic. This is the essence of the pragmatic Dutch approach to drug law enforcement. It is also the approach that many democracies take to enforcement of the sex laws.

These three sets of reform recommendations represent the highlights of my contributions and those of some of my learned colleagues to a comprehensive theoretical framework for a much needed fundamental rethinking of our drug laws and policies. There are many other sets of sensible wide-ranging reform principles that have been set out by insightful scholars and researchers over the years. To name the sources of only a few: Alfred R. Lindesmith, *The Addict and the Law;* Rufus King, *The Drug Hang-Up;* Edward M. Brecher and the editors of *Consumer Reports, Licit and Illicit Drugs;* National Commission on Marijuana and Drug Abuse [appointed by President Nixon], *Drug Use in America: Problem in Perspective;* and the Drug Abuse Council, *The Facts About 'Drug Abuse'.*

Allow me to add one more thought. While none of the sets of reform principles mentioned above, written by me or others, recommend outright legalization, I am now convinced that our society would be safer and healthier if all of the illegal drugs were fully removed from the control of the criminal law tomorrow morning at the start of business. I would be very worried about the possibility of future harm if that radical legal change took place but less worried than I am now about the reality of present harm being inflicted every day by our current laws and policies.

Beginning the Peace Process in the Drug Arena

However, there is no possibility of legalization of all drugs within the foreseeable future. I could be wrong about that pessimistic calculation but my suggestion is that we make the tough choice of focusing a good deal of our attention on practical steps that might be accomplished now within the realm of political reality. Of course, we should keep all of our grand theories and broad sets of principles in mind for the future and as present guides for more immediate action. Some pieces of the comprehensive principles will even be of some immediate value.

Thus I suggest that we now think not of total repeal of drug prohibition as occurred with alcohol prohibition in 1933. Rather, we should think of a gradual series of small steps that will, in effect, disengage forces and begin building peaceful relations in an arena torn by conflict and violence. This would be the equivalent of beginning the peace process that has been attempted in other shooting wars around the world in recent years. This process may be slow and painful but it may also be our only alternative to a more destructive drug war. Here are some of the steps we might take to begin that peace process in the drug arena.

1. *Organize opposition to extremist officials and policies.* It is highly likely that whoever is president, there will be powerful pressures to put extremists, once again, in drug policy positions within the federal government. Those of us who support drug law reform should recognize that even without changing a single law, it is possible to have more rational enforcement of the current laws. Accordingly, we should serve notice that we intend to combine forces and fight to prevent extremists, or wimps who toady to extremists, from once again occupying such positions as the heads of the White House drug policy office; of the Alcohol, Drug Abuse, and Mental Health Administration; of the National Institute on Drug Abuse; of the Food and Drug Administration; of the Customs Service; and of the Drug Enforcement Administration, among others. We may not be able to secure appointments for reformers, but we should attempt to combine forces so that fanatics are vetoed. Now, fanaticism or pseudo-fanaticism seem to be requirements for appointment.

In the same way, we can put maximum effort now not so much into repealing prohibition but rather into fighting extremist policies, some of which are mentioned in the suggestions that follow.

2. *Tolerance, compassion, and help for users and abusers.* An example of a fanatic is the present commissioner of customs. He is the major champion of Zero Tolerance, a principle that is alien to America and to rational police and prosecution procedures in any civilized country. For centuries, police and prosecution officials have used common sense and ethics in enforcing the law. Otherwise, all systems of law would collapse from overenforcement. The commissioner wants no drug violation ignored and wants all users to suffer some criminal penalty. The *National Law Journal* has just documented what many of us suspected: Nearly three-fourths of prosecutors surveyed reject zero tolerance (and one-fourth say marijuana should be decriminalized).

We should use every strategy at our command to oppose such policies, starting with opposition to appointments of extremists. In addition, we should encourage tolerance and compassion for users and abusers at the same time that we try to educate them to the dangers of drugs. When the government mounts attacks on users or suspected users, we should encourage legal action to prevent these attacks from invading rights. The Drug Policy Foundation is now developing a Medical-Legal Advocacy Project that seeks to mobilize legal talent in opposition to assaults on users. This will involve, for example, suits for damages in cases of mass random urine testing; or injunctions to stop such intrusions as just happened with Department of Justice lawyers. Another example would be support of Employee Assistance Programs, well-established methods that emphasize confidential treatment assistance rather than exposure and disgrace.

> 3. *Federal leadership and funds for treatment.* We should constantly point out to the public that users and abusers are members of our family, so to speak, and that we want to help, not punish, them. We should make alliances with leading police organizations and thinkers mutually to support a vast increase in treatment facilities for legal and illegal drug abuse. We can point out, as a model of enlightened police behavior, the recent action of the head of the Drugs Branch of the British Home Office, who campaigned to help a group of injecting addicts set up a new clinic for medical dispensation of narcotics.

Treatment is the one area in which positive drug legislation is possible during the next session of Congress. There are many hopeful treatment bills in the hopper, but none, to my knowledge, goes far enough. I think it might be politically acceptable to recommend that the federal government take a leadership role in demanding experiments with new treatment models supervised by ADAMHA and NIDA and fueled by a vast infusion of funds, perhaps working up to $3 billion per year by the early 1990s. The Reagan administration has cut treatment funds and put the pittance remaining into state block grants. Many congresspersons across the political spectrum oppose this penurious approach.

If possible, these experiments should allow for a wide array of models, including drug-free, drug maintenance, and needle exchange features. They should emphasize not just charitable treatment but also those paid for in whole or in part by the patients. Thus all classes would benefit and all classes might support these bills.

> 4. *AIDS treatment: a special priority.* AIDS is a greater threat to our survival than all of the drugs combined. The major engine for the transmission of AIDS is the heterosexual injecting addict. Drug reformers should stand solidly behind any

proposal that promises to provide better treatment for AIDS sufferers and that might curb the spread of the disease. Properly designed drug maintenance and needle-exchange programs should be advocated as essential elements in all AIDS-control strategies and bills. While it is sad to say, the AIDS threat makes for a much more compelling argument for decent treatment of addicts than a simple appeal to human compassion.

5. *Medicine for sufferers of more traditional diseases.* Making heroin and marijuana available as medicines for our sick people would seem to be a centrist proposal on which all sensible people could agree. Because of irrational fears of encouraging recreational use by our youth and others, even this most compassionate of proposed legislation may fail in Congress within the near future. If so, then we should work through other means than legislation for reform. Without changing a single word in existing control laws or executive regulations, FDA and DEA working together could see to it that heroin and marijuana were made available through doctors to most of those afflicted with cancer, glaucoma, multiple sclerosis, and other diseases who might be helped by these drugs. This availability could be part of a massive series of experiments in the control of pain and anxiety among our millions of sick people. An element in those experiments could be the more aggressive use of existing analgesics with less interference from the police.

Reformers should make clear to the new administration that they will fight the appointment of any new DEA or FDA head who does not show a willingness to be compassionate in this form to the sick people of the country. Of course, this will not occur unless the new president is convinced that he can allow this action without major political harm. Can we help convince him or the public that this is a proper action?

6. *Medical-legal court action.* For decades during the struggle for racial justice, legal action in the courts was the most effective path of reform. This may be the case in this struggle for rationality and compassion in the drug policy arena. The Drug Policy Foundation Medical-Legal Advocacy Project will coordinate legal assistance to patients and others who cannot afford a lawyer in cases that involve medicine and the law. We will continue our own legal work in the medical marijuana suit now being considered by a DEA Administrative Law Judge.

Reformers should seek to enlist major law firms and bar associations involved with these matters through the courts. The Drug Policy Foundation will actively push such alliances for action because they promise advances where all else has failed.

7. *Experiments with limited 'legalization'.* Working with police and prosecution organizations and leaders, we should encourage carefully researched experiments in limited or de facto legalization of possession and small sales of all drugs. This is a major part of the Dutch approach and is controlled by an extensive set of written guidelines prepared by the prosecutors and police with the support of the judges. In essence, all drugs remain illegal; but peaceful users and small sellers are left alone; blatant sellers and those who are violent or connected with organized crime are arrested. The results here could be a reversal of the swamping of the criminal justice system and jails with petty criminals, a reduction in street violence and police corruption, and greater overall efficiency for the police and the criminal justice system.

Carefully guided experiments might also take place with other models of limited legalization. The Alaskan approach might be more acceptable in some areas than the Dutch; namely, allow full legalization, not decriminalization, of growth and possession of marijuana for personal use in the privacy of the home. No other drugs are affected by this change based upon a State Supreme Court decision. We might also consider variation of the new law being proposed by the Oregon Marijuana Initiative: Upon the payment of a $50 annual tax, adults would be given a certificate by the county that allows them to grow and possess a small amount of marijuana for personal use. Again, all other drugs remain fully criminal.

Experiments also should be considered that would explore the industrial and commercial uses of the marijuana plant. Hemp has vast commercial potential as a fiber for rope and clothing, among other uses. It is possible that experiments will produce strains of marijuana that have a high fiber value and a low intoxication potential. In the current martial climate, research on such developments is not possible.

8. *Remember the legal drugs.* We must continue to support enlightened action that places greater legal and cultural controls on alcohol, tobacco, and caffeine. Positive steps are taking place here—more in the United States than any other country—and we drug policy reformers must support them. We also must emphasize that the greatest need for treatment remains in providing affordable help for legal drug abusers.

Select Bibliography

Abadinsky, Howard. *Drug Abuse: An Introduction*. Chicago: Nelson-Hall, 1989.

Alexander, Shana. *The Pizza Connection: Lawyers, Money, Drugs, Mafia*. New York: Weidenfeld and Nicolson, 1988.

Bakalar, James B., and Lester Grinspoon. *Drug Control in a Free Society*. Cambridge, England: Cambridge University Press, 1984.

Brecher, Edward M., and the editors of *Consumer Reports*. *Licit and Illicit Drugs*. Boston: Little, Brown, 1972.

Byck, R. (ed.) *Cocaine Papers: Sigmund Freud*. New York: New American Library, 1974.

Chatterjee, S. K. *Drug Abuse and Drug-Related Crimes*. Norwell, Ma: Kluwer, 1989.

Crafts, Dr. and Mrs. W. F., and M. and M. W. Leitch. *Intoxicating Drinks and Drugs, in all Lands and Times: A Twentieth-Century Survey of Intemperance, Based on a Symposium of Testimony from One Hundred Missionaries and Travellers*. Washington, DC: International Reform Bureau, 1900.

Drug Abuse Council, The. *The Facts about "Drug Abuse"*. New York: The Free Press, 1980.

Falco, Mathea, and Warren I. Cikins. *Toward a National Policy on Drug and AIDS Testing*. Washington, DC: Brookings Institution, 1989.

Fingarette, Herbert. *Heavy Drinking: The Myth of Alcoholism as a Disease*. Berkeley: University of California Press, 1988.

Friedman, David. *The Machinery of Freedom: Guide to a Radical Capitalism*. Second edition. La Salle: Open Court, 1989.

Furst, P. T. (ed.) *Flesh of the Gods: The Ritual Use of Hallucinogens*. New York: Praeger, 1972.

Grabowski, J. (ed.) *Cocaine: Pharmacology, Effects, and Treatment of Abuse*. National Institute on Drug Abuse, Research Monograph 50, 1984.

321

Grinspoon, Lester. *Marijuana Reconsidered*. Cambridge, Ma: Harvard University Press, 1971.

Grinspoon, Lester, and James Bakalar. *Cocaine: A Drug and Its Social Evolution*. New York: Basic Books, 1976.

Hamowy, Ronald (ed.) *Dealing With Drugs: Consequences of Government Control*. Lexington, Ma: Lexington Books, 1987.

Hawley, Richard A. *Drugs and Society: Responding to an Epidemic*. New York: Walker, 1988.

Hoffman, Abbie. *Steal This Urine Test*. New York: Penguin, 1987.

Huxley, Aldous. *The Doors of Perception*. New York: Harper and Row, 1970.

Inciardi, James A. *The War on Drugs: Heroin, Cocaine, Crime and Public Policy*. Mountain View, Ca: Mayfield, 1986.

Institute of Medicine, Division of Public Sciences Study. *Marijuana and Health*. National Academy Press, 1982.

Judson, Horace Freeland. *Heroin Addiction in Britain: What Americans Can Learn from the English Experience*. New York: Harcourt, Brace, Jovanovich, 1974.

Kaplan, John. *Marijuana—The New Prohibition*. New York: World Publishing, 1970.

———. *The Hardest Drug: Heroin and Public Policy*. Chicago: University of Chicago Press, 1983.

King, Rufus. *The Drug Hang-Up: America's Fifty-Year Folly*. New York: Norton, 1972.

Kleiman, Mark A. R. *Marijuana: Costs of Abuse, Costs of Control*. Westport, Ct: Greenwood, 1989.

Kozel, N. J., and E. H. Adams (ed.) *Cocaine Use in America: Epidemiology and Clinical Perspectives*. National Institute on Drug Abuse, Monograph 61, 1985.

Lee, David. *Cocaine Handbook: An Essential Reference*. Berkeley, Ca: And/Or Press, 1980.

Lee, Rensselaer W., III. *The White Labyrinth: Cocaine and Political Power*. New Brunswick, NJ: Transaction, 1989.

Lindesmith, Alfred R. *The Addict and the Law*. Bloomington, In: Indiana University Press, 1965.

———. *Addiction and Opiates*. Chicago: Aldine, 1968.

Mabry, Donald J. *The Latin American Narcotics Trade and U.S. National Security*. Westport, Ct: Greenwood, 1989.

McCormick, Michele. *Designer Drug Abuse*. New York: Franklin Watts, 1989.

MacDonald, Scott B. *Mountain High, White Avalanche: Cocaine and Power in the Andean States and Panama.* New York: Praeger, 1989.

Moore, Mark H. *Buy and Bust: The Effective Regulation of an Illicit Market in Heroin.* Lexington, Ma: Lexington Books, 1977.

Musto, David F. *The American Disease: Origins of Narcotic Control.* Expanded edition. London: Oxford University Press, 1987.

Nadelmann, Ethan Avram. 'Drug Prohibition in the United States: Costs, Consequences, and Alternatives'. *Science.* September 1st, 1989.

Nahas, Gabriel G. *Keep off the Grass.* Middlebury, Vt: Eriksson, 1985.

Nahas, Gabriel G., and Helene Peters. *Cocaine: The Great White Plague.* Middlebury, Vt: Eriksson, 1989.

Nahas, Gabriel G., and Harold M. Vuth. *How to Save Your Child from Drugs.* Middlebury, Vt: Eriksson, 1987.

National Commission on Marijuana and Drug Abuse. *Drug Use in America: Problem in Perspective.* Washington, DC: Government Printing Office, 1973.

National Commission on Marijuana and Drug Abuse. *Marijuana: A Signal of Misunderstanding.* Washington, DC: Government Printing Office, 1972.

Packer, Herbert. *The Limits of the Criminal Sanction.* Stanford: Stanford University Press, 1968.

Phillips, Joel L., and Ronald D. Wynne. *Cocaine: The Mystique and the Reality.* New York: Avon, 1980.

Peele, Stanton. *The Meaning of Addiction: Compulsive Experience and Its Interpretations.* Lexington, Ma: Lexington Books, 1985.

———. *The Diseasing of America: Addiction Treatment Out of Control.* Lexington, Ma: Lexington Books, 1989.

President's Commission on Organized Crime. *America's Habit: Drug Abuse, Drug Trafficking, and Organized Crime.* Washington, DC: Government Printing Office, 1986.

Quincey, Thomas De. *Confessions of an English Opium Eater.* First published 1822. Edited by Alethea Hayter. Harmondsworth, England: Penguin, 1971.

Raphael, Ray. *Cash Crop: An American Dream.* Mendocino, Ca: Ridge Times Press, 1985.

Richards, David A. J. *Sex, Drugs, Death and the Law: An Essay on Human Rights and Overcriminalization.* Totowa, NJ: Rowman and Littlefield, 1984.

Schwebel, Robert. *Saying No is Not Enough.* New York: Newmarket, 1989.

Sinclair, A. *Era of Excess: A Social History of the Prohibition Movement*. New York: Harper and Row, 1964.

Szasz, Thomas S. *The Manufacture of Madness: A Comparative Study of the Inquisition and the Mental Health Movement*. New York: Harper and Row, 1970.

———. *The Therapeutic State*. Buffalo: Prometheus, 1984.

———. *Ceremonial Chemistry: The Ritual Persecution of Drugs, Addicts, and Pushers*. Revised edition. Holmes Beach, Fl: Learning Publications, 1985.

———. *The Untamed Tongue: A Dissenting Dictionary*. La Salle: Open Court, 1990.

Trebach, Arnold S. *The Heroin Solution*. New Haven: Yale University Press, 1982.

———. (ed.) *Drugs, Crime, and Politics*. New York: Praeger, 1978.

———. *The Great Drug War*. New York: Macmillan, 1987.

Walker, William O. *Drug Control in the Americas*. Albuquerque: University of New Mexico Press, 1989.

Weil, Andrew. *The Natural Mind: A New Way of Looking at Drugs and the Higher Consciousness*. Boston: Houghton Mifflin, 1972.

Weil, Andrew, and Winifred Rosen. *Chocolate to Morphine: Understanding Mind-Active Drugs*. Boston: Houghton Mifflin, 1983.

Wisotsky, Steven. *Breaking the Impasse in the War on Drugs*. New York: Greenwood, 1986.

———. *Beyond the War on Drugs: Overcoming a Failed Public Policy*. Buffalo: Prometheus, 1990.

Wolff, Kay. *The Last Run*. New York: Viking, 1989.

Zinberg, Norman E. *Drugs, Set, and Setting: The Basis for Controlled Intoxicant Use*. New Haven: Yale University Press, 1984.

Zinberg, Norman E., and John A. Robertson. *Drugs and the Public*. New York: Simon and Schuster, 1972.

Index

Addams, Jane, 271–72
advertising restrictions, effects on consumption, 25
Afghanistan, 69
AIDS epidemic, 15; effect of legalization on, 286; relation to drug use, 23, 126–27, 131, 151, 206, 317–18
Air Force. *See* military
Alaska, state supreme court decision on marijuana, 113–14, 166, 319
Albernaz v. United States, 182, 193
alcohol: and violent crime, 22; costs of abuse of, 41–43; deaths linked to, 23–24, 84. *See also* Prohibition
Alcohol, Drug Abuse, and Mental Health Administration (U.S.), 316–17
Alcoholics Anonymous, 42
Alexander, Shana, 281
Amsterdam, 162. *See also* Netherlands
Anglin, Douglas, 39
Anti-Drug Abuse Act: of 1986, 194, 199; of 1988, 197
Anti-Narcotic Drug Act. *See* Harrison Act
Anti-Saloon League, 81
Aristotle, 105, 107, 110
Army. *See* Military
Australia, 311
autonomy, definition of, 119; arguments against legalization based

on, 119–122; arguments for legalization based on, 163–171. *See also* Mill, John Stuart: harm principle of

Bahamas, 186, 207
Baltimore, 312
Barry, Marion, 4, 6, 279, 284
Becker, Gary S., 3
Belle Terre v. Borass, 112
Belushi, John, 209
Bennett, Marguerite A., 63–76
Bennett, William, 8; as 'Drug Czar', 221–28, 235, 280–81; as Secretary of Education, 13, 288; letters from Milton Friedman, 7, 49–52, 57–59; response to Friedman, 53–56
Berent, Irwin M., 1–9
Bernstein, Sid, 3
Bewley, Thomas, 41
Bias, Len, 209, 303
Bill of Rights. *See* Constitution (U.S.)
Black market, in drug trade, xxi, 55. *See also* organized crime
Bloom, Floyd, 239
Boaz, David, 4, 6, 8, 198–99
Bolivia, 273; effects of drug war on, 50, 79, 84, 207–208
Bourne, Randolph, 258
Boxer Rebellion, 81, 249
Boyle, John, 29
Branch, Taylor, 297–308

Morse, Stephen, 80
Moslem Empire, hashish use in, 72, 248–49
Mothers Against Drunk Driving (MADD), 75
Moyer, Steny H., 4
Murray, Charles, 7
Musto, David, 130, 269–275

Nadelmann, Ethan A., 72, 284, 287; on costs of alcohol abuse, 41; on cocaine, 35–36; on morality of drug laws, 40–41; testimony before Congress, 6; writings favoring legalization, 5, 19–26, 65
Nahas, Gabriel G., 247–251
Narcotics Anonymous, 42
NASA, role in drug enforcement, 186
National Advisory Council for Drug Abuse Prevention, 28–30
National Commission on Marijuana and Drug Abuse, 201, 315
National Council on Alcoholism, 24
National Federation for Drug-Free Youth, 184
National Guard. *See* military
National Institute of Justice, 37
National Institute on Drug Abuse, 211; report on cocaine use, 24–25, 36–37, 235, 237–38, 280, 316–17
National Narcotics Border Interdiction System (NNBIS), 185–86
National Review, 3–4, 199. *See also* Buckley, William F.
National Temperance Society, 81
Navy. *See* military
Netherlands: laws on euthanasia, 119; legalization of drugs in, 162–63, 204, 212, 314, 319
New York City: cocaine use in, 37; drug related homicides in, 125;

heroin use in, 29, 238; law enforcement in, 305
Nicaragua, 298
nicotine. *See* tobacco
NIDA. *See* National Institute on Drug Abuse
1988 Omnibus Anti-Drug Abuse Act, 207
Nixon, Richard M., 28, 184, 238–39, 298, 315
Noriega, Manuel, 197
NORML, 6, 204
Nunn, Sam, 294

Opium Exclusion Act, 81–82
Oregon, 210, 319
organized crime, 140; during Prohibition, 92, 94, 96; effect of legalization on, 140, 284, 287, 299, 304–05; involvement in drug trade, 22, 50; President Reagan's remarks concerning, 183–85
Ostrowski, James, 8

Packer, Herbert, 190
Paris Adult Theatre I v. Slayton, 111
Partnership for a Drug-Free America, xxii
paternalism: legal paternalism, defined, 109, 168–169; examples of, in U.S. law, 66, 137; 'soft paternalism', 114, 119
Patton, George, 302
Pauling, Linus, xvii–xix
Pearson, Geoffrey, 33
People v. Woody, 167
perfectionism, 106–08
Peru, 274; drug use in ancient, 249; effects of drug war on, 50, 84, 207–08
Phelps, David, 196–97